CHINA

OPPOSING VIEWPOINTS®

Other Books of Related Interest in the Opposing Viewpoints Series:

American Foreign Policy
Israel
The Middle East
Problems of Africa
The Soviet Union
The Vietnam War

Additional Books in the Opposing Viewpoints Series:

Abortion
AIDS
American Government
The American Military
American Values
America's Elections
America's Prisons
The Arms Race
Biomedical Ethics
Censorship
Central America
Chemical Dependency
Civil Liberties
Constructing a Life Philosophy
Crime & Criminals
Criminal Justice
Death and Dying
The Death Penalty
Drug Abuse
Economics in America
The Environmental Crisis
The Health Crisis
Latin America & U.S. Foreign Policy
Male/Female Roles
The Mass Media
Nuclear War
The Political Spectrum
Poverty
Religion in America
Science and Religion
Sexual Values
Social Justice
Teenage Sexuality
Terrorism
War and Human Nature

CHINA

O P P O S I N G   V I E W P O I N T S®

David L. Bender & Bruno Leone, *Series Editors*

William Dudley & Karin Swisher, *Book Editors*

OPPOSING VIEWPOINTS SERIES ®

Greenhaven Press, Inc.   San Diego, CA

Library of Congress Cataloging-in-Publication Data

China : opposing viewpoints / William Dudley & Karin Swisher,
  book editors
        p.   cm. — (Opposing viewpoints series)
    Bibliography: p.
    Includes index.
    ISBN 0-89908-439-7 : $13.95. ISBN 0-89908-414-1 (pbk.) :
    $6.95
        1. China—History—1976-   2. China—Economic
conditions—1976-   3. Human rights—China. 4. China—
Foreign relations—United States. 5. United States—Foreign
relations—China. 6. China—Foreign relations—1976-   I.
Dudley, William, 1964-   . II. Swisher, Karin, 1966-   . III.
Series.
    DS779.2.C446 1989
    951.05—dc19
                                                    88-24296
                                                         CIP
                                                          AC

"Congress shall make no law...
abridging the freedom of speech,
or of the press."

First Amendment to the US Constitution

The basic foundation of our democracy is the first amendment
guarantee of freedom of expression. The *Opposing Viewpoints Series*
is dedicated to the concept of this basic freedom and the idea that
it is more important to practice it than to enshrine it.

Contents

Chapter 5: What Should US Policy Be Toward China?

Why Consider Opposing Viewpoints?

"It is better to debate a question without settling it than to settle a question without debating it."

Joseph Joubert (1754-1824)

The Importance of Examining Opposing Viewpoints

The purpose of the Opposing Viewpoints Series, and this book in particular, is to present balanced, and often difficult to find, opposing points of view on complex and sensitive issues.

Probably the best way to become informed is to analyze the positions of those who are regarded as experts and well studied on issues. It is important to consider every variety of opinion in an attempt to determine the truth. Opinions from the mainstream of society should be examined. But also important are opinions that are considered radical, reactionary, or minority as well as those stigmatized by some other uncomplimentary label. An important lesson of history is the eventual acceptance of many unpopular and even despised opinions. The ideas of Socrates, Jesus, and Galileo are good examples of this.

Readers will approach this book with their own opinions on the issues debated within it. However, to have a good grasp of one's own viewpoint, it is necessary to understand the arguments of those with whom one disagrees. It can be said that those who do not completely understand their adversary's point of view do not fully understand their own.

A persuasive case for considering opposing viewpoints has been presented by John Stuart Mill in his work *On Liberty*. When examining controversial issues it may be helpful to reflect on this suggestion:

> The only way in which a human being can make some approach to knowing the whole of a subject, is by hearing what can be said about it by persons of every variety of opinion, and studying all modes in which it can be looked at by every character of mind. No wise man ever acquired his wisdom in any mode but this.

Analyzing Sources of Information

The Opposing Viewpoints Series includes diverse materials taken from magazines, journals, books, and newspapers, as well as statements and position papers from a wide range of individuals, organizations and governments. This broad spectrum of sources helps to develop patterns of thinking which are open to the consideration of a variety of opinions.

Pitfalls To Avoid

A pitfall to avoid in considering opposing points of view is that of regarding one's own opinion as being common sense and the most rational stance and the point of view of others as being only opinion and naturally wrong. It may be that another's opinion is correct and one's own is in error.

Another pitfall to avoid is that of closing one's mind to the opinions of those with whom one disagrees. The best way to approach a dialogue is to make one's primary purpose that of understanding the mind and arguments of the other person and not that of enlightening him or her with one's own solutions. More can be learned by listening than speaking.

It is my hope that after reading this book the reader will have a deeper understanding of the issues debated and will appreciate the complexity of even seemingly simple issues on which good and honest people disagree. This awareness is particularly important in a democratic society such as ours where people enter into public debate to determine the common good. Those with whom one disagrees should not necessarily be regarded as enemies, but perhaps simply as people who suggest different paths to a common goal.

Developing Basic Reading and Thinking Skills

In this book, carefully edited opposing viewpoints are purposely placed back to back to create a running debate; each viewpoint is preceded by a short quotation that best expresses the author's main argument. This format instantly plunges the reader into the midst of a controversial issue and greatly aids that reader in mastering the basic skill of recognizing an author's point of view.

A number of basic skills for critical thinking are practiced in the activities that appear throughout the books in the series. Some of the skills are:

Evaluating Sources of Information The ability to choose from among alternative sources the most reliable and accurate source in relation to a given subject.

Separating Fact from Opinion The ability to make the basic distinction between factual statements (those that can be demonstrated or verified empirically) and statements of opinion (those that are beliefs or attitudes that cannot be proved).

Identifying Stereotypes The ability to identify oversimplified, exaggerated descriptions (favorable or unfavorable) about people and insulting statements about racial, religious or national groups, based upon misinformation or lack of information.

Recognizing Ethnocentrism The ability to recognize attitudes or opinions that express the view that one's own race, culture, or group is inherently superior, or those attitudes that judge another culture or group in terms of one's own.

It is important to consider opposing viewpoints and equally important to be able to critically analyze those viewpoints. The activities in this book are designed to help the reader master these thinking skills. Statements are taken from the book's viewpoints and the reader is asked to analyze them. This technique aids the reader in developing skills that not only can be applied to the viewpoints in this book, but also to situations where opinionated spokespersons comment on controversial issues. Although the activities are helpful to the solitary reader, they are most useful when the reader can benefit from the interaction of group discussion.

Using this book and others in the series should help readers develop basic reading and thinking skills. These skills should improve the reader's ability to understand what they read. Readers should be better able to separate fact from opinion, substance from rhetoric and become better consumers of information in our media-centered culture.

This volume of the Opposing Viewpoints Series does not advocate a particular point of view. Quite the contrary! The very nature of the book leaves it to the reader to formulate the opinions he or she finds most suitable. My purpose as publisher is to see that this is made possible by offering a wide range of viewpoints which are fairly presented.

David L. Bender
Publisher

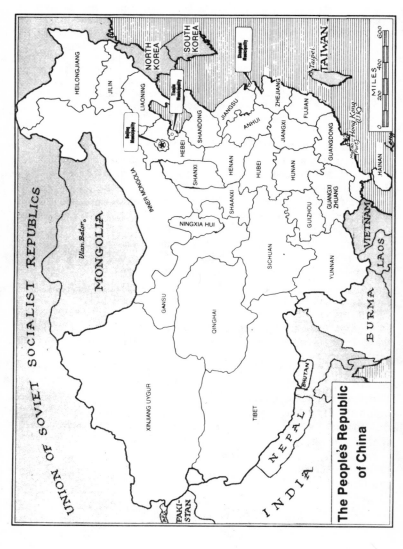

The People's Republic of China

Current History, September 1987. © 1987 Current History Inc.

Introduction

"One learns soon enough that only a fool understands the Chinese quickly."

Arthur Miller

An office worker in China attempting to file documents faces a problem. Nothing can be organized alphabetically. Each word in the Chinese language is one of more than forty thousand characters. The written Chinese language, one of the oldest in the world, and wonderfully suited for elegant essays and picturesque poetry, becomes a hindrance in today's Information Age. This dilemma is one example of something many Americans find hard to comprehend: how China's long heritage interferes with its attempt to function in today's complex and interrelated world.

For over two thousand years until 1911, China was bound under a continuous system of government and social philosophy. One trait of this long era was the philosophy developed by the Chinese sage Confucius and his followers. Confucius was concerned with how society should be organized. He postulated three master-subordinate relationships fundamental to civilization: ruler and subject, husband and wife, father and child. These social relationships become the cornerstones of Chinese society. Over the centuries dynasties would rise and fall, and China would expand, contract, break apart, and even be conquered by non-Chinese invaders. But the "idea" of China—the "middle kingdom" which was the epitome of culture, populated by extended patriarchal families, and ruled by a virtuous Confucian emperor who was the "Son of Heaven,"—remained the vision of most Chinese.

The social turbulence of China in the twentieth century can be seen as resulting from attempts to overthrow China's past. The abolishment of the imperial system in 1911 ended the Confucian vision of China, but there was nothing to replace it. The political and moral vacuum existed until 1949, when Mao Zedong led the Chinese Communist Party to power proclaiming a new vision of China. Mao's vision, like the one that preceded it, was complex. However, one element of this vision was the replacement of Confucian ideals with the creation of a "new socialist man" willing to "serve the people" and selflessly support Chinese communism. Mao's vision reached its zenith in the Cultural Revolution during

1966-69 and his campaign against the "four olds": old customs, old habits, old culture, and old thought. Teenage Red Guards, proclaiming themselves pure from the old China, repudiated their parents, toppled statues, burned books, destroyed temples and museums, and humiliated scholars, artists, and teachers, all in the name of advancing China's revolution by destroying the past.

The past, both recent and ancient, still looms over China. The Cultural Revolution is now officially condemned as a tragic waste, and the Chinese leadership today is reversing many of the goals and policies set by Mao Zedong, who died in 1976. Under the slogan of pursuing the "four modernizations," the government today stresses economic reform rather than social revolution as the means of escaping China's past. Mao's vision of China is rapidly fading. What to replace it with is the question facing China today.

China: Opposing Viewpoints features a variety of Chinese and foreign leaders, scholars, and observers debating China's directions in its economy, government, and foreign relations. The topics covered are Historical Debate: How Should China Modernize? Are China's Economic Reforms Significant? Does China Guarantee Human Rights? Is China a World Power? What Should US Policy Be Toward China? The editors have endeavored to include a wide spectrum of opinions about this complex nation whose future remains unclear.

Editor's Note: It is the editorial policy of Greenhaven Press to present viewpoints as they appeared in the original source without alteration. Therefore, the spelling of Chinese names may vary from viewpoint to viewpoint in this volume. All material written by Greenhaven editors is spelled consistently.

Historical Debate: How Should China Modernize?

Chapter Preface

For thousands of years the Chinese viewed themselves as the center of the civilized world. But in the nineteenth century China was shocked to find itself easily victimized by Western Europe and the United States. The inability to contend with these "barbarians" sparked a national debate over how China could regain its standing as a powerful and influential nation.

Some Chinese believed their country was still superior to the rest of the world except in the area of military technology. Impressed by the ships and guns Great Britain used to defeat China in the 1839 Opium War, they advocated learning Western science and technology as a means to greater military strength.

Others, especially those who studied or traveled abroad, argued that China needed more than just better ships and guns. They believed China needed fundamental social and cultural reforms. Many Chinese intellectuals were influenced by such Western ideas as democratic elections, the relative freedom of women, and Western schools. These reformers advocated complete Westernization as the way to make China strong and respected.

These were the challenges facing China at the time most of the viewpoints in this chapter were written. In many respects the questions they raise are still being debated in China today.

"What we then have to learn from the barbarians is only the one thing, solid ships and effective guns."

China Needs To Adopt Western Technology

Feng Kuei-fen

Feng Kuei-fen (1809-1874) was an imperial scholar and official. He was one of the first people in China to recognize the need to study Western countries. The following viewpoint is in two parts. In Part I, Feng advocates establishing special schools for Chinese scholars to study foreign languages and culture. In Part II, Feng emphasizes the need for China to modernize its military defenses. Written in 1860, Feng's essays express a confidence that China can soon catch up with the "barbarians."

As you read, consider the following questions:

1. What kinds of Western knowledge does the author emphasize as important?
2. Why does Feng believe China is weaker than the Western countries? What does he recommend?
3. What lesson does Japan hold for China, according to the author?

Excerpted by permission of the publishers from *China's Response to the West* by Ssu-yu Teng and John K. Fairbank, eds. Cambridge: Harvard University Press. Copyright © 1954 by the President and Fellows of Harvard College; © 1982 by S.Y. Teng and J.K. Fairbank.

I

The world today is not to be compared with that of the Three Dynasties (of ancient China). . . . Now the globe is ninety-thousand *li* around, and every spot may be reached by ships or wheeled vehicles. . . . According to what is listed on the maps by the Westerners, there are not less than one hundred countries. From these one hundred countries, only the books of Italy, at the end of the Ming dynasty, and now those of England have been translated into Chinese, altogether several tens of books. Those which expound the doctrine of Jesus are generally vulgar, not worth mentioning. Apart from these, Western books on mathematics, mechanics, optics, light, chemistry, and other subjects contain the best principles of the natural sciences. In the books on geography, the mountains, rivers, strategic points, customs, and native products of the hundred countries are fully listed. Most of this information is beyond the reach of our people.

Nowadays those familiar with barbarian affairs are called "linguists." These men are generally frivolous rascals and loafers in the cities and are despised in their villages and communities. They serve as interpreters only because they have no other means of making a livelihood. Their nature is boorish, their knowledge shallow, and furthermore, their moral principles are mean. They know nothing except sensual pleasures and material profit. Moreover, their ability consists of nothing more than a slight knowledge of the barbarian language and occasional recognition of barbarian characters, which is limited to names of commodities, numerical figures, some slang expressions and a little simple grammar. How can we expect them to pay attention to scholarly studies?

Need for Education

If today we wish to select and use Western knowledge, we should establish official translation offices at Canton and Shanghai. Brilliant students up to fifteen years of age should be selected from those areas to live and study in these schools on double rations. Westerners should be invited to teach them the spoken and written languages of the various nations, and famous Chinese teachers should also be engaged to teach them classics, history, and other subjects. At the same time they should learn mathematics. (Note: All Western knowledge is derived from mathematics. Every Westerner of ten years of age or more studies mathematics. If we now wish to adopt Western knowledge, naturally we cannot but learn mathematics. . . .)

I have heard that there are large collections of books in the Mei-hua shu-kuan [American Presbyterian Press] and in the Mo-hai shu-kuan [London Missionary Society's Printing Office]. Moreover, in 1847 the Russian barbarians presented us with more

The British, French, Russians and Germans carve up China—a turn-of-the-century French cartoon.

than one thousand books which are preserved in the Fang-lueh-kuan [Military Archives Office, in Peking]. These books should be sent to the new schools so that the valuable ones may be selected and translated. . . .

After three years all students who can recite with ease the books of the various nations should be permitted to become licentiates; and if there are some precocious ones who are able to make changes or improvements which can be put into practice, they should be recommended by the superintendent of trade to be imperially granted a *chu-jen* degree as a reward. As we have said before, there are many brilliant people in China; there must be some who can learn from the barbarians and surpass them. . . .

If we let Chinese ethics and famous [Confucian] teachings serve as an original foundation, and let them be supplemented by the methods used by the various nations for the attainment of prosperity and strength, would it not be the best of all procedures?

Controlling the Foreigners

Moreover, during the last twenty years since the opening of trade, a great many of the foreign chiefs have learned our written and spoken language, and the best of them can even read our classics and histories. They are generally able to speak on our dynastic regulations and government administration, on our geography and the state of the populace. On the other hand, our officers from generals down, in regard to foreign countries are completely uninformed. In comparison, should we not feel ashamed? The Chinese officials have to rely upon the stupid and silly "linguists" as their eyes and ears. The mildness or severity, leisureliness or urgency of their way of stating things may obscure the officials' original intent after repeated interpretations. Thus frequently a small grudge may develop into a grave hostility. At the present time the most important administrative problem of the empire is to control the barbarians, yet the pivotal function is entrusted to these people. No wonder that we understand neither the foreigners nor ourselves, and cannot distinguish fact from unreality. Whether in peace negotiations or in deliberating for war, we can never achieve the essential guiding principles. . . .

If my proposal is carried out, there will necessarily be many Chinese who learn their written and spoken languages; and when there are many such people, there will certainly emerge from among them some upright and honest gentlemen who thoroughly understand the fundamentals of administration, and who would then get hold of the essential guiding principles for the control of foreigners.

II

The most unparalleled anger which has ever existed since creation of heaven and earth is exciting all who are conscious in their minds and have spirit in their blood; their hats are raised by their hair standing on end. This is because the largest country on the globe today, with a vast area of 10,000 *li*, is yet controlled by small barbarians. . . . According to a general geography by an Englishman, the territory of our China is eight times larger than that of Russia, ten times that of America, one hundred times that of France, and two hundred times that of England. . . . Yet now we are shamefully humiliated by those four nations in the recent treaties—not because our climate, soil, or resources are inferior to theirs, but because our people are really inferior. . . . Why are they small and yet strong? Why are we large and yet weak? We must try to discover some means to become their equal, and that also depends upon human effort. Regarding the present situation there are several major points: in making use of the ability of our manpower, with no one neglected, we are inferior to the barbarians; in securing the benefit of the soil, with nothing wasted, we are inferior to the barbarians; in maintaining a close relationship between the ruler and the people, with no barrier between them, we are inferior to the barbarians; and in the necessary accord of word with deed, we are also inferior to the barbarians. The way to correct these four points lies with ourselves, for they can be changed at once if only our Emperor would set the general policy right. There is no need for outside help in these matters. . . .

What we then have to learn from the barbarians is only the one thing, solid ships and effective guns. When Wei Yuan discussed the control of the barbarians, he said that we should use barbarians to attack barbarians, and use barbarians to negotiate with barbarians. Even regardless of the difficulties of languages and our ignorance of diplomatic usages it is utterly impossible for us outsiders to sow dissension among the closely related barbarians. . . . In my opinion, if we cannot make ourselves strong but merely presume on cunning and deceit, it will be just enough to incur failure. Only one sentence of Wei Yuan is correct: "Learn the strong techniques of the barbarians in order to control them.". . .

Learn from the Barbarians

The method of self-strengthening lies in learning what they can do, and in taking over what they rely upon. Moreover, their possession of guns, cannon, and steamships began only within the last hundred years or so, and their progress has been so fast that their influence has spread into China. If we can really and thoroughly understand their methods—and the more we learn, the more improve—and promote them further and further, can we not expect that after a century or so we can reject the barbarians and stand on our own feet?

Li Hung- Chang, *Defense of Building Steamships*, 1872.

Funds should be assigned to establish a shipyard and arsenal in each trading port. Several barbarians should be invited and Chinese who are good in using their minds should be summoned to receive their instructions so that they may in turn teach many artisans. When a piece of work is finished and is indistinguishable from that made by the barbarians, the makers should be given a *chu-jen* degree as a reward, and be permitted to participate in the metropolitan examination on an equal footing with other scholars. Those whose products are superior to the barbarian manufacture should be granted a *chin-shih* degree as a reward, and be permitted to participate in the palace examinations on the same basis as others. The workers should be double-paid so as to prevent them from quitting.

Our nation has emphasized the civil service examinations, which have preoccupied people's minds for a long time. Wise and intelligent scholars have exhausted their time and energy in such useless things as the eight-legged essays [highly stylized essays for the civil service examination, divided into eight paragraphs], examination papers, and formal calligraphy. . . . Now let us order one-half of them to apply themselves to the pursuit of manufacturing weapons and instruments and imitating foreign crafts. . . . The intelligence and wisdom of the Chinese are necessarily superior to those of the various barbarians, only formerly we have not made use of them. When the Emperor above likes something, those below him will pursue it even further, like the moving of grass in the wind or the response of an echo. There ought to be some people of extraordinary intelligence who can have new ideas and improve on Western methods. At first they may learn and pattern after the foreigners; then they may compare and try to be their equal; and finally they may go ahead and surpass them—the way to make ourselves strong actually lies in this. . . .

The Japanese Example

Two years ago the Western barbarians suddenly entered the Japanese capital to seek trade relations, which were permitted. Before long the Japanese were able to send some ten steamships of their own over the western ocean to pay return visits to the various countries. They made many requests for treaties which were also granted by these countries, who understood Japan's intentions. Japan is a tiny country and still knows how to exert her energy to become strong. Should we, as a large country, alone accept defilement and insult throughout all time? . . . We are just now in an interval of peaceful and harmonious relations. This is probably an opportunity given by heaven for us to strengthen ourselves. If we do not at this point quickly rise to this opportunity but passively receive the destiny of heaven, our subsequent regret will come too late. . . . If we live in the present day and speak of rejecting the barbarians, we should raise the question as to what instruments we can reject them with. . . .

Some suggest purchasing ships and hiring foreign people, but the answer is that this is quite impossible. If we can manufacture, can repair, and can use them, then they are our weapons. If we cannot manufacture, nor repair, nor use them, then they are still the weapons of others. When these weapons are in the hands of others and are used for grain transportation, then one day they can make us starve; and if they are used for salt transportation, one day they can deprive us of salt. . . . Eventually we must consider manufacturing, repairing, and using weapons by ourselves. . . . Only thus will we be able to pacify the empire; only thus can we play a leading role on the globe; and only thus shall we restore our original strength, and redeem ourselves from former humiliations.

"Now there is not a single one of the Chinese people's sentiments, customs, or political and legal institutions which can be favorably compared with those of the barbarians."

Adopting Western Technology Alone Is Not Sufficient

Wang T'ao and T'an Ssu-t'ung

As the nineteenth century drew to a close more Chinese started to criticize the pace of modernization. Some argued that China must not only use Western technology to modernize, but also adopt Western systems of government, law, and education. The following viewpoint is by two people who develop this argument. Part I is by Wang T'ao (1828-1897), a pioneer journalist who traveled to Europe and had much contact with foreigners. Part II is a personal letter by T'an Ssu-t'ung (1865-1898), in which he responds to a friend who had asked his views on China and the West. T'an was an imperial scholar who was executed in 1898 by court officials who considered his views dangerous to the government.

As you read, consider the following questions:

1. Why does Wang believe China's modernization was superficial?
2. In what areas was it particularly important for China to modernize, according to the authors?

Excerpted by permission of the publishers from *China's Response to the West* by Ssu-ya Teng and John K. Fairbanks, eds. Cambridge: Harvard University Press. Copyright © 1954 by the President and Fellows of Harvard College; Copyright © 1982 by S.Y. Teng and J.K. Fairbanks.

I

If Confucius were born today we may be certain that he would not stubbornly believe in antiquity and oppose making changes. . . .

First, the method of selecting civil servants should be reformed. The examination essays up to the present day have gone from bad to worse. . . . And yet we are still using them to select scholars. . . .

Secondly, the method of training soldiers should be reformed. Now our army camps and water forces have only names registered on books, but no actual persons. The authorities consider our troops unreliable, and then they recruit militia, who can be assembled but cannot be disbanded. . . . This is called 'using the untrained people to fight,' which is no different from driving them to their deaths. . . .

Thirdly, the empty show of our schools should be reformed. Now district directors of schools and sub-directors of schools are installed, one person for a small city, and two for a larger city. It is a sheer waste. . . . Such people are usually degenerate, incompetent, and senile and have little sense of shame. They are unfit to set the example for scholars. . . .

Set the Foundation

He who rules the empire should establish the foundation and not merely mend the superstructure. . . . Formerly we thought that the foundation of our wealth and strength would be established if only Western methods were respected or adopted and that the result would be achieved immediately. . . . Now in all the coastal provinces there have been established special factories to make guns, bullets, and ships. Young men have been selected and sent to study abroad. Seen from the outside, the effort is really great and fine. Unfortunately, however, we are still copying the superficialities of their methods, getting the terminology (of Western civilization) but little actual substance. The ships which were formerly built at Foochow were entirely based on old methods of Western countries, beneath contempt, to those who know. As to things made in other places, for the trick of moving a machine or valve we must rely on the instruction of Westerners. Yet, if we watch the bearing of the Chinese manufacturers, they already feel noisily pleased with themselves. They usually believe that their thinking and wisdom are sufficient to match those of the Westerners, or that they have even surpassed them.

In general (the advantage of) guns lies in the fine technique of discharging them, that of ships in the ability to navigate them. . . . The handling of effective weapons depends upon the people. . . . But the so-called able minds of our people are not necessarily able, and so-called competent ones are not necessarily competent. They are merely mediocrities who accomplish something through the aid of others.

Therefore, the urgent problem of our nation today lies primarily in the governance of the people; next in the training of soldiers; and in these two matters the crucial thing to aim at is the accumulation of men of ability. Indeed, superficial imitation in practical matters is certainly not as effective as arousing genuine intellectual curiosity. The polishing and pounding in factories is definitely not as important as the machining of people's minds.

II

Your letter says that during the last several decades Chinese scholars and officials have been trying to talk about "foreign matters," but that they have achieved absolutely nothing and, on the contrary, they have been driving the men of ability in the empire into foolishness, greed, and cheating. Ssu-t'ung thinks that not only do you not know what is meant by "foreign matters," but also that you are ignorant of the meaning of discussion. In China, during the last several decades, where have we had genuine understanding of foreign culture? When have we had scholars or officials who could discuss them? If they had been able to discuss foreign matters, there would have been no such incident as we have today [the defeat of China by Japan]. What you mean by foreign matters are things you have seen, such as steamships, telegraph lines, trains, guns, cannon, torpedoes, and machines for

---

Rotten Traditions

Those who advocate no change frequently claim, "We follow the ancients, follow the ancients." Do they know that from prehistoric, ancient, medieval and modern times down to the present day, there have been many hundreds of thousands and myriads of changes? . . . I have investigated this tendency from ancient times, when one family received the mandate to make laws and establish systems and have them followed for several generations, and yet what their descendants had to obey and put into effect was inevitably different from what their ancestors did. Nevertheless the prince and the people, the upper and lower classes always stubbornly thought that "our laws today were used by our ancestors to rule the Empire, and it was well governed." They obstinately observed them, following tradition without discrimination. Gradually as time moved on the tradition changed from bad to worse, everything became neglected and finally was so rotten that it was beyond repair. . . . Those who insist that there is no need for reform still say, "Let us follow the ancients, follow the ancients." They coldly sit and watch everything being laid waste by following tradition, and there is no concern in their hearts.

Liang Ch'i-ch'ao, *A General Discussion of Reform*, 1896.

---

weaving and for metallurgy; that's all. You have never dreamed of or seen the beauty and perfection of Western legal systems and political institutions. . . . All that you speak of are the branches and foliage of foreign matters, not the root. . . .

We have more than one arsenal, and those at Tientsin, Shanghai, and Nanking are the oldest; but at the time when we need guns and cannon, there are no guns and cannon. We have more than one shipyard, and those at Port Arthur and Foochow are the largest; but at the time when we need ships, there are no ships. Helplessly we have to purchase these things from foreign countries. But the foreigners know that China has no machinery to test the quality of ships and weapons, and no way to distinguish between good and bad, so they sell to China, for an exorbitant price, weapons which have already been abandoned. . . . And Chinese diplomatic envoys in foreign countries seek a share in the profit. When they receive a remittance and dispatch the officers to make the purchase, they ask for a fee. Consequently, the higher the price, the poorer the weapons. . . . In this way China has wasted several decades. Yet you still consider Chinese scholar-officials to be learning about foreign matters. Are you not overestimating the various authorities and wishing to wash off their blame? . . .

What Should Be Done?

We should extend the telegraph lines, establish post offices to take charge of postal administration, supply water, and burn electric or gas lamps for the use of the people. When the streets are well kept, the sources of pestilence will be cut off; when hospitals are numerous, the medical treatment will be excellent. We should have parks for public recreation and health. We should have a holiday once every seven days to enable civil and military officials to follow the policy of (alternation between) pressure and relaxation. We should thoroughly learn the written and spoken languages of all countries so as to translate Western books and newspapers, in order to know what other countries are doing all around us, and also to train men of ability as diplomats. We should send people to travel to all countries in order to enlarge their points of view and enrich their store of information, to observe the strengths and weaknesses, the rise and fall, of other countries; to adopt all the good points of other nations and to avoid their bad points from the start. As a result there will be none of the ships and weapons of any nation which we shall not be able to make, and none of the machines or implements which we shall not be able to improve. We should be exact about our units of measure, examine our legal system, and unify our moral standards and customs. When our legal system is established, our culture will be kept intact. . . .

Your idea of despising our enemies arises because you think that they are still barbarians. This is a common mistake of the scholars and officials of the whole empire and they must get rid of it. A proverb says, "Know yourself and know your enemy." We must first make ourselves respectable before we despise others. Now there is not a single one of the Chinese people's sentiments, customs, or political and legal institutions which can be favorably compared with those of the barbarians. Is there any bit of Western culture which was influenced by China? Even if we beg to be on an equal footing with the barbarians, we still cannot achieve it, so how can we convert them to be Chinese? . . . Hereafter, Ssu-t'ung will seek more and new knowledge and will not confine himself to what has been mentioned above. If you do not scorn me as crazy, I have even better policies which I would like to explain to you in full. The first is how to raise funds for reform. . . . The big mansions and the high buildings (of temples or monasteries) can be made into parliaments, schools, and other public offices. . . .

Examine Old Customs

Why must problems be studied? Because our society is now undergoing a period in which its foundations are shaken. Many customs and systems which were not questioned have become difficult issues owing to their failure to meet the needs of circumstance and satisfy the people; therefore we cannot but thoroughly study them, cannot but ask whether or not the old solutions were wrong; if they were wrong, wherein the mistake lies; and when the mistake is discovered, whether there is a better solution, or whether there is any way that will better meet the demands of the present time.

Hu Shih, *The Significance of New Thought*, 1919.

In the preceding lines I have talked about seeking men of ability through change in our school system and in the civil service examinations, and yet the most valuable thing is to have men to shoulder the responsibility at the beginning of the reform. There is nothing better than to urge the gentry leaders of all counties, prefectures, and districts to promote the ideas of abolishing temples and monasteries or of gathering stockholders to open mines or of installing machinery, etc., . . . Anyone who is outstanding in achievement or in any type of service or in any economic enterprise which will yield a profit shall be given special honors and ranks, or be allowed to become a member of parliament, and be subsidized and protected by the officials in order to bring his work to a successful conclusion.

"The English newspapers . . . state that the teachings of Confucius lie at the bottom of our inflexible conservatism. In this they are greatly mistaken."

China Needs To Affirm Its Cultural Values

Chang Chih-tung

Chang Chih-tung (1837-1909) was a famous scholar and government official. He was appointed governor of several Chinese provinces, and in his last years supervised the Ministry of Education. Chang took a position between conservatives who were against any modernization and radicals who advocated thorough Westernization. His views are perhaps best summarized by his slogan "Chinese learning for the fundamental principles, Western learning for practical application." In the following viewpoint, Chang argues that China must reform, but that China also must affirm traditional Confucian teachings regarding government and morality.

As you read, consider the following questions:

1. How does the author distinguish between true and false Confucianism?
2. Why does Chang believe that scholars should learn Chinese history and philosophy before studying foreign countries?
3. How are Chinese and Western learning different, according to the author?

Chang Chih-tung, *China's Only Hope*, translated by Samuel I. Woodbridge. New York: Fleming H. Revell Company, 1900.

An old saying runs: "If a man will not understand in what misfortune consists, disgrace is sure to follow; but if he will only face the difficulty, happiness will ensue."

In no period of China's history has there arisen an emergency like the present. It is a time of change, and His Imperial Highness, the Emperor of China, has accepted the situation by altering somewhat the system of civil and military examinations and by establishing schools. New plans are being formed for the welfare of the country by Chinese philanthropists, but these plans differ both in degree and kind. There are some who hold that the new learning will save us; others maintain that its acceptation will abrogate our old doctrines, and that we ought to hold fast the patrimony of our sages. Who can tell which is right? The Conservatives are evidently off their food from inability to swallow, whilst the Liberals are like a flock of sheep who have arrived at a road of many forks and do not know which to follow. The former do not understand what international intercourse means, the latter are ignorant of what is radical in Chinese affairs. The Conservatives fail to see the utility of modern military methods and the benefits of successful change, while the Progressionists, zealous without knowledge, look with contempt upon our widespread doctrines of Confucius. Thus those who cling to the old order of things heartily despise those who even propose any innovation, and they in turn cordially detest the Conservatives with all the ardor of their liberal convictions. It thus falls out that those who really wish to learn are in doubt as to which course to pursue, and in the meantime error creeps in, the enemy invades our coast, and, consequently, there is no defence and no peace. . . .

Three Necessities

We would here state that there are now three things necessary to be done in order to save China from revolution. The first is to *maintain the reigning Dynasty;* the second is to *conserve the Holy Religion;* and the third is to *protect the Chinese Race.* These are inseparably connected; in fact they together constitute one; for in order to protect the Chinese Race we must first conserve the Religion, and if the Religion is to be conserved we are bound to maintain the Dynasty. . . .

Our Holy Religion has flourished in China several thousand years without change. The early Emperors and Kings embellished our tenets by their noble examples and bequeathed to us the rich legacy which we now possess. The sovereigns were the teachers. The Han, the T'ang and all the Chinese Dynasties to the Ming [embracing a period of 1800 years], honored and revered the religion of Confucius. Religion is the government, and the Emperors of our Dynasty honor Confucianism with a still greater reverence. It was the sages who purged the heresy from the

Classics and handed them down to us in compiled form. The Emperors themselves follow the truth and then instruct all in the Empire, so that everyone that has breath knows how to honor and how to love. For government and religion are inseparably linked together and constitute the warp of the past and present, the woof of intercommunication between China and the West.

Preserve Moral Standards

As for China's old moral standards, they are not yet lost sight of by the people of China. First come Loyalty and Filial Devotion, then Kindness and Love, Faithfulness and Justice, then Harmony and Peace. The Chinese still speak of these ancient qualities of character. But since our domination by alien races and since the invasion of foreign culture which has spread its influence all over China, a group intoxicated with the new culture has begun to reject the old morality, saying that the former makes the latter unnecessary. They do not understand that we ought to preserve what is good in our past and throw away only the bad. China now is in a period of conflict between old and new currents and a large number of our people have nothing to follow after.

Sun Yat-sen, *The Three Principles of the People,* 1924.

The foundations of our State are deep and durable. Protected by Heaven, the superstructure will certainly stand secure! But supposing this absurd gossip about the partition of China by Europeans were true and the country were cut up, be it ever so exalted and excellent, would foreigners respect the Holy Doctrine of Confucius? Far from it. The Classics of the Four Philosophers would be thrown out as refuse, and the Confucian cap and gown would never more cherish the hope of an official career. Our clever scholars would figure as clergymen, compradores, and clerks, whilst the common people would be required to pay a poll-tax and be used as soldiers, artisans, underlings, and servants. That is what would happen. And the more menial our people became, the more stupid they would be; until being both menial and stupid, they would become reduced to wretched poverty and at last perish miserably. Our Holy Religion would meet the same fate that Brahmanism in India did. Its adherents would be found skulking away, or crouching among the cavernous hills, but clinging fast the while to some tattered remnants of the truth! The Flowery People would become like the black Kwun Lun of the Southern Ocean, the life-long slaves of men, vainly seeking an escape from the curses and blows of their masters. . . .

In order to render China powerful, and at the same time preserve our own institutions, it is absolutely necessary that we should utilize Western knowledge. But unless Chinese learning is made the basis of education, and a Chinese direction given to thought, the strong will become anarchists, and the weak, slaves. Thus the latter end will be worse than the former. The English newspapers have recently been ridiculing us for not reforming, and they state that the teachings of Confucius lie at the bottom of our inflexible conservatism. In this they are greatly mistaken. Those who have translated the Four Books and Five Classics into foreign languages, have missed the true intent of Confucianism by accepting the explanations of inefficient Chinese instructors who know nothing whatever of our doctrine. These newspapers get their information from these translated books, and ridicule what they know nothing about. The superficial Chinese commentaries which pass current for truth, the unconnected, non-cohesive eight-legged essays, the effete philosophies, countless antiquarian works, false but high-sounding poetry of China, are not Confucian learning. . . .

Confucian learning consists in the acquisition of extensive literature and the strict observance of what is right; in the profound and careful meditation of the old in order to understand the new; in the making of one's self the peer of heaven by means of perfect sincerity and thus influencing men in all things for good.

Confucian government consists in rendering honor to whom honor is due, and filial piety to whom filial piety is due; in first providing a sufficiency for the people, and afterward instructing them; in preparing for war in time of peace, and in doing things at the proper time and in the proper manner. Confucius is equal to the thousand sages and the hundred kings. He is the co-equal and the co-worker with heaven and earth in nourishing and transforming men and things. How, then, can it be said that he is like the effete and inoperative "scholar" of to-day? . . .

Combining Western Methods with Chinese Foundation

Our scholars to-day should become conversant with the Classics, in order to understand the real intent of the early sages and philosophers in establishing our Religion; and a knowledge of history should be acquired in order to become familiar with our Chinese governmental methods and customs in past generations. The literary relics of our schoolmen should be reviewed to profit withal, in learning and literature. After this is done, our deficiency in books can be supplied from Western sources, and our government ills be cured by Western physicians. In this way, China can derive benefit from foreign countries, without incurring the danger of adopting Western methods that would be prejudicial to her best interests. A person who wishes to become strong and well must first get up an appetite. This obtained, he will enjoy all the good things set before him. To heal a disease the doctor must first make a diagnosis, and afterward prescribe the proper medicine. In like manner a thorough knowledge of Chinese must be obtained before Western learning is introduced. In Western educational institutions a daily study of the Bible is compulsory. This shows a respect for the Christian religion. The students in the lower schools first learn Latin in order to preserve what is ancient; and in order to observe the proper sequence of things, a thorough knowledge of the country's geography and a general acquaintance with that of other countries is required. The literature of their schools extols the excellence of their ancient Emperors' governments; and both in public and private the notes of their music swell forth in praise of the bravery and prosperity of the fatherland. These things manifest the patriotism of Western people.

Learn Chinese Foundation

If we wish to receive the benefit of Western methods, we must first acquire a knowledge of Confucius, Mencius, Ch'eng and Chu [i.e., Neo-Confucianism], and keep it as the foundation to make people thoroughly familiar with filial piety, younger-brotherhood, loyalty, sincerity, ceremony, righteousness, integrity, a sense of shame, obligations and the teachings of the sages and moral courage, in order to understand and demonstrate the foundation, before we can learn the foreign spoken and written languages for some practical use.

Wen-ti, quoted in *China's Response to the West*, 1954.

If the Chinese student is not versed in Chinese literature he is like a man who does not know his own name. Attempts to govern without a knowledge of Chinese, will be like trying to ride a horse without a bridle, or steer a boat without a rudder. Without a basis of native literature the Chinese who acquires this Western learning, will loath his country in proportion as his scientific knowledge increases; and, although his knowledge may be perfected to a high degree, how can our country employ him if he does not know Chinese? . . .

Three Mistakes

There is a class of Chinese who despise foreign methods, and without examining their excellences, contemptuously fling them aside with the remark that they are not specially mentioned in the Six Classics and the Histories of China. But what old method will suit the present day emergency? We challenge all these cavillers to produce an Ever Victorious Army from the ancient drill, or protect our coast with old Chinese gunboats instead of with armored cruisers. By not adopting foreign methods we block our own way; that is, we render ourselves proud and bigoted obstructionists, who sooner or later will perish through our own stupidity.

There is a second class who partly understand foreign methods and attempt to reconcile every discrepancy by saying that our Classics already contain all Western learning. Who boast, for instance, that algebra is an original product of China [called Tsie Ken Fang] and hence are unwilling to study mathematics. They also brag that modern firearms are handed down from the Yuan Dynasty [A.D. 1200] and that their models were copied by foreign countries when they were forcibly pacified by the Chinese; and will not, in conseqence, examine the merits of foreign arsenals, etc. This drivel is pure self-deception. What do we mean by self-deception? That which causes men to be overcome without even seeking the truth.

Still another class is drowned in Western methods. They combine Chinese and "Western" into one, and say there is no appreciable distinction between the two. They state that the "Spring and Autumn Classic" of Confucius is International Law, and that the Confucian Religion agrees with the Religion of Jesus. This is being self-bound. What is being self-bound? Becoming deceived, deranged, and losing what has already been attained. . . .

Conclusion

To sum up: Chinese learning is moral. Western learning is practical. Chinese learning concerns itself with moral conduct. Western learning, with the affairs of the world. What matters it, then, whether Western learning is mentioned in the Classics or not, if it teaches nothing repugnant, or antagonistic, to the genius of our books? If the Chinese heart throbs in unison with the heart of the sages, expressing the truth in irreprovable conduct, in filial piety, brotherly love, honesty, integrity, virtue; if government is loyalty and protection, then let government make use of foreign machinery and the railway from morning to night, and nothing untoward will befall the disciples of Confucius.

"The manifold needs of China . . . will be met permanently, completely, only by Christian civilization."

China Needs To Adopt Western Values

Arthur H. Smith

Arthur H. Smith (1845-1932) was a Christian missionary who, after arriving in China in 1872, spent over forty years there. He was later highly popular in America as a lecturer and author, and his opinions about China were typical of many missionaries and Americans during this time. In the following viewpoint, he argues that China lacks the ability to reform by itself, and that merely learning Western science and technology will not help. Smith attacks Confucianism and concludes that China lacks a moral center that can be filled only by the values of Christian civilization.

As you read, consider the following questions:

1. What does the author believe about Confucianism?
2. Why is improved science and technology not enough for China, according to the author?
3. How might the author of the opposing viewpoint respond to Smith?

Arthur H. Smith, *Chinese Characteristics*. Fleming H. Revell Company, 1894.

What the Chinese lack is not intellectual ability. It is not patience, practicality, nor cheerfulness, for in all these qualities they greatly excel. What they do lack is Character and Conscience. . . .

Chinese society resembles some of the scenery in China. At a little distance it appears fair and attractive. Upon a nearer approach, however, there is invariably much that is shabby and repulsive, and the air is full of odors which are not fragrant. No photograph does justice to Chinese scenery, for though photography has been described as "justice without mercy," this is not true of Chinese photography, in which the dirt and the smells are omitted. . . .

Making Comparisons

That many of the evils in Chinese society . . . are also to be found in Western "nominally Christian lands," we are perfectly aware. Perhaps the reader may have been disappointed not to find a more definite recognition of this fact, and some systematic attempt at comparison and contrast. Such a procedure was in contemplation, but it had to be given up. The writer's acquaintance with any Western country except his own is of an altogether too limited and inadequate character to justify the undertaking, which must for other reasons have failed. Let each reader make his own running comparisons as he proceeds, freeing himself as far as he may be able from "the bias of patriotism," and always giving the Chinese the benefit of the doubt. After such a comparison shall have been made, the very lowest result which we should expect would be the ascertained fact that the face of every Western land is towards the dawning morning of the future, while the face of China is always and everywhere towards the darkness of the remote past. A most pregnant fact, if it is a fact, and one which we beg the reader to ponder well; for how came it about?

The needs of China, let us repeat, are few. They are only Character and Conscience. Nay, they are but one, for Conscience *is* Character. It was said of a famous maker of pianos that he was "like his own instruments—square, upright, and grand." Does one ever meet any such characters in China? . . .

Christianity vs. Confucianism

The fairest fruit of Christian civilization is in the beautiful lives which it produces. They are not rare. Hundreds of records of such lives have been produced within the present generation, and there are thousands upon thousands of such lives of which no public record ever appears. Every reader must have known of at least one such life of single-hearted devotion to the good of others, and some have been privileged to know many such, within the range of their own experience. How are these lives to be accounted for, and whence do they draw their inspiration? . . . No human institution can escape from the law, inexorable because divine: "By their

35

fruits ye shall know them." The forces of Confucianism have had an abundant time in which to work out their ultimate results. We believe that they have long since done all that they are capable of doing, and that from them there is no further fruit to be expected. They have achieved all that man alone can do, and more than he has done in any other land, under any other conditions. And after a patient survey of all that China has to offer, the most friendly critic is compelled, reluctantly and sadly, to coincide in the verdict, "The answer to Confucianism is China."

Three Theories on China's Reform

Three mutually inconsistent theories are held in regard to reform in China. First, that it is unnecessary. This is no doubt the view of some of the Chinese themselves, though by no means of all Chinese. It is also the opinion adopted by certain foreigners, who look at China and the Chinese through the mirage of distance. Second, that reform is impossible. This pessimistic conclusion is arrived at by many who have had too much occasion to know the tremendous obstacles which any permanent and real reform must encounter, before it can even be tried. To such persons, the thorough reformation of so vast a body as the Chinese people appears to be a task as hopeless as the galvanizing into life of an Egyptian mummy. To us, the second of these views appears only less unreasonable than the first; but if what has been already said fails to make this evident, nothing that could here be added would be sufficient to do so.

Lack of Trust

No student, informed on the subject, can doubt that China has the brain and the brawn vastly to increase her wealth. As yet, under the heathen conditions these physical and mental assets cannot be adequately applied to the development of the Creator's boundless gifts. As yet the people have not learned to trust each other. Thus as a race they do not take to large-scale commercial or industrial organization. "Each for himself is safer," they argue.

Charles Ernest Scott, *China From Within*, 1917.

To those who are agreed that reform in China is both necessary and possible, the question by what agency that reform is to be brought about is an important one, and it is not surprising that there are several different and inharmonious replies.

Can China Reform Herself?

At the very outset, we have to face the inquiry, Can China be reformed from within herself? . . .

An intelligent British official, who knows "the terrible *vis iner-*

tiae of Oriental apathy and fatalism—that dumb stupidity against which Schiller says even the gods are powerless"—and who knows what is involved in permanent "reform," would have been able to predict the result with infallible precision. In referring to certain abuses in southwest China, connected with the production of copper, Mr. Baber remarks: "Before the mines can be adequately worked, Yunnan must be peopled, the Lolos must be fairly treated, roads must be constructed, the facilities offered for navigation by the upper Yangtze must be improved—in short, China must be civilized. A thousand years would be too short a period to allow of such a consummation, unless some force from without should accelerate the impulse." To attempt to reform China without "some force from without," is like trying to build a ship in the sea; all the laws of air and water conspire to make it impossible. It is a principle of mechanics that a force that begins and ends in a machine has no power to move it.

Between Tientsin and Peking there is a bend in the Peiho, where the traveler sees half of a ruined temple standing on the brink of the bank. The other half has been washed away. Just below is an elaborate barrier against the water, composed of bundles of reeds tied to stakes. Half of this has been carried away by the floods. The gods stand exposed to the storms, the land lies exposed to inundation, the river is half silted up, a melancholy type of the condition of the Empire. There is classical authority for the dictum that "rotten wood cannot be carved." It must be wholly cut away, and new material grafted upon the old stock. China can never be reformed from within. . . .

Are Science and Culture Enough?

There are many friends of China well acquainted with her condition. . . . In their view, China needs Western culture, Western science, and . . . "funded civilization." The Chinese have been a cultured nation for millenniums. They had already been civilized for ages when our ancestors were rooting in the primeval forests. In China, if anywhere on the globe, that recipe has been faithfully tried. There is in culture as such nothing of a reformatory nature. Culture is selfish. Its conscious or unconscious motto is, "I, rather than you." As we daily perceive in China, where our boasted culture is scouted, there is no scorn like intellectual scorn. If Chinese culture has been unable to exert a due restraining influence upon those who have been so thoroughly steeped in it, is it probable that this result will be attained by a foreign exotic?

Of science the Chinese are unquestionably in the greatest need. They need every modern science for the development of the still latent resources of their mighty Empire. This they are themselves beginning clearly to perceive, and will perceive still more clearly in the immediate future. But is it certain that an acquaintance with science will exert an advantageous moral influence over the Empire? What is the process by which this is to take place? No science lies nearer to our modern advancement than chemistry. Would the spread of a general knowledge of chemistry in China, therefore, be a moral agency for regenerating the people? Would it not rather introduce new and unthought-of possibilities of fraud and violence throughout every department of life? Would it be quite safe, Chinese character being what it is, to diffuse through the Empire, together with an unlimited supply of chemicals, an exact formula for the preparation of every variety of modern explosives?

China Needs Guidance

China has always been the largest, and, in view of its present unexampled transition, must be considered to be the most important mission field in the world. In such a time of national awakening old things readily pass away and all things become new. There has long been in China an unconscious sense of dissatisfaction with China's past, but this feeling has now become acute and all-pervasive. There is everywhere a readiness to listen to preaching and to teaching upon almost any subject, such as was formerly unknown. . . . China is reconstructing her civilization, not out of the ruins, but out of the materials of the old. She needs guidance and help upon every point and in every place. Much of this help must come from abroad and much more must be developed from within. The profoundest need of the Christian Church in China is such an infilling of God's Spirit as shall fit it for the great task of evangelizing the entire Chinese race.

Arthur H. Smith, *The Uplift of China*, 1907.

By "funded civilization" are meant the material results of the vast development of Western progress. It includes the manifold marvels resulting from steam and electricity. This, we are told, is what China really needs, and it is all that she needs. Railways from every city to every other city, steam navigation on her inland waters, a complete postal system, national banks, coined silver, telegraphs and telephones as nerves of connection—these are to be the visible signs of the new and happy day for China.

Perhaps this was the half-formed idea of Chang Chih-tung, when in his memorial on the subject of railways he affirmed that they will do away with many risks incidental to river transport, "such as stealing by the crews." Will the accumulation, then, of funded civilization diminish moral evils? Do railways ensure honesty in their employees, or even in their managers? . . . Is funded civilization an original cause by itself, or is it the effect of a long train of complex causes, working in slow harmony for great periods of time? Would the introduction of the ballot box into China make the Chinese a democratic people, and fit them for republican rule? No more will funded civilization produce in the Chinese Empire those conditions which accompany it in the West, unless the causes which have produced the conditions in the West are set in motion to produce the like results in China. Those causes are not material, they are moral.

Failure To Follow Western Models

How is it that with the object-lessons of Hong Kong, of Shanghai and other treaty ports before them, the Chinese do not introduce "model settlements" into the native cities of China? Because they do not wish for such changes, and would not tolerate them if they were introduced. How is it that with the object-lesson of an honest administration of the Imperial Maritime Customs before their eyes for nearly a third of a century, the government does not adopt such methods elsewhere? Because, in the present condition of China, the adoption of such methods of taxation of Chinese by Chinese is an absolute moral impossibility. British character and conscience have been more than a thousand years in attaining their present development, and they cannot be suddenly taken up by the Chinese for their own, and set in operation, like a Krupp gun from Essen, mounted and ready to be discharged.

The Need for Christianity

The forces which have developed character and conscience in the Anglo-Saxon race are as definite and as certain facts of history as the landing of Julius Caesar in Britain, or the invasion of William the Conqueror. These forces came with Christianity, and they grew with Christianity. In proportion as Christianity roots itself in the popular heart these products flourish, and not otherwise. . . .

In order to reform China the springs of character must be reached and purified, conscience must be practically enthroned and no longer imprisoned in its own palace like the long line of Japanese Mikados. It is a truth well stated by one of the leading exponents of modern philosophy, that "there is no alchemy by which to get golden conduct from leaden instincts." What China needs is righteousness, and in order to attain it, it is absolutely necessary that she have a knowledge of God and a new conception of man, as well as of the relation of man to God. She needs a new life in every individual soul, in the family, and in society. The manifold needs of China we find, then, to be a single imperative need. It will be met permanently, completely, only by Christian civilization.

"The Nationalist Revolution is the only upright and bright road."

Nationalism Can Revitalize China

Chiang Kai-shek

Chiang Kai-shek became leader of the Kuomintang, or Nationalist party, following the death in 1925 of founder Sun Yat-sen. He wrote the following viewpoint in 1943, at a time when China was locked into war with the Japanese who had invaded China in 1937. Chiang was fighting not only Japanese invaders, but also the Communists under Mao Zedong who had established themselves in northern China. In the following viewpoint, Chiang attacks the Communists as "feudal warlords" who hinder China's development, and calls for support of the "Three People's Principles" of Nationalism, Democracy and the People's Livelihood.

As you read, consider the following questions:

1. What does the author believe is crucial for China's "national reconstruction"?
2. How does Chiang depict the Communists?
3. What is Chiang's attitude toward democracy?

Chiang Kai-shek, *China's Destiny*. New York: Roy Publishers, 1947.

Five thousand years ago, the Chinese nation established itself on the continent of Asia. Other states established five thousand years ago are now only matters of historical record. China is not merely the only ancient state still in existence, but also, in company with other peace-loving and anti-aggressor states, is fighting an unprecedented war for justice and righteousness, and for the freedom and liberation of mankind. We are now advancing on the broad road to a brilliant victory and everlasting peace. . . .

During the last hundred years, China's national position and the morale of the people deteriorated to such an extent that an unprecedented situation developed. Territories required for the survival of the Chinese nation experienced the painful process of partition. The oppression and bondage of the unequal treaties further undermined the vitality of the Chinese state and the nation. A survey of our long history of five thousand years reveals the alternative rise and fall of states and the survival and extinction of nations. Yet the national decay during the last hundred years reached a point unequaled in our history. The state and the nation became weakened and encountered inner crises in the political, economic, social, ethical, and psychological spheres, until the basis of rebirth and recovery was almost destroyed.

Sun Yat-sen and the KMT

If the Father of our Country [Sun Yat-sen] had not promoted the Three People's Principles and led our National Revolution, China would have suffered the same fate as Korea, and would have been swallowed up by the Japanese invaders with their methods of "nibbling like a silkworm or swallowing like a whale." Fortunately, Sun Yat-sen, with his prophetic foresight, applied his great courage and wisdom to the task of establishing China's freedom and equality, and of arousing the whole nation. He fought for forty years, directing the common aspirations of all the Chinese people into the right channels. On his deathbed, he designated the abolition of the unequal treaties as the first objective of the Chinese Nationalist Revolution, and left to us, the comrades who survived him, and to the citizens of the entire country, the accomplishment of this great task. We have continued to fight till this day, and have finally succeeded in the first step. Thus the opportunity for the recovery of the nation and the hope of the rebirth of the state are now presented to the citizens of the entire country. I, Chiang Kai-shek, have been identified from the beginning with restarting the Republic of China on the road to independence and freedom. . . .

The Need for Social Transformation

It is clear that the success or failure of national reconstruction hinges upon the transformation of social customs and public morale. This transformation depends upon those people in the villages, counties, provinces, and the whole country that have knowledge, will power, determination, and a sense of responsibility. They must assume leadership and cause the people to carry out their mission constantly and unquestioningly, so that the successful reform of social customs may be achieved. . . .

I want here to carry this discussion a step further. It should be understood that the transformation of social customs and public morale and the practical work of national reconstruction are the most important enterprises in the rehabilitation of the nation, and require constant effort. If a single individual struggles along in isolation, his achievements cannot be great or enduring. Therefore, all adult citizens and ambitious young men in every village, district, province, and the entire country must be part of a common structure and a general organization for national reconstruction and individual effort. Only when each individual works within such a general organization can we accomplish what Sun Yat-sen described as: ''Use each individual's few years of mortal life to establish the immortal foundation for the countless ages of the state.''

From *20th Century China* by Edmund Clubb. Copyright © 1978 Columbia University Press. Used by permission.

If China's adult citizens cannot unite on a large scale, our unity cannot long endure, and we shall experience the humiliation and shame of being a "pan of loose sand" and be laughed at for our "five minutes of boiling blood." We should recognize that if we cannot unite together, it is because of selfishness, and that in order to avoid selfishness, there is nothing better than to become public spirited. When unity cannot long endure, it is because of dishonesty, and to avoid dishonesty nothing is better than being sincere. A single thought directed toward the public good will enable us to reach the stage of "all men are brothers and oneness with all things." A single thought of sincerity will enable us to see clearly through a project from beginning to end. And only the Three People's Principles are based upon absolute public good and developed from absolute sincerity. Thus the ideology of the Kuomintang is all-embracing, and the activities of the Kuomintang are "a choice of the best and a retention of the original.". . .

China's Destiny

Although the people of the entire country already understand the movement to avenge the national humiliation and make the state strong, there are still divergent views as to the direction to be followed in national reconstruction and in the establishment of private enterprises. We have today attained the first step in the abolition of the unequal treaties, and the accomplishment of the Three People's Principles and the Nationalist Revolution is now an immediate prospect. I think that, beginning today, patriots of all groups that have the will to revolution ought to think deeply, subject themselves to a thorough self-examination, and then shoulder to shoulder and hand in hand, go forward with faith in the Three People's Principles, join the Kuomintang, and become close and sincere comrades. It should be recognized that the present is an opportunity that occurs "only once in a thousand years," but it is also without question a situation so critical that it may be likened to "an enormous weight hanging by a single hair." Speaking specifically, China's former destiny, her rise or fall, her prosperity or decay, depended upon whether or not the unequal treaties could be abolished. But now that the unequal treaties have been abolished, China's destiny hereafter will depend upon whether or not internal politics can be unified, and whether or not the strength of the state can be centralized. In other words, China's destiny formerly depended upon external affairs, and was controlled by foreign imperialists. But her destiny hereafter depends entirely on internal affairs, and rests in the hands of our entire citizenry. If our internal affairs are unified, if the strength of our state is centralized, and if, in addition, all the citizens can join in a united effort, then China's destiny may be epitomized by the following words: "Be sincere and united, uphold the

Government and obey the law"; and in that event, China's destiny will be independence and liberty. Otherwise it will be epitomized by another set of words: "Cheating, dishonesty, violation of the law, and chaos," and will be characterized by a return to feudal warlordism and military partitioning, thus destroying unity and preventing reconstruction. In such an event, China's destiny will decline and become extinct. China will not merely continue to be a subcolony, but the descendants of the Chinese nation for generations to come will be perpetually enslaved, with no chance to regain independence and with no hope for revival. . . .

Great Difficulties Make a Nation

For the rebirth of a people certain factors are necessary. Of these one is that the people should go through a period of trials and tribulations.

The most important, however, is that the people must have full confidence in their national destiny. The possession of such confidence makes them aware of their responsibility and gives them strength to carry out their historic mission.

The Chinese have a culture and a history of more than five thousand years. They are now being threatened with extinction by the ruthless aggression of Japan. In this unprecedented crisis, their national spirit has risen to the occasion: the longer they fight, the more determined becomes their will to survive and conquer.

The ancients have a saying: "Great difficulties make a nation." How true this is! Out of her tribulations and suffering, China will surely emerge a stronger nation. This is the conviction in the heart of every true son of China, as it is also the belief of everybody the world over.

Chiang Kai-shek, *China Shall Rise Again*, 1940.

My Compatriots! With the survival or destruction of the state, and the happiness or misfortune of the nation thus clearly placed before us, we must choose our course now. The international situation and the trend of the times do not permit us to hesitate and remain undecided. Therefore, our whole citizenry, particularly those revolutionary fighters that wish to serve the state for the sake of independence and freedom for the nation, for the elimination of our humiliation, for strengthening the state, and for the sake of preventing future generations from falling into the tragic condition of slavery, should all join together within the Kuomintang in order to fulfill our responsibilities and duties. . . .

So long as the Kuomintang remains in existence, so long will China continue to exist. If China today did not have the Kuomintang, there would be no China. Had the Revolution of the Kuomintang been defeated, it would have meant the complete defeat of the Chinese state. Briefly speaking, China's destiny rests entirely with the Kuomintang. If there was no Kuomintang, or if the Kuomintang should fail in its task, China would have nothing on which to depend. Without the Kuomintang, not only would China not have been one of the four Great Powers in the world, but she would certainly have been partitioned by the other powers, and the name of China would not be seen on the map of the world.

We should all recognize, therefore, that from the standpoint of the state's organic life, if there had been no Three People's Principles, China's work of national reconstruction would have lost its guiding principle. Thus, the Three People's Principles are the soul of the state. From the standpoint of the state's organic activity, if there was no Kuomintang, China's work of national reconstruction would have lost its motivating power. The Kuomintang is, therefore, the state's blood stream [artery], and the *San Min Chu I* Youth Corps provides the new corpuscles in that blood stream. If all the revolutionary elements and the ambitious youth of the country really wish to live and die with the state, share the glory and humiliation with the nation, regard the enterprise of the state as their own enterprise, and the life of the nation as their own life, they should, as a body, join the Kuomintang and the *San Min Chu I* Youth Corps. Only then can they fulfill a citizen's supreme responsibility and attain the most well-rounded life. And only then can we fulfill our great mission of jointly building the state. . . .

I believe that if we all take an objective attitude toward the Kuomintang, use the facts of past history as evidence and analyze it in the light of the present changeable international situation, and examine it in reference to the country's future, we shall then realize that in China only the Three People's Principles constitute a comprehensive and profound ideology; that the Nationalist Revolution is the only upright and bright road; and that, furthermore, the Kuomintang was the motivating power that guided the Revolution and founded the Republic, and is now the main artery for the revival of the Chinese nation and the building of the state.

The Communist Traitors

Aside from this, during the period of military rule and political tutelage, those that endeavor to organize armed forces and to partition territory, no matter under what name or with whatever strategy, may be described if not as warlords, then at the very least as feudal. Are those disguised warlords and new feudalists beneficial or harmful to the nation and to the Revolution? Everyone severely condemned those that formerly controlled armies and the territory-grabbing warlords as counter-revolutionary. Can we now call these disguised warlords and new feudalists genuine revolutionaries? If the anti-revolutionary forces based upon the partition of territories by force and feudal warlordism remain in existence for a single day, then for that day the politics of the state cannot be placed on the right track and the period of military rule also cannot be ended. Not only is there no way to inaugurate the period of constitutional government, but the work of political tutelage also cannot be carried out. The hindrance and damage to the state and the Revolution caused by such a situation is immeasurable.

The Need for Nationalism

What is the standing of our nation in the world? In comparison with other nations we have the greatest population and the oldest culture, of four thousands years' duration. We ought to be advancing in line with the nations of Europe and America. But the Chinese people have only family and clan groups; there is no national spirit. Consequently, in spite of four hundred million people gathered together in one China, we are in fact but a sheet of loose sand. We are the poorest and weakest state in the world, occupying the lowest position in international affairs; the rest of mankind is the carving knife and the serving dish, while we are the fish and the meat. Our position now is extremely perilous; if we do not earnestly promote nationalism and weld together our four hundred millions into a strong nation, we face a tragedy—the loss of our country and the destruction of our race. To ward off this danger, we must espouse Nationalism and employ the national spirit to save the country.

Sun Yat-sen, *The Three Principles of the People*, 1924.

Moreover, the Great Powers—Soviet Russia, Great Britain, the United States, and other nations—all hope that our nation will be liberated and become progressive; that our state will become independent and free. Therefore, they have voluntarily agreed to relinquish the special privileges and extensive influence that they had enjoyed for the past hundred years under the unequal treaties. How is it then that our own internal parties and groups are not willing to abandon their evil habits of partitioning territory by armed force and give up their attitude of feudal warlordism? How can they still be called Chinese citizens? How can they be spoken of as a political party? In what country in the world is there a political party that follows a policy of armed force and illegal seizure of territory, obstructs the unification of its own country, and prevents the governmental system from entering upon its proper course? Is this not counter-revolutionary? Is it not an obstacle to the Revolution? If such obstacles to the Revolution are not voluntarily withdrawn, will they not ruin the state and harm the nation? They will not only ruin the state and harm the nation, but eventually will ruin themselves by ruining others.

I have always maintained that the Nationalist Government should adopt a lenient attitude toward all various opinions and disagreements within the country, and should seek to harmonize them through reasonable methods. But if there is no willingness thoroughly to alter the habit of feudal warlordism, and abandon completely the partition of territory by force of arms, then no matter how lenient our attitude may be, it cannot produce any result and no reasonable solution can be found. I believe that we are all patriots who love our country, and that no matter how much we may have fought each other in the past, there is no reason why we cannot give up our personal prejudices and animosities for the sake of the life of the state and the future of the nation. This would allow our internal politics to be unified and our Government to proceed along the right road, so that foreigners would not look down upon us as a backward nation and inferior people. . . .

A Time for Unity

We revolutionaries must speak the truth and perform real work. We should always remember the saying: "Sincere reproofs grate on the ears, and good medicine is bitter to the mouth." You who gather together in organizations that purport to be revolutionary but in fact destroy the Revolution, that purport to be patriotic but in fact injure the country, are not only harming the state and the nation and injuring the revolutionary reconstruction of the state, but are also harming your own futures and dooming your personal enterprises to failure. I wish most honestly and frankly to warn everyone again: If you cling to your old habits and maintain your past attitude, you will only obstruct your own future, hinder your own enterprise, prevent the strength of the state from being completely centralized, and the work of national reconstruction from being satisfactorily carried out. This will not be of the slightest benefit to you and will cause incalculable damage to the state and the nation. We should realize that today the destiny of our country hangs in the balance between life and death. Not a single person can be permitted to throw himself away; not a single ounce of strength can be wasted. I hope, therefore, that everyone, for the benefit of the state and the survival of the nation, with one mind and one purpose, will join together with faith in the Three People's Principles, and unite together within the organization of the Kuomintang.

"Except for the Communist Party, no political party . . . is equal to the task of leading China's two great revolutions."

Communism Can Revitalize China

Mao Zedong

Mao Zedong was the leader of the Chinese Communist party. He defeated the forces of Chinese leader Chiang Kai-shek and became leader of China in 1949. Mao ruled until his death in 1976. The following viewpoint was written in 1939 when Mao was leading the Communist party against the Japanese and Chiang Kai-shek's Nationalists from his base in northern China. In the following viewpoint Mao summarizes his view of Chinese history and his vision of China under Communist rule. He argues that traditional Chinese culture has exploited the majority of China's people, and that it must be replaced with the new ideology of Communism.

As you read, consider the following questions:

1. What are the characteristics of traditional Chinese society, according to the author?
2. What was the impact of imperialism, according to Mao?
3. What kinds of revolutions does Mao describe?

Mao Zedong, "The Chinese Revolution and the Chinese Communist Party" (December 1939), *Selected Works*, II. Beijing: Foreign Language Press. Reprinted with permission.

Although China is a great nation and although she is a vast country with an immense population, a long history, a rich revolutionary tradition and a splendid historical heritage, her economic, political and cultural development was sluggish for a long time after the transition from slave to feudal society. This feudal society, beginning with the Chou and Chin Dynasties, lasted about 3,000 years.

The Feudal Society

The main features of the economic and political system of China's feudal era were as follows:

(1) A self-sufficient natural economy predominated. The peasants produced for themselves not only agricultural products but most of the handicraft articles they needed. What the landlords and the nobility exacted from them in the form of land rent was also chiefly for private enjoyment and not for exchange. Although exchange developed as time went on, it did not play a decisive role in the economy as a whole.

(2) The feudal ruling class composed of landlords, the nobility and the emperor owned most of the land, while the peasants had very little or none at all. The peasants tilled the land of the landlords, the nobility and the royal family with their own farm implements and had to turn over to them for their private enjoyment 40, 50, 60, 70, or even 80 per cent or more of the crop. In effect the peasants were still serfs.

(3) Not only did the landlords, the nobility and the royal family live on rent extorted from the peasants, but the landlord state also exacted tribute, taxes and *corvee* services from them to support a horde of government officials and an army which was used mainly for their repression.

(4) The feudal landlord state was the organ of power protecting this system of feudal exploitation. . . .

It was under such feudal economic exploitation and political oppression that the Chinese peasants lived like slaves, in poverty and suffering, through the ages. Under the bondage of feudalism they had no freedom of person. The landlord had the right to beat, abuse or even kill them at will, and they had no political rights whatsoever. The extreme poverty and backwardness of the peasants resulting from ruthless landlord exploitation and oppression is the basic reason why Chinese society remained at the same stage of socio-economic development for several thousand years.

The principal contradiction in feudal society was between the peasantry and the landlord class.

The peasants and the handicraft workers were the basic classes which created the wealth and culture of this society.

The ruthless economic exploitation and political oppression of the Chinese peasants forced them into numerous uprisings against landlord rule. There were hundreds of uprisings, great and small, all of them peasant revolts or peasant revolutionary wars. . . . The scale of peasant uprisings and peasant wars in Chinese history has no parallel anywhere else. The class struggles of the peasants, the peasant uprisings and peasant wars constituted the real motive force of historical development in Chinese feudal society. For each of the major peasant uprisings and wars dealt a blow to the feudal regime of the time, and hence more or less furthered the growth of the social productive forces. However, since neither new productive forces, nor new relations of production, nor new class forces, nor any advanced political party existed in those days, the peasant uprisings and wars did not have correct leadership such as the proletariat and the Communist Party provide today; every peasant revolution failed, and the peasantry was invariably used by the landlords and the nobility, either during or after the revolution, as a lever for bringing about dynastic change. Therefore, although some social progress was made after each great peasant revolutionary struggle, the feudal economic relations and political system remained basically unchanged.

It is only in the last hundred years that a change of a different order has taken place.

Social Contradictions

The contradiction between imperialism and the Chinese nation and the contradiction between feudalism and the great masses of the people are the basic contradictions in modern Chinese society. . . . These contradictions and their intensification must inevitably result in the incessant growth of revolutionary movements. The great revolutions in modern and contemporary China have emerged and grown on the basis of these basic contradictions.

Mao Zedong, *The Chinese Revolution and the Chinese Communist Party*, 1939.

As explained above, Chinese society remained feudal for 3,000 years. But is it still completely feudal today? No, China has changed. After the Opium War of 1840 China gradually changed into a semi-colonial and semi-feudal society. Since the Incident of September 18, 1931, when the Japanese imperialists started their armed aggression, China has changed further into a colonial, semi-colonial and semi-feudal society. We shall now describe the course of this change.

Chinese feudal society lasted for about 3,000 years. It was not until the middle of the 19th century, with the penetration of foreign capitalism, that great changes took place in Chinese society. . . .

It is certainly not the purpose of the imperalist powers invading

China to transform feudal China into capitalist China. On the contrary, their purpose is to transform China into their own semi-colony or colony.

China Is a Colony

To this end the imperialist powers have used and continue to use military, political, economic and cultural means of oppression, so that China has gradually become a semi-colony and colony. They are as follows:

(1) The imperialist powers have waged many wars of aggression against China, for instance, the Opium War launched by Britain in 1840, the war launched by the Anglo-French allied forces in 1857, the Sino-French War of 1884, the Sino-Japanese War of 1894, and the war launched by the allied forces of the eight powers in 1900. After defeating China in war, they not only occupied many neighbouring countries formerly under her protection, but seized or "leased" parts of her territory....

(2) The imperialist powers have forced China to sign numerous unequal treaties by which they have acquired the right to station land and sea forces and exercise consular jurisdiction in China, and they have carved up the whole country into imperialist spheres of influence.

(3) The imperialist powers have gained control of all the important trading ports in China by these unequal treaties and have marked off areas in many of these ports as concessions under their direct administration. They have also gained control of China's customs, foreign trade and communications (sea, land, inland water and air). Thus they have been able to dump their goods in China, turn her into a market for their industrial products, and at the same time subordinate her agriculture to their imperialist needs.

(4) The imperialist powers operate many enterprises in both light and heavy industry in China in order to utilize her raw materials and cheap labour on the spot, and they thereby directly exert economic pressure on China's national industry and obstruct the development of her productive forces.

(5) The imperialist powers monopolize China's banking and finance by extending loans to the Chinese government and establishing banks in China. Thus they have not only overwhelmed China's national capitalism in commodity competition, they have also secured a stranglehold on her banking and finance.

(6) The imperialist powers have established a network of comprador and merchant-usurer exploitation right across China, from the trading ports to the remote hinterland, and have created a comprador and merchant-usurer class in their service, so as to facilitate their exploitation of the masses of the Chinese peasantry and other sections of the people.

(7) The imperialist powers have made the feudal landlord class as well as the comprador class the main props of their rule in China. . . .

(8) The imperialist powers supply the reactionary government with large quantities of munitions and a host of military advisers, in order to keep the warlords fighting among themselves and to suppress the Chinese people.

(9) Furthermore, the imperialist powers have never slackened their efforts to poison the minds of the Chinese people. This is their policy of cultural aggression. And it is carried out through missionary work, through establishing hospitals and schools, publishing newspapers and inducing Chinese students to study abroad. Their aim is to train intellectuals who will serve their interests and to dupe the people.

(10) Since September 18, 1931, the large-scale invasion of Japanese imperialism has turned a big chunk of semi-colonial China into a Japanese colony.

The Need for Communism

Communism is at once a complete system of proletarian ideology and a new social system. It is different from any other ideology or social system, and is the most complete, progressive, revolutionary and rational system in human history. The ideological and social system of feudalism has a place only in the museum of history. The ideological and social system of capitalism has also become a museum piece in one part of the world (in the Soviet Union), while in other countries it resembles "a dying person who is sinking fast, like the sun setting beyond the western hills", and will soon be relegated to the museum. The communist ideological and social system alone is full of youth and vitality, sweeping the world with the momentum of an avalanche and the force of a thunderbolt. The introduction of scientific communism into China has opened new vistas for people and has changed the face of the Chinese revolution. Without communism to guide it, China's democratic revolution cannot possibly succeed, let alone move on to the next stage. This is the reason why the bourgeois die-hards are so loudly demanding that communism be "folded up". But it must not be "folded up", for once communism is "folded up", China will be doomed. The whole world today depends on communism for its salvation, and China is no exception.

Mao Zedong, *On New Democracy*, 1940.

These facts represent the other aspect of the change that has taken place since the imperialist penetration of China—the blood-stained picture of feudal China being reduced to semi-feudal, semi-colonial and colonial China.

It is thus clear that in their aggression against China the imperialist powers have on the one hand hastened the disintegration of feudal society and the growth of elements of capitalism, thereby transforming a feudal into a semi-feudal society, and on the other imposed their ruthless rule on China, reducing an independent country to a semi-colonial and colonial country. . . .

The Kuomintang

The national revolutionary struggle of the Chinese people has a history of fully one hundred years counting from the Opium War of 1840, or of thirty years counting from the Revolution of 1911. It has not yet run its full course, nor has it yet performed its tasks with any signal success; therefore the Chinese people, and above all the Communist Party, must shoulder the responsibility of resolutely fighting on. . . .

The Chinese bourgeoisie, which is also a victim of imperialist oppression, once led or played a principal role in revolutionary struggles such as the Revolution of 1911, and has participated in revolutionary struggles such as the Northern Expedition and the present War of Resistance Against Japan. In the long period from 1927 to 1937, however, its upper stratum, namely, the section represented by the reactionary clique within the Kuomintang, collaborated with imperialism, formed a reactionary alliance with the landlord class, betrayed the friends who had helped it—the Communist Party, the proletariat, the peasantry and other sections of the petty bourgeoisie—betrayed the Chinese revolution and brought about its defeat. At that time, therefore, the revolutionary people and the revolutionary political party (the Communist Party) could not but regard these bourgeois elements as one of the targets of the revolution. . . .

The Tasks of the Chinese Revolution

Imperialism and the feudal landlord class being the chief enemies of the Chinese revolution at this stage, what are the present tasks of the revolution?

Unquestionably, the main tasks are to strike at these two enemies, to carry out a national revolution to overthrow foreign imperialist oppression and a democratic revolution to overthrow feudal landlord oppression, the primary and foremost task being the national revolution to overthrow imperialism.

These two great tasks are interrelated. Unless imperialist rule is overthrown, the rule of the feudal landlord class cannot be terminated, because imperialism is its main support. Conversely, unless help is given to the peasants in their struggle to overthrow the feudal landlord class, it will be impossible to build powerful revolutionary contingents to overthrow imperialist rule, because the feudal landlord class is the main social base of imperialist rule in China and the peasantry is the main force in the Chinese revolution. Therefore the two fundamental tasks, the national revolution and the democratic revolution, are at once distinct and united. . . .

Why China Needs Communism

To complete China's bourgeois-democratic revolution (the new-democratic revolution) and to transform it into a socialist revolution when all the necessary conditions are ripe—such is the sum total of the great and glorious revolutionary task of the Chinese Communist Party. Every Party member must strive for its accomplishment and must under no circumstances give up halfway. Some immature Communists think that our task is confined to the present democratic revolution and does not include the future socialist revolution, or that the present revolution or the Agrarian Revolution is actually a socialist revolution. It must be emphatically pointed out that these views are wrong. Every Communist ought to know that, taken as a whole, the Chinese revolutionary movement led by the Communist Party embraces the two stages, *i.e.*, the democratic and the socialist revolutions, which are two essentially different revolutionary processes, and that the second process can be carried through only after the first has been completed. The democratic revolution is the necessary preparation for the socialist revolution, and the socialist revolution is the inevitable sequel to the democratic revolution. The ultimate aim for which all communists strive is to bring about a socialist and communist society. A clear understanding of both the differences and the interconnections between the democratic and the socialist revolutions is indispensable to correct leadership in the Chinese revolution.

Except for the Communist Party, no political party (bourgeois or petty-bourgeois) is equal to the task of leading China's two great revolutions, the democratic and the socialist revolutions, to complete fulfillment. From the very day of its birth, the Communist Party has taken this twofold task on its own shoulders and for eighteen years has fought strenuously for its accomplishment.

It is a task at once glorious and arduous. And it cannot be accomplished without a bolshevized Chinese Communist Party which is national in scale and has a broad mass character, a party fully consolidated ideologically, politically and organizationally. Therefore every Communist has the duty of playing an active part in building up such a Communist Party.

Distinguishing Primary from Secondary Sources

A critical thinker must always question sources of information. One important question historians ask is whether their information comes from *primary* or *secondary* sources.

Primary sources are firsthand or eyewitness accounts of events and usually appear in the form of personal letters, documents, or speeches. Secondary sources are usually based on one or more primary sources, and can appear in newspapers, encyclopedias, and similar types of publications. A letter from a nineteenth-century missionary in China describing the town in which he or she lives is an example of a primary source. A book examining the lives and attitudes of Chinese missionaries would be an example of a secondary source.

This activity is designed to test your skills in distinguishing between primary and secondary sources. Listed below are a number of possible sources concerning China's efforts to modernize. *Place a P next to those descriptions you believe are primary sources. Place an S next to those you believe are secondary sources.*

If you are doing this activity as a member of a class or group, discuss and compare your evaluation with other members of the group. If you are reading this book alone, you may want to ask others if they agree with your evaluation.

P = *primary*
S = *secondary*

1. A collection of letters written by a missionary's wife about a Chinese village.

2. A history of China written by an American professor who was born and raised in China by missionary parents.

3. An 1839 British newspaper's account of the Opium War.

4. Text of the treaty signed after the first Opium War.

5. A speech by Mao Zedong on foreign imperialism and the Opium War.

6. The autobiography of Henry Pu-yi, China's last emperor.

7. The film *The Last Emperor*, in which the life of Henry Pu-yi is depicted.

8. Viewpoint 1 in this chapter.

9. An analysis compiled by a study group at Harvard University which examines US relations with China during Chiang Kai-shek's rule.

10. A critique of Sun Yat-sen's *Three Principles of the People*.

11. Official report of the first Chinese Communist Party meeting in 1921.

12. An Emperor's edict in 1901 calling for educational reform.

13. Wall posters put up in 1900 calling for the removal of foreigners from China.

14. A Japanese account of China's 1911 revolution.

15. A book by a British professor called *China and the West, 1840-1900*.

16. Edgar Snow's *Red Star over China*, a 1938 book based on his visits to the Chinese communist leadership in Yanan.

17. Newsreel film from 1939 covering the Sino-Japanese War.

18. Viewpoint 5 in this chapter.

2 CHAPTER

Are China's Economic Reforms Significant?

Chapter Preface

In 1967, at the beginning of the Cultural Revolution, Deng Xiaoping was removed from power by Mao Zedong and publicly ly denounced as a "capitalist roader," a person who would betray China's communist revolution. After Mao's death in 1976, Deng maneuvered himself back into power and began to foster reforms in China's economy that to some people proved Mao's fear to be well-founded. Today many people in China and America are debating the economic and social changes China has made in recent years.

Some of the reforms Deng has introduced include the dismantling of the large rural communes; the rise of markets where peasants can sell their excess produce directly to consumers; the end of the "iron rice bowl" system of guaranteed lifetime employment by the state; the attempt to reduce government control of industry; the relaxation of constraints on private enterprises; the encouragement of foreign trade and investment; and the reopening of stock markets.

These changes have been praised by many Chinese who have seen their living standards rise, by many Americans excited by the prospect of a communist country embracing capitalism, and by foreign investors with an eye on the large China market. The reforms have not been without critics, however, both in and out of China. Some observers have argued that China's reforms are superficial—that the government is paying lip service to capitalist free market strategies while maintaining bureaucratic control of the economy. Other critics have been blamed capitalism for ills that have befallen China, including inflation, unemployment, and social inequality.

The authors in the following chapter debate both the intent and impact of China's economic reforms.

58

"I believe that China will be the first communist state ever to revert to capitalism."

China's Reforms Are Significant

Charles R. Smith

China's recent economic reforms have led some people to believe that China is evolving from communism to capitalism. In the following viewpoint, Charles R. Smith examines such reforms as the development of privately-owned businesses, decollectivized agriculture, a stock market, and business management courses. He concludes that China is moving toward a capitalist system. Smith is publisher of *The China Newsletter*, a Hong Kong-based monthly newsletter that analyzes Chinese affairs.

As you read, consider the following questions:

1. What examples of Chinese capitalism does Smith describe?
2. According to the author, why has China changed its economic system?
3. Why does the author believe that China will continue its reforms?

Charles R. Smith, "Down the Capitalist Road," *Reader's Digest*, December 1986. Reprinted with permission.

When peasant Zhang Xiangheng began growing medicinal herbs on his private plot in Hubei Province, his annual income jumped to more than 2300 renminbi ($1200), about five times the average in China. Appalled by such capitalistic excess, more than 1000 locals gathered at a mass-accusation rally to denounce Zhang. However, *People's Daily,* the Communist Party's official newspaper, rallied to his defense, declaring: "The more peasants like Zhang there are, the better off we will be."

Authorities in a village in Jiangsu Province decided the neighborhood needed a new hotel. Their novel financing method could not have been more capitalistic: sell shares to the villagers. According to press reports, tens of thousands of farmers lined up to apply for share allocations. The "novel" idea caught on. A few months ago, the first stock exchange since 1949 opened in Shanghai.

In Beijing, China's capital, free markets flourish. A short walk from the mausoleum housing Communist Party Chairman Mao Zedong's body, one can see peasants and workers selling fruit and vegetables, clothing, homemade kitchenware. As *The China Letter* recently put it: "Roll over, Chairman Mao!"

Going Capitalist

I believe that China will be the first communist state ever to revert to capitalism. Because such sweeping change cannot be made overnight—even in a dictatorship—most of China is still communist. But communism in the People's Republic is yesterday's idea. Though still ritually invoking Lenin's name, Beijing has mobilized the formidable force of Chinese nationalism in support of one of the most dramatic turnarounds in history. "While political reforms lag behind liberal economic reforms," notes economist Jude Wanniski, "there is exciting promise for the future."

China is altering its economic approach so drastically because the Chinese leadership has learned an economics lesson the hard way. For 28 years, Mao waged a war against the principles of a free economy—and lost badly. He sought to prove that a billion people, denied financial incentives, would nevertheless labor harder for the state than Westerners work for themselves. The result was one of history's worst examples of national self-damage.

According to a Western diplomat, by the time Mao died in 1976, production figures had plummeted and one-quarter of China's state-owned enterprises were losing money. Grain production, for example, was less than it had been two decades earlier, forcing China to spend about $1 billion on food imports, money that would have been better used to buy productive machinery. Millions were unemployed, and average income had dropped significantly.

Taking somber stock of the Mao era, the nation's ruling group turned to their most prominent anti-Maoist, Deng Xiaoping. Deng had been purged, then reinstated, from high Party standing so often that he had come to be called "the iron yo-yo."

Under Mao, a favored slogan was: "Better a poor society under socialism than a rich society under capitalism."

"That's absurd!" said Deng. "Who cares whether a cat is black or white? So long as it catches mice, it's a good cat!"

Once in power, Deng carried out some economic experiments in his native Sichuan, China's largest province. "It doesn't matter if we put profits in command a little," he explained. Beginning in 1978, Sichuan factories were free to retain some profits and spend them as they saw fit; they could also hire their own workers, reward them, and fire lazy or redundant staff.

The Second Step

It cannot be said that China has been transformed from a socialist into a capitalist country. However, it can be stated that in order to carry out its development, China has decided to accept ideas and try methods that are typical of capitalism. . . .

Deng Xiaoping and his disciples realize that the first step in the modernization of China was the agrarian revolution carried out by Mao, which triumphed at the end of the 1940s. But they believe that the second step will be the reforms they advocate, which encourage private initiative as a means toward prosperity and progress. This is the motor that has propelled economies of other nations in the Far East that are very close to China not only geographically but also culturally and ethnically.

Enrique Chirinos Soto, *World Press Review*, January 1988.

Most factories slipped into higher gear immediately. Learning that China was about to buy oil pipes from foreign suppliers, the Seamless Steel Tube Plant in Chengdu, Sichuan's capital, began making the pipes with its unused capacity. Part of the factory's extra revenues from this new market went into steelworkers' bonuses—22 percent of the average annual salary (and more than 60 percent for one workaholic employee).

The Sichuan Experiment

Since 80 percent of Chinese work on the land, the experiment was extended to agriculture. In 1980, Sichuan Province made an extra 822,000 acres of land available to its peasants to add to their small, "private plots" and farm as they wished.

In the first year of the "Sichuan Experiment," profits from "reformed" or quasi-capitalist factories were up 24 percent, compared with 14 percent for "unreformed" enterprises. During Mao's

Cultural Revolution (1966-76), Sichuan had become a famine-ridden, food-importing province; now its farm lands produce more than 76 million tons of grain annually, twice the province's needs.

The Sichuan Experiment spread through China like a prairie fire. From 1980 to 1985, China's real growth reached 11 percent a year in both agriculture and industry. As light-industrial production took off, a flood of new consumer products changed China's way of life. Overnight, brightly colored clothing replaced the shapeless blue, black, gray or khaki uniforms of former times. In 1978, China produced only about 300 washing machines for home use. By the end of [1985] annual production was more than eight million and rising rapidly.

In Tianjin last May [1986], China's first international department store opened. More than 15,000 foreign products are on display—French shoes, Japanese fishing rods, British bicycles. Familiar U.S. consumer products are part of the avalanche. Coca-Cola, for example, is now available throughout China, even at foodstalls on the Great Wall. And Kentucky Fried Chicken will shortly become the first U.S. fast-food company to have restaurants in the People's Republic.

The Responsibility System

In the 1970s, the inhabitants of Hongqiao commune (now a township) on Shanghai's outskirts suffered all the ills of rural China—irregular food supplies, poverty and little hope for the future. Under the new "responsibility system," the township must still consign a certain amount of its cabbages, tomatoes and other vegetables to the government. Once that quota is filled, however, Hongqiao may sell the rest of its produce for whatever price it can get in Shanghai's free markets.

Meanwhile, Hongqiao's new entrepreneurs have been establishing factories whose products range from export-quality suits to semiconductors. Between 1982 and 1985, the township's agricultural and industrial production tripled.

A Hongqiao woman was recently quoted in *The Asian Wall Street Journal* as saying: "We've seen changes in everything in the past five years. Now we have running water, a television, refrigerator, washing machine. Next we're going to get an air conditioner. Our food is better too—now we can eat like city folk."

No Turning Back

At Dalian in Manchuria, the National Center for Industrial Science and Technology Management Development houses the world's most improbable business school. Outside stands a massive statue of Mao. Over the main staircase inside is a by no means inappropriate exhortation from Karl Marx himself: "Only those who do not fear fatigue can hope to climb to the summit."

In the building's classrooms, high-powered teams of U.S.

business executives and professors offer Chinese managers a 26-week program in business administration called Enterprise Managers. Texts include translations of books ultra-leftists condemn as "poisonous weeds": Adam Smith's *The Wealth of Nations,* Paul Samuelson's *Economics,* Milton and Rose Friedman's *Capitalism and Freedom* and *Free to Choose.*

All this "capitalist roading" does not please die-hard communists. But it seems unlikely there are enough Marxist and Maoist dogmatists remaining in power to prevent it. I would not wish to be the unreconstructed Maoist who tries to tell the people: "Comrades, we're returning to the joyous struggle and poverty of building a New Socialist Man. Forget about saving for those refrigerators!"

The United States and China are very different countries and won't always see eye to eye. But the expansion of Soviet interests in the Asia-Pacific region has brought China and the United States ever closer. Indeed, we regularly exchange intelligence about Soviet activities.

As China continues to embrace capitalism, it will want a world that is safer for economic development. Accordingly, the world will be better off.

"Market freedoms are being used to shore up a fundamentally antimarket system."

China's Reforms Are Superficial

Ross Terrill

Sichuan Province is well-known as one of the centers of China's economic reforms. In the following viewpoint, Ross Terrill describes some of the changes he sees there. He argues that despite the existence of much market activity, the government still maintains economic control, and China as a whole cannot be described as capitalist. He concludes that the future of China's reforms is highly uncertain. Terrill's many books on China include *800,000,000: The Real China* and *The Future of China: After Mao.*

As you read, consider the following questions:

1. What economic activities does Terrill describe? What significance does he attach to them?
2. According to the author, what are the two main innovations in China's economy?
3. What are the limitations of China's economic reforms, according to Terrill?

Ross Terrill, "Penny Capitalism," *The New Republic*, June 16, 1986. Reprinted by permission of THE NEW REPUBLIC, © 1986, The New Republic, Inc.

A freshly painted announcement in the middle of Chongqing, a city of hills and ferries and fog, once Chiang Kaishek's wartime capital, proclaims: "Our company, noting that Chongqing's bus service is inadequate, has obtained new vehicles from Japan, with very soft and comfortable seats, and we are starting to offer buses to the following places. . . ." Such private service companies flourish under China's new economic policies. "Test our service," the announcement ends, and that is just the mood of the Chinese consumer, for whom a choice of products and services is a welcome novelty.

In Chengdu, the Sichuan capital, my driver parks the Toyota by a billboard that reads: LEAVE HOME FOR WORK HAPPILY, RETURN HOME FROM WORK SAFELY. It used to urge: CARRY THROUGH REVOLUTION TO THE END.

A Chinese Market

Balconies are festooned with rust-colored peppers suspended on hooks and clothes drying on sticks. Below them is a flurry of salesmanship. Vendors are eager to sell me everything from the green vegetable *qing cai* to life insurance, toy telephones, and gaudy glazed tiles that reflect a widespread zeal to upgrade one's apartment. Skinned rabbits hang in pathetic stiffness on hooks in the open air. "Buy one, they're cheap," says a grinning boy, promoting his wares as no one does in the half-empty state shops behind the rows of newly built private stalls. Rakish young men in Sichuan-style mustaches and caps worn jauntily at an angle sell black-market cigarettes, successfully driving a rapier of private commerce through the ribs of a ponderous supply mechanism that lags eternally behind demand. Among the movies advertised on the billboards are *Pink Skirts in the Street, You Can Get Rich, Jade Butterfly,* and *Gypsy Boy*.

Here is a photocopy shop, its subversive possibilities forgotten in the rush to satisfy the market. "I wasn't earning enough at my factory job," the proprietor explains, "so I managed to buy a secondhand machine through a friend in a government unit." Copies are 20 cents. People bring job applications, wills, draft contracts, sample exam answers.

A line of people of all ages inches forward to buy lottery tickets. I jostle into position and buy my ticket for 60 cents. This is no small affair: my number is above one million. "First prize is a motorbike," says the attendant, looking very pleased. "The next four lucky numbers receive a 20-inch color TV."

All of this is exciting to one whose China trips used to consist of nodding with glazed eyes at sermons of political rectitude and dodging arrows of "anti-imperialist" indignation.

The countryside of Sichuan, China's most populous province, with 104 million people, is just as business-minded as the cities.

Gary Brookins. Reprinted with special permission of NAS, Inc.

On a drive from Chengdu toward Mount Omei, a famous Buddhist retreat, the narrow, twisting road is alive with commerce. A faded but still-legible sign is painted in white characters on a decrepit barn: IN AGRICULTURE LEARN FROM DAZHAI. For all its relevance now, it might as well be an ad for a New York nightclub. Equality and collective responsibility, the crown jewels of the Dazhai "model," are relics of a mocked past. Today's watchwords are initiative, profit, and *inequality*. If some get rich first, the government argues, others will be able to follow.

I meet one farmer who has grown so wealthy from growing potted plants that he has beggars at his gate. He has just donated 10,000 yuan ($4,000) to the local school system. I meet another newly rich farmer, Mr. Ge Ji, a small sharp-featured man with quick gestures, in a village of the Yi race in southern Sichuan. "Are you the richest man in Zhaojue?" I ask him. "One of the richest," he says with a grin. Ge runs a brick and tile kiln that was handed over to him after it went broke as a state-run unit. This made him a "specialized household"—essentially a family business.

We sit in the living room of his large, mud-walled, tiled home, which like most Yi houses has no windows. In the manner of Yi hospitality, he fetches beer and boiled eggs. Last year Ge and his

66

household of six people took in 32,000 yuan ($12,800), a seven-fold increase over 1982. Net profit was 11,800 yuan, after paying 9,500 yuan to his 34 employees and other outlays—no tax. "Mr. Ge, you've done well, and the government is pleased with you," I say. "Wouldn't China be better off if all the villages moved to a specialized household pattern?"

"If 80 percent did," he replies, "China could become prosperous."

Post-Mao Innovations

The post-Mao rulers of Sichuan, who are proud that Deng Xiaoping is Sichuanese, and who point out that former Chinese premier, Zhao Ziyang, formerly party boss of Sichuan, worked out many of China's reforms on Sichuan soil, are staking the political, social, even cultural future of the province on what the governor sums up for me as a "shift from a self-sufficient to a commercial economy."

There are two main innovations: the mechanism of prices takes the place of some aspects of the previous planning system; and economic units (especially in the countryside) have much more responsibility for choosing what they will produce, husbanding resources, and marketing products. The result is not capitalism— the means of production are not in private hands—but a state-sponsored commercialization. Will the changes stick? Unfortunately, tokenism seems built into the reforms, and market freedoms are being used to shore up a fundamentally antimarket system.

In Chongqing, I chat with an executive of Min Sheng shipping, a revival of a famous pre-Liberation company whose assets were confiscated by the Communists in 1954. "State-owned shipping companies are jealous of us," Mr. Luo tells me, drumming his fingers on a cluttered desk overlooking the Yangzi River. "Sometimes they even try to sabotage us."

Min Sheng has been extremely successful over the past year, and it is expanding like bamboo after spring rain. "We're starting passenger service on the Yangzi," Luo says, referring to the long haul of nearly 2,000 kilometers downstream to Shanghai. "At present, buying boat tickets is hard and slow. We're going to sell tickets by mail. We also found out that people don't like having to eat on the floor. On our boats, food will be taken to your seat or compartment. Our boat staff will be trained in a special school."

To a degree, the more successful the new Min Sheng company is, the greater will be its vulnerability. I ask Mr. Luo if he could be confiscated again. "No, now we are so small," he replies. But what if Min Sheng grows large again?

In Xichange, a warm, flower-bedecked city in southern Sichuan, two businesswomen, Chen and Zhou, aged 17 and 20, sit me down in their tiny but thriving shop on a tree-lined street. They were unable to find jobs on leaving high school. Their solution is "Overseas Chinese Fashion Store," which is full of dresses, rings, and scarves that the proud vendors call "trendy [*shi mao*]."

"Being unemployed is awful," says Zhou, who has painted fingernails and a stylish hairdo. "I hated being dependent on my parents."

"Five of us got together," Chen explains. "An old retired man, two younger men who have other jobs as well, and us two." All five are from families with relatives abroad, and no doubt gained business acumen from their upbringing.

"Our capital was 40,000 yuan ($16,000) when we started last year," Chen continues. "In the first full year we had 7,000 yuan sales and 1,000 yuan profit—70 percent of that goes for our wages." The government has offered them free rent and electricity and no taxes for three years.

Lessons of History

Those steeped in history can recall that whenever Marxist governments get into economic trouble, they seek support from capitalist nations and at the same time allow economic incentives to bail out the failures of socialism. Even Lenin, faced with economic difficulties resulting from his socialist policies, adopted the "New Economic Policy," which allowed elements of free enterprise to enter the Soviet Union's economy. When the economy began to grow, Lenin clamped down on this limited economic freedom, returning to socialist/communist policies while initiating a further tightening in the political sphere.

There is nothing to indicate that the Chinese experience will be any different. . . .

Deng's economic policies have fallen far short of initiating a free market economy in China.

Donald S. Senese, *The Freeman,* July 1987.

I asked her if there is any danger that policies might turn against private businesses. "I don't think so. Not in the short run, anyway—you see the unemployment problem is so great, the government has to encourage such small business." Meanwhile both girls study at night in case they ever need to get into college.

Here are the limitations of Deng's reforms: Min Sheng shipping is safe only as long as it doesn't succeed too well. The two business girls are given freedom because the Communist Party doesn't know any other way to arrest severe urban unemployment.

At times the Communist leaders speak as if scales had just fallen from their eyes. "We made housing a *welfare industry*," cries the governor of Sichuan, "whereas it should be profitable." The mayor of Chongqing sounds like a Texas tycoon railing against too much government regulation: "Rents are too low! There's no incentive to construct housing. Goodness, would *you* build new apartments in Chongqing if it takes, as it would take given present rentals, more than 100 years to recover your investment?" "Look," says Lin Ling, a leading research economist in Chengdu, in a tone of exasperation, "we aren't concerned with the exact differences between socialism and capitalism—we just want economic progress."

Other results of the commercialization of Sichuan are less expected than the undoubted if modest increases in efficiency and prosperity. Public services sag in the countryside. "No one wants to be a teacher anymore," a teacher laments to me. "My three children are interested only in a business career." The decline of political supervision—excellent for economic life—opens the door to crime and delinquency.

Politics and People

The two biggest problems are that politics tugs against economics, and that in China there are simply too many people. The logic of the economic reforms requires an autonomy for the economic sphere. But the Communist guardians fear this would chip away at their political power. "Economic autonomy" means nothing if the central ministries insist on fixing prices, as they sometimes do. Marxist ideas have faded, but the monopoly on power of the Leninist Party has not—so politics, if not a very ideological politics, still dominates every realm of life.

As for the population problem, the Chinese economy has repeatedly grown at a respectable rate only to see the per capita results fall flat because of the high birth rate. Family planning is belatedly starting to take hold, but there are over 500 million more people in China today then when the Communists came to power in 1949. Sheer numbers prevent expectations being realized, which in turn intensifies political control. The Communists take no chances with a disgruntled populace.

When Deng goes, the military—which has been left behind by the new "commercial economy"—will for a time become the cutting edge of political resistance to full-fledged economic reforms. The men and women of the gun tend to favor traditions and security and seniority—all at a discount in the post-Mao era. If the Politburo is split when Deng passes, the military will throw its considerable weight on the side of curbing the "excesses" of the economic reforms.

Surface Changes

Even today, and even in Sichuan, where many of the reforms began, much of the new economic activity remains "penny capitalism": a business spirit, rather than a business system. It is a mere commercial layer upon the face of an unchanged beast—Leninism—just as the boxlike stalls in the city streets are a gaudy mask of commerce hiding the skeletal line of gray stores of state socialism behind them. It seems to many thoughtful Chinese, and to me, that the government is not bent on a fundamental change of economic system, but on hanging on to its own political power by offering bread and circuses to a long-suffering people.

The clear verdict cannot yet be given, because the leaders themselves are focused on method more than on ultimate goal. The vehicle is hurtling but no one is too sure where the road leads. To be sure, Deng's people are fairly openminded. But thus far the world has seen no case of sustained rapid economic growth under a Communist Party's auspices, or of economic change bringing about the dismantling of an established Leninist political system. "Does Deng intend the economic changes to produce political change?" I ask a Chengdu intellectual. "Look," he replies, "if he thought the economic reforms would lead to a change of the political system, he wouldn't have unleashed those reforms."

My try at the lottery in Chengdu was aborted. Before it was time for the draw, the government came out with some new regulations. "Units are using lotteries to make unreasonable profits," says the preamble, "which are then distributed in bonuses for themselves." It goes on to hint that lotteries are a "pollution" from the West. The lottery, like much else in Sichuan, and in the China of 81-year-old Deng Xiaoping, hangs in the balance.

"Our achievements in the last few years have proved the correctness of our policies of reform."

Reforms Have Helped China

Deng Xiaoping

Although he lacks an official title, Deng Xiaoping is viewed by the Chinese and the world as the single most powerful man in China. Deng was general secretary of the Communist Party Central Committee in the 1950s. During China's Cultural Revolution he was disgraced and removed from office in 1967 and again in 1976. He reappeared after Mao Zedong's death in 1976, and by the end of 1978 was recognized by the Chinese press as China's "paramount leader." Under his leadership China embarked on its programs of economic reform. In the following viewpoint, he describes some of these reforms in agriculture, industry, and foreign trade, and concludes that they have helped China's economy and standard of living.

As you read, consider the following questions:

1. Why does Deng believe that reforms were necessary?
2. What does he consider to be the reforms' greatest success?
3. How does Deng evaluate China's trade with other countries?

Deng Xiaoping, "We Shall Speed Up Reform," in *Fundamental Issues in Present-Day China*. Beijing, China: Foreign Languages Press, 1987. Reprinted with permission.

China is now carrying out a reform. I am all in favour of that. There is no other solution for us. After years of practice it turned out that the old stuff didn't work. In the past we copied foreign models mechanically, which only hampered the development of our productive forces, induced ideological rigidity and kept people and grass-roots units from taking any initiative. We made some mistakes of our own as well, such as the Great Leap Forward and the "cultural revolution," which were our own inventions. I would say that since 1957 our major mistakes have been "Left" ones. The "cultural revolution" was an ultra-Left mistake. In fact, during the two decades from 1958 through 1978, China remained at a standstill. There was little economic growth and not much of a rise in the people's standard of living. How could we go on like that without introducing reforms? So in 1978, at the Third Plenary Session of the Eleventh Central Committee, we formulated a new basic political line: to give first priority to the drive for modernization and strive to develop the productive forces. In accordance with that line we drew up a series of new principles and policies, the major ones being reform and the open policy. By reform we mean something comprehensive, including reform of both the economic structure and the political structure and corresponding changes in all other areas. By the open policy we mean both opening to all other countries, irrespective of their social systems, and opening at home, which means invigorating the domestic economy.

Reforming the Countryside

We introduced reform and the open policy first in the economic field, beginning with the countryside. Why did we start there? Because that is where 80 per cent of China's population lives. An unstable situation in the countryside would lead to an unstable political situation throughout the country. If the peasants did not shake off poverty, it would mean that the majority of the people remained poor. So after the Third Plenary Session of the Eleventh Central Committee, we decided to carry out rural reform, giving more decision-making power to the peasants and the grass-roots units. By so doing we immediately brought their initiative into play. And by adopting a policy of diversifying agriculture, we substantially increased not only the output of grain but also the output of cash crops. The rural reform has achieved much faster results than we had anticipated. Frankly, before the reform the majority of the peasants were extremely poor, hardly able to afford enough food, clothing, shelter and transportation. Since the rural reform began they have shown their initiative. Bearing local conditions in mind, they have grown grain and cash crops in places suited to them. Since the peasants were given the power to decide for themselves what to produce, they have brought about a dramatic change in the rural areas. The reform was so successful that in many places it yielded tangible results within just one year. The peasants' income has increased substantially, sometimes even doubling or quadrupling. Of course, not everyone was in favour of reform at the outset. In the beginning two provinces took the lead: Sichuan—my home province—led by Comrade Zhao Ziyang, and Anhui, led by Comrade Wan Li. . . . We worked out the principles and policies of reform on the basis of the experience accumulated by these two provinces. For one or two years after we publicized these principles and policies, some provinces had misgivings about them and other didn't know what to think, but in the end they all followed suit. The Central Committee's policy was to wait for them to be convinced by facts.

Achievements of Reform

Reform and the open policy have broken down the rigid economic structure and revitalized the economy. The socialist commodity economy has grown vigorously and with irresistible momentum. The coastal areas from south to north are forming a vast forward strip open to the outside world. The enthusiasm of the masses has been brought into play, and this has further liberated the productive forces.

Reform and the open policy have also further emancipated the minds of the people, battering down many old concepts that have long stifled their thinking. It is becoming a trend for people to seek change, to blaze new trails and to stress practical results.

Zhao Ziyang, report delivered at the Thirteenth National Congress of the Communist Party of China, October 25, 1987.

Generally speaking, once the peasants' initiative was brought into play, the rural reform developed very quickly. Our greatest success—and it is one we had by no means anticipated—has been the emergence of a large number of enterprises run by villages and townships. They were like a new force that just came into being spontaneously. These enterprises engage in the most diverse endeavours, including both manufacturing and trade. The Central Committee takes no credit for this. The annual output value of these village and township enterprises has been increasing by more than 20 per cent every year for the last several years. In the first five months of [1987] their output value has been greater than in the corresponding period last year. This increase in village and township enterprises, particularly industrial enterprises, has provided jobs for 50 per cent of the surplus labour in the countryside. Instead of flocking into the cities, the surplus farm workers have been building up a new type of villages and townships. If the Central Committee made any contribution in this respect, it was only by laying down the correct policy of invigorating the domestic economy. The fact that this policy has had such a favourable result shows that we made a good decision. But this result was not anything that I or any of the other comrades had foreseen; it just came out of the blue. In short, the rural reform has produced rapid and noticeable results. Of course, that doesn't mean all the problems in the countryside have been solved.

The success of the reform in the countryside emboldened us to apply the experience we had gained from it to economic restructuring in the cities. That too has been very successful, although it is more complicated than rural reform.

Opening China's Doors

In the meantime, the policy of opening China's doors to the outside world has produced the results we hoped for. We have implemented that policy in various ways, including setting up special economic zones and opening 14 coastal cities. Wherever the open policy has been implemented there have been notable results. First we established the Shenzhen Special Economic Zone. It was the leaders of Guangdong Province who came up with the proposal that special zones be established, and I agreed. But I said they should be called special *economic* zones, not special *political* zones, because we didn't want anything of that sort. We decided to set up three more special zones in addition to Shenzhen: Zhuhai and Shantou, both also in Guangdong Province, and Xiamen in Fujian Province. I visited Shenzhen a couple of years ago and found the economy flourishing there. The Shenzhen people asked me to write an inscription for them, and I wrote: "The development and experience of the Shenzhen Special Economic Zone prove the correctness of our policy of establishing such zones." At the time a number of people of different political persuasions, from Hongkong journalists to Party members, were sceptical about that policy. They didn't think it would work. But the Shenzhen Special Economic Zone has achieved remarkable successes since it was established almost eight years ago. This zone is an entirely new thing, and it is not fair for the people who run it not to be allowed to make mistakes. If they have made mistakes, they were minor ones. The people in Shenzhen reviewed their experience and decided to shift the zone's economy from a domestic orientation to an external orientation, which meant that Shenzhen would become an industrial base and offer its products on the world market. It is only two or three years since then, and already the situation in Shenzhen has changed greatly. The comrades there told me that more than 50 per cent of their products were exported and that receipts and payments of foreign exchange were in balance. I am now in a position to say with certainty that our decision to establish special economic zones was a good one and has proved successful. All scepticism has vanished. Recently a comrade told me that the Xiamen Special Economic Zone is developing even faster than Shenzhen. When I visited Xiamen in 1984, there was only an airport surrounded by wasteland. Great changes have taken place there since then. Now we are preparing to make all of Hainan Island a special economic zone. Hainan Island, which is almost as big as Taiwan, has abundant natural resources, such as iron ore and oil, as well as rubber and other tropical and subtropical crops. When it is fully developed, the results should be extraordinary.

Our achievements in the last few years have proved the correctness of our policies of reform and of opening to the outside world. Although there are still problems in various fields, I don't think they'll be too hard to solve, if we go at it systematically. Therefore, we must not abandon these policies or even slow them down. One of the topics we have been discussing recently is whether we should speed up reform or slow it down. That's because reform and the open policy involve risks. Of course we have to be cautious, but that doesn't mean we should do nothing. Indeed, on the basis of our experience to date, the Central Committee has been considering to accelerate the reform and our opening to the outside world.

"The downside of market-led growth . . . [is] evident. Many peasants . . . are now landless laborers. Inflation is high and unemployment is a major problem."

Reforms Have Harmed China

Richard Levy

Richard Levy has visited China five times between 1978 and 1987, and has written articles for *China Quarterly* and *Modern China.* In the following viewpoint, he expresses concern over China's new economic policies. Writing from a socialist perspective, he describes the negative effects arising from China's reforms, including inflation, unemployment, crime, corruption, and political alienation.

As you read, consider the following questions:

1. How does the author describe China's economy before the reforms?
2. What were some common complaints among the Chinese people, according to the author?
3. What does Levy fear might happen in China?

Richard Levy, "China Goes To Market," *Dollars & Sense*, April 1988. Reprinted with the permission of *Dollars & Sense* magazine, 1 Summer Street, Somerville, MA 02143.

China has now been living with the economic reforms initiated by former Premier Deng Xiaoping for ten years. The reforms, which introduced market principles into China's socialist economy, have been uniformly hailed by the West.

The signs of growth are everywhere. The cities bustle with economic activity. Brightly colored clothes have replaced the uniform blues and grays and televisions blare from many homes. Kentucky Fried Chicken and other foreign enterprises dot the streets of Beijing and other cities. The air of optimism is pervasive, reflecting widespread popular support for the reforms.

While the optimism was contagious, I was still left uneasy by what I saw during a visit [in 1987]. The downside of market-led growth was also evident. Many peasants, who used to be members of agricultural collectives, are now landless laborers. Inflation is high and unemployment is a major problem. Corruption is rampant. Prostitutes work the fancy tourist hotels. Money-changers in search of foreign currency pester foreigners constantly.

I returned to the United States ambivalent about China. On the one hand, the need for a higher standard of living is clear. For all they had achieved, Mao's policies seemed to have exhausted their potential. New economic policies were clearly needed. On the other hand, the economic reforms enacted under Deng's leadership embrace market principles in such an uncritical manner as to give any socialist pause. The only thing that was clear was that China today is a very different country from the one I first visited in 1978.

Going to Market

The introduction of profitability as the primary criterion in economic decisionmaking is the principle guiding most of the reforms. Factories are now responsible for making a profit, and collectivized agriculture is being disbanded in favor of individual plots in an effort to boost production.

For China's highly centralized, planned economy, such changes were quite radical. Prior to the reforms, a national plan allocated raw materials and assigned output quotas to each factory. China's collectivized agriculture operated in a similar fashion. Each collective had a production quota, made work assignments to its members, and sold all surplus produce to the government at fixed prices. The government guaranteed employment, though frequently with long delays; provided cheap, if crowded, housing; and ensured an adequate supply of cheap food in the cities through state subsidies. Health care and education were very inexpensive and widely available.

The results were both impressive and unsatisfactory. Food production managed to keep up with the population increase of some 400 million people between 1949 and 1976. A heavy industrial base and infrastructure were built. And housing, education, and medical care expanded dramatically. Between 1958 and 1976, industry grew an average of 10% per year, while agricultural production rose 2.2% annually. Although the standard of living remained low, Mao's economic policies ensured basic necessities to nearly all.

Despite its achievements, the Chinese economy had serious problems. Labor productivity grew only marginally, product quality was frequently low, and central planning created inefficiencies. One Communist Party member told me that on his collective farm they were not allowed to sell their products to the commune across the road because of the prohibition against commodity exchange. Instead, they had to make the exchange through the county bureaucracy, a process that frequently took so long that the produce had rotted by the time the transaction was complete.

The Rise of Inflation

The elderly woman grabbed her ration coupons and went to stand in line at a Beijing market at 1:30 in the morning. She wanted to buy government-subsidized pork for a relative's wedding. Five hours later, when the woman reached the front of the queue, the pork was sold out, and she didn't have enough money to buy the pricier meat on the free market. "Everything is too expensive, and nothing is available," she said, "How can we go on like this?"

Beijing once dismissed it as an affliction of degenerate capitalism, but the Chinese are struggling with inflation. Official figures show an 11 percent price rise during the first quarter [1988], but the real rate may be twice that. Across the country, people wait on line for eggs, sugar and other subsidized staples. Prices are soaring for scarce clothing, soap and home appliances. . . . Leader Deng Xiaoping's efforts to build a more modern, market-driven economy are behind the current crisis.

Dorinda Elliott, *Newsweek*, May 30, 1988.

To address the problems in industry, Chinese leaders implemented the "responsibility system," in which each enterprise functions more as an independent economic unit and is responsible for generating a surplus. Under the new system, factory managers and technical experts have greater authority to make production decisions independent of both the central plan and the factory's workers. No longer allocated raw materials, managers buy supplies and bargain for the best prices. Managers can make independent decisions about what to produce, and they can sell their products to the highest bidder. If they generate a surplus, they must pay a percentage to the central government as taxes.

They can then reinvest the remaining surplus as they see fit. They can even develop satellite plants and linkages with other factories.

In rural areas, collective land is being divided up among collective members. Peasant families bid for government contracts granting them exclusive use of a tract of land for periods of 15 years or longer. The government awards the contracts to those families who promise the highest payback. Families that do not win contracts are effectively forced off the land and must find other ways to make a living, either working in local industry, starting small enterprises, or, more commonly, working as hired laborers for peasants with land.

Because the peasants who receive land are free to meet their obligations to the government either in cash or in kind, they are increasingly able to determine what they grow. They can then sell their produce either to the government, at considerably higher prices than before the reforms, or on the private market. Peasants can hire laborers, with wages negotiated between the two parties, and they can sell their land contracts to other peasants.

Riding the Boom

Largely as a result of the reforms, the Chinese economy is booming. GNP [Gross National Product] grew 9% [in 1987] after even faster growth in previous years. Industrial output rose 14.5% in 1987, up slightly from the 11% growth rate of the previous year. After several years of double-digit growth rates in agriculture, growth slowed [in 1987] to a still-respectable 4%. Between 1978 and 1984, the production of basic grains increased 34%. Because of China's relatively egalitarian income distribution, the boom is translating into improved standards of living for most Chinese, with incomes rising fastest in rural areas.

To the traveler, the most noticeable change in China is less rising income levels than changes in the style of living. Several of my friends in working class jobs had acquired refrigerators, televisions, tape recorders, washing machines, bottled gas stoves, and sitdown flush toilets since my last visit in 1983. One couple was about to move—their second move in three years—into a larger apartment, of which they would be 40% owners.

Among the people I talked to, there was widespread support for the reforms, in large part because political reforms have accompanied the economic changes. People now feel freer to say what they want and to organize their time as they please. In many ways, the popular support for the reforms is a direct reaction to the excesses of the Cultural Revolution, when "capitalist" thoughts and actions—everything from using profitability as the key criterion in production to wearing high heels—left people open to criticism and punishment.

But there is discontent too. The most common complaint I heard was about inflation, a phenomenon previously unknown to most Chinese. Prior to the reforms, prices were stable, with the government absorbing all fluctuations that in a market economy would have led to price increases. Since the reforms, inflation has become chronic. In 1983, prices rose 8.5%. Since then, inflation has risen even faster. While official estimates put the inflation rate at 10% for 1987, other sources say it was twice that. Food prices jumped an estimated 20% between August 1986 and August 1987.

By paying higher prices for farm products while maintaining needed food subsidies, the government is now running a substantial deficit. It can only resolve the dilemma by cutting the prices paid to farmers, undermining the reforms, or by raising consumer food prices, which is both politically unpopular and highly inflationary. So far, the government has moved slightly towards the latter course of action.

Discontent

The economic changes introduced by China's senior leader, Deng Xiaoping, have created more competitiveness—as the hard-driving Guangdongese, who lead the nation in exports and innovation, have proven—but also have created more inequalities, jealousies and tensions.

A survey by China's Economic Reform Research Institute found that 86 percent of urban residents say that "Reform should enable us more speedily to increase our income."

"Up to now," the report argues, "reform has brought more risks and instability to the populace."

The report notes that most complaints are concerned with unequal opportunities. Often a taxi driver's salary can quadruple that of a university professor's.

"If this state of affairs continues for long," the report says, "the discontent will be further aggravated."

The Washington Post, quoted in the Minneapolis *StarTribune,* May 21, 1988.

Rising food prices represent a decrease in the "social wage"— the benefits provided to workers at no direct cost. Housing prices are increasing, and in the areas where the government is allowing a private housing market, I saw advertisements for private housing at rents twenty times the government rate. Education is becoming a more elite institution, as affirmative action policies for peasants and working class children are abandoned. In Shanghai textile factories, a friend told me health and safety conditions have deteriorated considerably. The rural medical system is also falling apart. Childhood diseases such as measles and diphtheria have once again become common in the last ten years. Students in Shanghai recently protested when a student died after he was refused medical care because he couldn't pay for it.

Social Problems

In rural areas, the move away from collective farming has undermined certain types of production and increased income disparities. Irrigation systems are falling apart as the burden of maintaining and developing them falls on individual peasants who are unwilling or unable to keep them up. The absence of collective investment is compounded by a drop in government spending on agriculture. The shift to smaller plots has also left most farms too small for mechanization, and I read stories about farm equipment lying idle in state warehouses because no one could afford to buy it or use it effectively.

For factory workers in the cities, the changes have been dramatic as well. Workers now have to find their own jobs and are no longer guaranteed life-long employment. They can be laid off, fired, or have their benefits reduced by decisions of the factory leadership. In an attempt to instill a stronger work ethic, piecework compensation is now the norm instead of monthly salaries. The responsibility system, in some cases, has led to heartless management decisions. I spoke to one retired man who had lost his retirement income when the factory managers decided to cut costs by eliminating payments to retirees.

The emergence of a stronger money economy, with the accompanying influx of both foreign currency and foreign products, has created new incentives for corruption. On a daily basis, bribes are necessary to complete many common interactions with government officials. An ex-Red Guard told me he was outraged to witness his brother paying off a health inspector to pass his restaurant. "People weren't entirely pure before," he told me, "but it was never like this." On a grander scale, ministerial officials allowed a forest nearly the size of the state of California to burn to the ground because they weren't bribed to use their fire-fighting equipment. There has also been a generalized increase in street crime, virtually unheard of in pre-reform China.

Political Alienation

Perhaps the thing that disturbed me most about post-reform China was the alienation of the Chinese people from the political process that is shaping their lives. In the China of the 1970s, people were encouraged (some would even say forced) to participate in the political process. That's what the Cultural Revolution was all about.

Now, Chinese leaders seem to dissuade popular involvement in decisionmaking. Despite minor differences between the so-called pragmatists and conservatives, all of whom opposed the

Cultural Revolution, they seem to see economic development as a technical, basically non-political process which must take precedence over issues of economic and social justice. The Chinese people, jaded by the political upheavals of the Cultural Revolution, seem willing to go along, at least for now.

Decreased women's rights, worsening pollution, and increased health hazards on the job are tolerated as the costs of increasing profitability. Corruption is seen as an issue of bad individuals rather than as a class issue where those with money buy influence and consolidate their own positions. The entire issue of people organizing their lives and relations with other people on the basis of money, rather than organizing their economic lives around social relationships, is accepted as the natural process of economic development.

What Is Socialism?

The Western press hails the reforms as the return of capitalism to China. Most of the people I talked with, while quite familiar with the concept of a capitalist road, weren't so sure. Neither was I. But if this is the beginning of capitalism in China, it will certainly look far different from other capitalist societies because the country is starting from such an egalitarian base.

Still, the leadership's uncritical adoption of market principles, packaged as the further development of Chinese socialism, left me cold. I came away convinced that a process of market-led capital accumulation might be necessary to get China off the economic plateau it has reached. But to sell it as socialism, rather than a necessary retreat from socialism, is another thing.

The leadership muddle over what is capitalism and what is socialism has trickled down to the society at large. Many people idolize and idealize the United States, to the point where some in the upper strata are undergoing operations to make their eyes look "Western."

The Ills of Capitalism

The reforms are clearly popular now during the market-led boom. But I left China wondering what the atmosphere would be like after the country has experienced its first market-led downturn. For the majority of Chinese people, the ills of capitalism are still an abstraction. They have no direct experience with booms that turn to busts or capital accumulation that tends to concentrate in the hands of a few.

The reforms have spurred unprecedented short-term economic expansion. The danger is that the price for such growth may be a system that combines the worst of a bureaucratically controlled society like the Soviet Union with the worst of economically polarized societies like India and the Philippines.

"The tides surge strongly toward closer links with the United States and other countries that can deliver what China needs most—markets and technology."

Western Influence Inspired China's Reforms

Mary Lord, Maureen Santini, and Robert A. Manning

China's reforms have sparked much American media attention as analysts speculate what impact these reforms will have on China, the US, and the world. In the following viewpoint, Mary Lord, Maureen Santini, and Robert A. Manning argue that China's reforms are inspired by Western capitalism, and that China will develop closer ties to the US to take advantage of Western markets, technology, and ideas. Lord, Santini, and Manning are correspondents for *U.S. News & World Report*, a weekly newsmagazine.

As you read, consider the following questions:

1. What is the legacy of Mao Zedong, and how does it influence reforms in China today, according to the authors?
2. Why do the authors believe China will continue to strengthen ties with the West?
3. According to the authors, what might affect the future of China's reforms?

Mary Lord, Maureen Santini, and Robert A. Manning, "China: New Long March, New Revolution," *U.S. News & World Report*, Copyright, September 8, 1986, U.S. News & World Report.

Ten years after Mao Tse-tung's death, his successors have committed a billion Chinese to a new revolution. Domestic reforms range from unprecedented touches of personal freedom to experiments with capitalism. In foreign affairs, China is breaking out of isolation to become a global force.

Deng Xiaoping, the paramount leader, and other reformers already may have passed the point of no return. Whatever emerges from the new long march will be nothing like the China envisioned by Chairman Mao. Yet China forges ahead, careful step by careful step, with what U.S. Ambassador Winston Lord calls "the boldest and most important domestic adventure . . . in the world today."

China today has a tentative form of capitalism tucked inside a looser, if still authoritarian, Communist wrapper. Now comes the question of whether the pragmatic Deng, still active at 82, will make even bolder political and economic strokes to retool China into a modern world power. Without further reforms, economic stagnation could set in—potentially explosive in a land where people now hope for better lives after generations of shrinking horizons.

Links with the West

For this and other reasons, the tides surge strongly toward closer links with the United States and other countries that can deliver what China needs most—markets and technology. Much depends on what happens after Deng's death. "They have crossed the river," says political scientist Seweryn Bialer of Columbia University, a recent visitor. "It's a question of whether they lead the revolution, or it leads them."

Few Communist states have gone China's economic route. Unlike Hungary, whose economy also has moved from strict collectivism, China lacks a safety net. Moscow is not standing in the wings to prop up Peking should China's fortunes suddenly darken—as could happen with a massive crop failure.

The ghost of Mao, who died Sept. 9, 1976, slows those eager for too rapid change. That makes the task confronting Deng and fellow reformers both epic and paradoxical: How to honor Mao's memory yet exorcise his doctrine.

Mao's Legacy

No one dares repudiate completely the leader who gave the Chinese Communists their first real claim to legitimacy. It was Mao who humbled Chiang Kai-shek's Nationalists in 1949, stampeding them into exile in Taiwan. It was Mao who pledged egalitarianism, Mao who ended China's myopic fixation on East Asia.

Yet is was also Mao whose turn toward repression made him the bloody equal of Soviet leader Joseph Stalin. During his cultural revolution, tens of thousands were executed. Millions of the best and brightest—a whole intellectual generation—were exiled to rural labor brigades. Doctors sweated in rice paddies, poets mucked out cesspools.

But from this national agony came a resolve to recapture the commercial enterprise and cultural eminence demonstrated by China over 4,000 years of civilization. Already, China has been remarkably transformed from the gloom and Spartan isolation of that period. In Peking, banners praising Mao have yielded to signs extolling appliances from Japan, once an implacable enemy. Even the baggy trousers and blouses dictated by Mao have given way to more-stylish clothing, permitted by official decree since 1982. Street vendors formerly assailed as decadent now freely work in the cities. Construction cranes thrust skyward as cities brace for hotels and office buildings. Peking displays the ultimate incongruity of a Kentucky Fried Chicken outlet.

China's Progress

To gauge China's progress in this brief period, a visitor need only talk to businessman Zhang Xiaobin or journalist Qin Benli, survivors of Mao's excesses who now flourish. They show the hopeful face of a new China. "We lost a lot of time but we learned how to survive," Zhang says. "We are lucky to start our company at this time." Qin, too, endured years of forced labor, finally emerging to launch the *World Economic Herald,* the freest of all newspapers in China. "We're still in the experimental stage," he says. "We feel there should be an environment in which people feel free to speak."

The Iacocca Craze

The best-selling author in Beijing [during 1987] is not Mao Tse-tung, Deng Xiaoping or the Communist Party's new leader, Zhao Ziyang. It is Lee Iacocca. The Chrysler chairman's autobiography has sold to hundreds of thousands of Chinese readers. A Chinese translation has been put out by seven different publishers, all eager to tap the insatiable market for America's new Horatio Alger story. . . .

The Iacocca craze tells better than any speech where China is headed. Not every young Chinese wants to grow up to be Lee Iacocca, but a startling number would like to go that way. "What's wrong with being a millionaire?" asked one bold college graduate.

Harrison E. Salisbury, *U.S. News & World Report,* February 8, 1988.

Like millions of others, these Chinese hope for much more. Yet much more probably would require further relaxation of the party's grip on the economy and government. Each step will require bold decisions that risk the state's Marxist underpinnings.

How matters ultimately work out also rests on whether Deng can resolve the tensions his program has caused. So far, he has managed. Deng weathered one more attack on his leadership this summer [1986], when conservatives blamed China's rapid economic expansion and foreign links for spawning crime and other social ills.

In his defense, Deng could point to annual wages that have risen 58 percent for rural industrial workers and much higher for those in cities. Peasant income has doubled since 1981, while yearly farm production expands now at the rate of 7 percent. Exports have grown from $7 billion to $27.4 billion over the past few years. A few farmers even have become wealthy, moving into homes that testify to the truth of a post-Mao slogan: "To get rich is glorious."

Such successes help free Deng to pursue politically sensitive reforms, such as management autonomy and price decontrol. But pitfalls are there, waiting in Mao's long shadow. A lost generation, deprived of schooling by the cultural revolution, cries for redress. A neglected urban infrastructure badly needs repair. The farm system still cannot get perishable produce to market. Just to draw abreast of leading developing nations by the year 2000, overall Chinese productivity must increase at least 5.5 percent annually, a rate matched in modern times only by South Korea and Greece.

The Four Modernizations

Deng's "four modernizations"—agriculture, industry, science and technology, and the military—provide his framework. In each, he seeks to erase dogmas, irrationality and inefficiencies of Mao's era and, at deliberate speed, transform the Middle Kingdom into a shining new state.

Deng launched his revolution in the countryside, permitting families in 1979 to farm leased land for profit. Encouraged by the results, he quickly moved to free some prices of government control, then followed with limited reforms in the urban workplace. At the same time, he began to put increased emphasis on both Western investment and production of television sets, refrigerators and other consumer goods long denied the average Chinese. Within six years of Mao's death, China was well launched on a new course.

For the 80 percent of Chinese living in rural areas, life has been made easier and more productive. The proportion of rural population living in poverty fell from 31 percent in 1979 to 6 percent today. Food production is 2½ times the level of 1960, providing a higher standard of living for workers. In a country historically racked by periodic famine, people now have enough to eat.

A skimpy diet has become richer in protein—most families eat eggs daily now—and Chinese show the result in physical stature. Since household farming began replacing collective agriculture,

China on the Move

Behrendt, printed with permission of Cartoonists & Writers Syndicate.

China for the first time has enough grain both to export and to feed a population that is 10 times Japan's, 60 times Taiwan's.

Under old production schemes, farmers were told what to grow. Now, most sign crop contracts with the state or regional planning commissions. The benefits are manifest in abundant fruit sold at roadside stalls, in houses filled with appliances and in taxes the state can levy on the profits.

Prosperity has its price, however. Grain production has begun to slip again, the result of too many farmers' planting more-lucrative crops. And despite rewards, some 100 million rural workers are expected to leave their farms by 1996 to take up higher-paying jobs in industry and other sectors.

Making industry more efficient, autonomous and responsive to market demand has been difficult. The first step lay simply in opening three major cities—or special economic zones—to foreign traders in 1979. The number has since expanded to encompass 73 small and medium-sized areas competing with each other for business. . . .

Price reforms, launched in 1985, and attempts to break the "iron rice bowl"—the practice of rewarding workers regardless of the quality of their output—have proved equally tricky. When government controls were lifted, meat prices immediately shot up by 30 percent, while the cost of eggs increased sixfold.

Experiments in contract work and bonus systems, quality control and five-day workweeks are starting to erode collective-employment patterns. Since its inception in 1982, a contractual labor system has pulled in 3.5 million persons, 5 percent of the work force. In Manchuria, Shenyang's automobile industry recently advertised for foremen. And in Shanghai's pioneer, model textile factory No. 17, independent managers promote quality through contests, rewards for suggestions and annual bonuses worth up to four times a worker's wages. . . .

Capitalism?

None dares call it capitalism, but the brisk pace of financial reform suggest nothing else so strongly. China even recorded its first Western-style bankruptcy in August when an instrument factory abruptly closed. "The ultimate paradox," a Western scholar mused, "is when bankruptcy is progress."

There are other capitalistic touches. In Shenyang, China's first "stock market" has been opened. . . . Set up by Shenyang Investment Trust to handle a lottery and local manufacturers' bonds, the exchange seeks to pump hard cash into local industry hungry for capital.

In Peking, Zhang Jibing, 58, operates his Tianqiao department store almost like a board chairman might run a company in the West. He no longer must beg permission from political bosses for every order. Although the state owns half his stock, Zhang personally contracts for the more than 10,000 products on sale. "We now pay a lot of attention to quality," he says. "Our business depends on our reputations. This spring breeze of reforms gives us a new force for doing business.". . .

Deng is moving as quickly as he can in the hope of insuring that his policies endure after his death, something Mao failed to achieve. He began by hammering away at the personality cult and one-man rule of Mao, stressing that new programs were not his but the party's. Next he broadened upper ranks by swapping the post of Party Chairman for an 11-member Secretariat. . . .

China's Western tilt almost certainly will continue, if only out of sheer economic necessity. "Who can supply the technology, the investment, the management skills that China needs for modernization?" asks a senior U.S. official. "Certainly not the Soviet Union. We can." One measure of this phenomenon: Chinese-Soviet trade is about a quarter of U.S.-China commerce.

Already, China is leagues ahead of the other Communist giant, the Soviet Union, in social and economic daring. Only now, with the rise of Mikhail Gorbachev, do the Soviets show even faint signs in the same direction. Their chances of succeeding may be considerably less.

For one reason, says Columbia's Bialer, the homogeneity of Chinese society permits a degree of decentralization that would be difficult for Moscow. For the Soviet Union to take comparable actions could encourage its many nationalities—and the nations of its Eastern European empire—toward greater independence. Moreover, Bialer says, China has no superpower aspirations, while the Soviet Union, facing pressure from the United States, needs central control to maintain its status. . . .

China's Future

For all that has changed in China, much stays the same. Many of its people—perhaps even hundreds of millions—are still beyond the reach of the reforms that have been made.

The future may turn less on ideology than on the ability of Deng and those who follow to alter the ancient feudal traditions that helped Mao launch his peasant's revolution. Mistrust of outsiders is little changed since Marco Polo first set foot in China, and a farmer still refuses to build a house higher than the neighbors' lest he be responsible for raining troubles on their heads. "Feudalism retains a hold on the ideology of today's China," says Su Shaozhi, one of his country's leading political scientists. "Unless there is a great change in the people's way of thinking, neither political nor economic reform will be successful."

But the richer China gets, the more chance there is of converting hearts and minds—and cementing policies. Outsiders like the World Bank find plenty of cause for optimism in the world's most populous nation. However, the Chinese are like the tethered cormorant birds they use to catch fish. They can snag a tasty bite but rarely are permitted a swallow. Policy liberalizations have been followed by clampdowns, campaigns against "spiritual pollution" and reversals on such simple items as lotteries. . . .

No one knows the price of failure and the vagaries of power in Peking better than Deng, who has fallen three times in his political life only to rise again. If nothing else, he can content himself with knowing that he has provided China with a guiding set of principles as it faces an uncertain future.

"The policies of the post-Mao regime . . . are not making China 'more like us.' . . . They are making China more like the Soviet Union."

Soviet Influence Inspired China's Reforms

Maurice J. Meisner

Maurice J. Meisner is a professor of history at the University of Wisconsin-Madison. His books include *Mao's China and After.* In the following viewpoint, he argues that China's reforms are inspired more by Soviet communism than by Western capitalism. By restructuring the Communist Party to include younger members, strengthening party discipline, and emphasizing technical expertise over social equality, Meisner believes that Chinese leader Deng Xiaoping has shown many resemblances to the Soviet dictator Josef Stalin.

As you read, consider the following questions:

1. How do media images of China and the Soviet Union differ, according to the author? What reasons does he give for these differences?
2. In what ways do Deng Xiaoping's policies resemble those of Josef Stalin, according to Meisner?
3. What impact does Meisner believe Deng's reforms have had on Sino-Soviet relations?

Maurice J. Meisner, "The Wrong March," *The Progressive*, October 1986. Reprinted by permission from *The Progressive*, 409 East Main St., Madison, Wisconsin 53703.

The People's Republic of China—product of the greatest and most radical of modern revolutions—has gained some politically astonishing champions in recent years. Among the more notable is William Safire, *The New York Times*'s designated conservative, who has hastened to celebrate "the rejection of Marxism and embrace of capitalism by the government of a billion Chinese." Another and even more unlikely convert is *Time* magazine, whose editors have selected Deng Xiaoping (China's "paramount leader," in the delicate phrase favored by Western journalists) as its "Man of the Year," not once but twice. This double if somewhat dubious honor previously had been bestowed on only one other Chinese: Chiang Kai-shek. . . .

Fashion . . . calls for the American media to praise China. Images of "Red China" as the land of "blue ants" and "red hordes" have vanished from the popular press. In their place are new portraits more pleasing to Western eyes. China's new leaders are pictured as soberminded "pragmatists" who have abandoned "ideology" in favor of "modernization."

The China Market

Beijing's "open-door" policy, welcoming foreign trade and investment (and also more naked forms of exploiting Chinese labor in "special economic zones"), is cause for Western celebration, conjuring up old visions of a limitless "China market" and the profits to be made therein. (The term "open door," so intimately associated with the annals of Western imperialism in China, is a rather curious choice on the part of the Chinese government; that the leaders of the People's Republic should have resurrected it may be attributed to a fit of historical absent-mindedness or a deliberate attempt to appeal to Western greed.)

American journalists, eager to demonstrate that avarice is a universal human characteristic, are much enchanted by the Chinese discovery of the "magic of the market," reproducing from the official Chinese press success stories of Chinese entrepreneurs who have heeded their government's injuction to "get rich." The reappearance of street peddlers and noodle vendors—few of whom become rich and most of whom eke out the barest of existences much in the fashion of their counterparts in other Third World lands—is offered as evidence of the rebirth of liveliness in Chinese cities. Chinese arts and crafts, not long ago banned under the "Trading with the Enemy Act," are advertised in publications catering to affluent American readers—and sold at Bloomingdale's at inflated prices.

U.S. citizens are naturally eager to visit a country that garners such rave reviews. It offers the double attraction of being "exotic" and becoming "more like us." The Beijing government, willing to sacrifice a bit of national pride in exchange for foreign currency, has spared no effort to satisfy tourist tastes. . . .

The contrast between Western media portraits of China and the Soviet Union is striking. The popular media treat Americans to a Russia full of drunken and slothful workers laboring in antiquated factories, an inefficient and virtually collapsing economy whose creaky functioning is dependent on the purchase (or theft) of Western technology, long lines of shabbily clad consumers queued up to buy the bare essentials of life at perpetually ill-stocked state stores, a ubiquitous KGB dispatching untold numbers of dissidents to labor camps or psychiatric hospitals, and an overbearing bureaucracy staffed by officials whose incompetence is matched only by their venality.

Close Soviet Ties

Perhaps even more disconcerting to the Western world is the revival of another set of ties between the younger Chinese leaders and their Soviet counterparts. Many Chinese leaders were trained either in the Soviet Union or by Soviet experts on Chinese soil. A conservative estimate numbers Chinese students who studied in the Soviet Union or other Eastern bloc countries in the 1950s at about 20,000, but there were perhaps hundreds of thousands receiving similar training in China under Marxist tutelage. . . .

Today many of these leaders occupy important positions in the party, the military, and the administration, both in Beijing and in the provinces. To them, socialist concepts are recognizable and acceptable, but they really do not understand the West. They may respond to Western concepts with hesitancy, if not outright rejection.

David Chen, *The World & I*, April 1987.

By contrast, the media portray a China dominated by enterprising and prospering peasants newly freed from collectivistic bondage, innovative entrepreneurs who have rediscovered the wonders of the market, reform-minded leaders who wisely hope their country will learn the ways and techniques of Western capitalism, and masses of consumers purchasing a vast array of products hitherto denied them. The dominant American image of the Soviet Union is the Gulag; that of China, a happy tourist strolling atop the Great Wall.

These images of Russia and China bear little relation to their respective social realities; the first is caricature, the second a romanticized vision. By any reasonable standard of judgment, and certainly by the standards which Americans usually apply to judge other lands, it is the Soviet Union that should get a comparatively favorable press. Soviet citizens enjoy a material standard of life that the Chinese people can only dream of achieving sometime in the next century—if, in the unlikely event, the policies that proceed under the title of the Four Modernizations actually yield what Chinese leaders promise.

A Leninist State

China, moreover, remains a Leninist Party-State where the realm of semi-freedom, while widening in recent years, is still considerably more restrictive than it is in Russia. Chinese authorities, for instance, would never tolerate the writings of an independent and critical historian of the stature of Roy Medvedev, much less permit him to publish his works abroad. And if the Soviet regime engaged in mass public executions of alleged criminals following summary trials, as has become a regular practice of the Chinese state in recent years, one can easily imagine the condemnations of barbarous and uncivilized behavior that would flow from Western pens. But in China, where the practice has become routine, the events are reported in matter-of-fact fashion (if at all) as salutary measures to maintain social order. . . .

It is, then, an irony of contemporary history that the policies of the post-Mao regime, almost universally praised by Western observers, are not making China "more like us." They are making China more like the Soviet Union. In political organization, social structure, and ideology, China under Deng Xiaoping has come to resemble Soviet Russia far more closely than was the case under Mao Zedong.

Positive Accomplishments

A discussion of China's current "Soviet"—or one might say "neo-Stalinist"—tendencies must be prefaced by noting the many positive accomplishments of the post-Mao era. Hundreds of thousands of political prisoners have been released from jails and labor camps, often with due apologies and sometimes honors. Many of the more repressive and obscurantist orthodoxies in cultural and intellectual life have been denounced or ignored. This has permitted a significantly wider (if still limited) realm of freedom for artistic and intellectual expression. Many of the political abuses performed under the name of "class struggle" and the pernicious system of "class labels" have been terminated.

Policies emphasizing the development of agriculture and the production of consumer goods have corrected many of the economic imbalances inherited from the Mao period, yielding a significant (if unequally distributed) rise in an abysmally low material standard of life. These have been progressive developments by any reasonable standard of judgment and should be welcomed by all who are concerned with the welfare of the Chinese people.

But along with these changes, which have been widely reported and universally applauded, certain basic social and political patterns have emerged—patterns that are less visible and less salutary and bear a distinctively Soviet imprint. The much-celebrated economic reforms of the post-Mao years are considerably less innovative than advertised. Virtually all have precedents in the Soviet Union or Eastern Europe.

Such "reforms" as strict managerial authority in the factories and the principle of enterprise profitability, for example, were among Stalin's "socialist" innovations in the 1930s. The market-oriented economic policies are, largely, eclectic borrowings from the "market socialisms" of Hungary and Yugoslavia. And even as the leaders of the People's Republic experiment with the market—an instrumentality notorious for its unruly behavior and unintended consequences—China is clearly moving closer to the Soviet Union in many other areas of social life.

Renewing Old Friendships

Economic cooperation between the two giant communist states also has been progressing steadily. The visit by Ivan Arkhipov, the architect of Soviet economic cooperation in the 1950s, rekindled friendly contacts between old friends as the genuine bear hug between him and President Li Xiannian eloquently testified. Joint ventures, for several years the hallmark of cooperation between China and the capitalist world, are also featured in the new Sino-Soviet relationship. Moscow, for example, is actively assisting the Chinese in renovating or redesigning many old Soviet-style factories, which still outnumber the plants built by the West or with Western assistance.

What is startling to the outside world is the reemergence of a comradely spirit between Chinese leaders and their Soviet counterparts. The Li-Arkhipov embrace was symbolic of the comradeship forged in the impoverished days of the 1950s.

David Chen, *The World & I,* April 1987.

One such area of "Sovietization" or "Stalinization" has been the refashioning of the Chinese Communist Party in accordance with firm Leninist organizational principles and methods of discipline, making the Chinese Party structurally and functionally more similar to its Russian counterpart. The post of Party chairman has been abolished in favor of a revived secretariat and the position of Party secretary-general, the Stalinist-invented office which Deng Xiaoping occupied in the 1950s before Mao abolished it.

Changing the Communist Party

Far more important than Soviet-style organizational changes has been the changing social composition of the Party. In recent years, the Party has emphasized the recruitment and promotion of technical specialists and university graduates, replacing millions of purged "leftists." Here, Deng Xiaoping, who has often complained that Party members lacked modern technological knowledge and specialized skills, has followed directly in Stalin's footsteps. In the 1930s Stalin ordered the Soviet Party to recruit new members from among professionals, technical specialists, and intellectuals.

As Benjamin Schwartz once observed, Stalin stressed the "social-engineering" function of the Communist Party, in striking contrast to Mao Zedong, who was concerned with the moral and political virtues of Party members. "If Mao was to find the Party insufficiently Red," Schwartz wrote, "Stalin found it insufficiently expert." Deng Xiaoping, like Stalin, also finds the Party insufficiently expert—and has adopted Stalin's solution to remedy the deficiency. Thus the "red/expert" dichotomy, so long an agonizing dilemma for Chinese Communists, has now been resolved in eminently Soviet fashion.

The changing social composition of the Chinese Communist Party has been accompanied by a broader effort to rationalize the functioning of the bureaucracy. The essential aim of what is advertised as "political reform" in post-Mao China is not democracy, although much democratic rhetoric and, indeed, some genuine Party democrats exist. Rather, as Deng Xiaoping candidly sums it up, the aim is to make state bureaucrats "better educated, professionally more competent, and younger."...

Rise of Elitism

The elitist character of the effort is nowhere more strikingly apparent than in the 1985 announcement that the regime had selected 1,000 especially talented and well-educated officials in their forties and fifties to form a pool from which the future leaders of China will be drawn. Such measures have little to do with—and indeed are totally antithetical to—the professed aim of "socialist democratization."

Along with Soviet-style political developments, the position of urban elites has been consolidated and institutionalized. In recent years, the government has gone to great lengths to raise the material and social status of intellectuals, technical specialists, factory managers, and professionals. It grants them considerable autonomy within their respective spheres of expertise in exchange for political loyalty—or, for that matter, apolitical loyalty. As a consequence, an elite of urban bureaucrats, intellectuals, and professionals has emerged as the most reliable political supporters of the post-Mao regime—and, indeed, its essential social base.

The phenomenon is similar to a characteristic feature of Soviet society since the 1930s. Also similar to the Soviet pattern is the revamped and expanded university system, which serves to foster and perpetuate the privileges and status of urban elites. Having abandoned the more egalitarian features of Maoist educational policies, the "new" education system is, in fact, largely a refurbished version of the elitist and Soviet-modeled system adopted in the People's Republic in the early 1950s. . . .

Soviet Marxism

Official Chinese Marxist theory, now purged of its more radical Maoist features, has in recent years increasingly come to resemble the orthodox Soviet version of Marxism-Leninism. Having abandoned the Maoist view of socialism as a continuous process of social and human transformation demanding progressive reductions in social inequalities, post-Maoist ideologists have found it convenient to return to the simplistic Soviet definition of socialism: "public ownership" of the major means of production and the principle of "payment according to work." This flexible formula has the advantage of permitting wide latitude in social and economic practice while retaining the ideological claim to socialism.

The development of socialism itself is now viewed through the prism of an economically deterministic interpretation of Marxism. The Chinese have adopted the long-standing Soviet orthodoxy (first formulated by Stalin) that the combination of modern economic development and Communist political power more or less automatically guarantees the achievement of ever higher stages of socialism and the eventual arrival of a Communist society.

Social Inequality

One of the more prominent features of Chinese communist ideology in recent years has been condemnations of what is called "the fallacy of egalitarianism," to which many of the evils of the Maoist era are attributed. The stridency of these Chinese denunciations is reminiscent of Stalin's infamous campaigns against egalitarian ideals.

The most pronounced similarities between China's post-Mao regime and the Soviet Union are in the realm of social policies, and they bear a Stalinist imprint—albeit without the terror that accompanied virtually all of Stalin's pursuits. The noted Sovietologist Moshe Lewin has described Stalin's post-1933 social policies as "a set of classical measures of social conservatism, law-and-order strategies, complete with a nationalist revival, trying to instill values of discipline, patriotism, conformism, authority, and orderly careerism." The characterization is as applicable to Deng Xiaoping as it is to Stalin—and, of course, to Stalin's successors. It is likely to apply to Deng's successors, as well.

As post-Mao China has moved closer to the Soviet Union in both theory and practice, relations between the two countries have become increasingly friendly. Whereas Chinese leaders in Mao's time condemned the Soviet Union as "revisionist," "capitalist," and even "fascist," the new leaders of the People's Republic recognize Russia as "socialist"—one among a variety of national forms of "socialism." Moscow, in turn, has generally welcomed the changes wrought by Deng Xiaoping, praising the Chinese leader for his "economic common sense," and his efforts at "de-Maoification."

Sino-Soviet trade and cultural relations have grown markedly over the past half-decade, and a recent agreement provides for the dispatch of Russian technicians to oversee the modernization of the aging Chinese industrial plant built with Soviet assistance in the 1950s. What remains of the Sino-Soviet dispute are purely issues of conflicting national self-interest—Vietnamese troops in Cambodia, Russian troops in Afghanistan, and old border disputes in Central Asia.

Stalinization and China's Future

Sovietization, or Stalinization, is, of course, not the only force at work in this period of the history of the People's Republic. It is part of an eclectic (if not necessarily contradictory) mixture of tendencies which include processes of de-Stalinization, the rationalization of the Stalinist component of Maoism, and a significant (if weakening) movement for democratic socialism. To these one must add the unleashing of market forces whose social results are especially unpredictable—although it can be predicted that market relationships will not be allowed to threaten the bureaucracy's control over economic and political life.

But a Soviet-type pattern of development is clearly among the more powerful tendencies molding the post-Mao era. The tendency has been little noted, not because it is particularly obscure but for reasons of political expediency among Western journalists and scholars alike. But it is a development that is too important to be ignored—especially by those who are celebrating (or lamenting) the birth of capitalism in China and those who praise the current Beijing leaders as "Marxist materialists" laying the necessary economic foundations for socialism.

Recognizing Statements That Are Provable

From various sources of information we are constantly confronted with statements and generalizations about social and moral problems. In order to think clearly about these problems, it is useful if one can make a basic distinction between statements for which evidence can be found and other statements which cannot be verified or proved because evidence is not available, or the issue is so controversial that it cannot be definitely proved.

Readers should be aware that magazines, newspapers, and other sources often contain statements of a controversial nature. The following activity is designed to allow experimentation with statements that are provable and those that are not.

The following statements are taken from the viewpoints in this chapter. Consider each statement carefully. *Mark P for any statement you believe is provable. Mark U for any statement you feel is unprovable because of the lack of evidence. Mark C for any statements you think are too controversial to be proved to everyone's satisfaction.*

If you are doing this activity as a member of a class or group, compare your answers with those of other class or group members. Be able to defend your answers. You may discover that others will come to different conclusions than you. Listening to the reasons others present for their answers may give you valuable insights in recognizing statements that are provable.

P = provable
U = unprovable
C= too controversial

1. Deng Xiaoping has twice been selected as *Time* magazine's "man of the year."

2. The post-Mao reforms are making China more like the Soviet Union, not the US.

3. Sino-Soviet trade has grown rapidly over the past half-decade.

4. Deng Xiaoping and other reformers already may have passed the point of no return.

5. China today has a tentative form of capitalism tucked inside a looser Communist wrapper.

6. China's economic activity is a mere commercial layer upon the face of an unchanging socialist system.

7. In Beijing, banners praising Chairman Mao have yielded to billboards extolling appliances from Japan, once an implacable enemy.

8. The first US fast-food company to have restaurants in China is Kentucky Fried Chicken.

9. The shift to smaller land plots has left most farms too small for mechanization.

10. There are 500 million more people in China today than in 1949.

11. The Maoist themes of equality and collective responsibility are relics of a mocked past.

12. The emergence of a stronger money economy has created new incentives for corruption.

13. In 1986 the first Chinese stock exchange since 1949 opened in Shanghai.

14. The Cultural Revolution was all about encouraging people to participate in the political process.

15. There is exciting promise for China's future.

16. The provinces where reforms were first tried out were Sichuan and Anhui.

17. The achievements of the past few years have proved the correctness of the economic reforms.

Periodical Bibliography

The following articles have been selected to supplement the diverse views presented in this chapter.

Burton Abrams	"Real Life Behind China's Changes," *Reason*, May 1987.
A. Doak Barnett	"Ten Years After Mao," *Foreign Affairs*, Fall 1986.
Gordon H. Chang	"Perspectives on Marxism in China Today," *Monthly Review*, September 1986.
Howard G. Chua-Eoan	"One for the Money, One Goes Slow," *Time*, April 11, 1988.
Tod O. Clare	"The Business Challenge in China," *Vital Speeches of the Day*, October 15, 1986.
Stephen Endicott	"Of Rice and Riches," *New Internationalist*, April 1987.
Marshall I. Goldman	"China's Apprenticeship in the World Economy," *Technology Review*, January 1988.
David S.G. Goodman	"China: The Transition to the Post-Revolutionary Era," *Third World Quarterly*, January 1988.
Ed A. Hewett and Harry Harding	"Reforms in China and the Soviet Union," *The Brookings Review*, Spring 1988.
William H. Hinton	"Dazhai Revisited," *Monthly Review*, March 1988.
Alisa Joyce	"China Takes the Reformist Road," *The Nation*, December 19, 1987.
John Kohan	"Two Crossroads of Reform," *Time*, November 9, 1987.
Nicholas D. Kristof	"In China the Buck Starts Here," *The New York Times Magazine*, December 20, 1987.
Arthur Schlesinger Jr.	"At Last: Capitalistic Communism," *The Wall Street Journal*, August 4, 1987.
Donald J. Senese	"China's 'Free Enterprise' Experiment," *The Freeman*, July 1987.
Wang Fang	"Economic Truths and Economic Practice," *Socialist Affairs*, 1/1987.
Zhou Minyi	"Emancipation of the Mind and Reform," *Beijing Review*, June 6-12, 1988.

Does China Guarantee Human Rights?

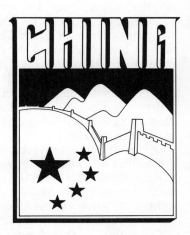

Chapter Preface

Cultural perceptions are an important part of the question of whether China provides human rights for its citizens. Some scholars have argued that China cannot be judged by American standards of human rights. They argue that for centuries Chinese culture has emphasized the duties owed to society, rather than individual self-fulfillment. One reflection of this can be seen in the Chinese language; the Chinese word for "freedom" has unsavory connotations, and there is no Chinese word for "privacy." Thus, some people in and out of China conclude that what Americans view as violations of basic rights are not viewed as such by Chinese citizens.

Others disagree, however, with this conclusion. They state that the desire for freedom is universal, and that the human rights standards outlined in the 1948 United Nations Declaration ought to be guaranteed throughout the world. Critics of China's human rights record point to the 1986/1987 university student demonstrations as evidence that Chinese people desire human rights.

The authors in this chapter debate several controversial human rights issues from both Chinese and American perspectives.

"The Chinese citizens' rights stipulated in the Constitution are superior to Western bourgeoisie's concepts of individual human rights."

China Supports Human Rights

Shen Baoxiang, Wang Chengquan, and Li Zerui

In the following viewpoint, Shen Baoxiang, Wang Chengquan, and Li Zerui state that China's socialist system is more capable of providing human rights than the Western capitalist system. They argue that the concept of individual human rights as it has developed in the West has enabled wealthy nations and people to exploit poorer countries and people. Shen, Wang, and Li are legal workers who write for *The Beijing Review*, an official Chinese newsweekly.

As you read, consider the following questions:

1. According to the authors, what is wrong with Western ideas on human rights?
2. What do the authors believe are the main threats against human rights?
3. How has China supported human rights, according to the authors?

Shen Baoxiang, Wang Chengquan, and Li Zerui, "On the Question of Human Rights in the International Realm," *Beijing Review*, July 26, 1982. Reprinted with permission.

The notion of human rights was first raised by Westerners two or three centuries ago. To challenge the privileges and religious authority of feudal aristocrats and the clergy in the Middle Ages, enlightened bourgeois thinkers at that time created the theory of natural rights and championed such human rights as freedom, equality and the pursuit of happiness. This theory became a powerful ideological weapon for the new emerging bourgeoisie in its fight against feudal autocracy.

The 1776 US Declaration of Independence declared that "all men are created equal, that they are endowed by their Creator with certain unalienable Rights, that among these are Life, Liberty and the Pursuit of Happiness." This was the first time that the bourgeoisie affirmed its demand for and stand on human rights in a political programme. . . .

The theory and slogan of human rights played a fairly progressive role in a historical period and reflected characteristics of that time, and they have exerted widespread influence in the capitalist world for a long time. Human rights were supposed to pertain to all human beings. However, this bourgeois slogan expressed the new bourgeoisie's claims in the most ordinary form of rights. In the name of human rights, the bourgeoisie replaced the feudal lords' hierarchy and hereditary privileges by those derived from its control of money. The rights of freedom refer mainly to the freedom to possess private property. The rights to pursue happiness refer, in fact, to the right to exploit labourers as much as possible and to pursue wealth. Marx pointed out: "The rights of men themselves are considered as privilege." . . .

New Developments

Rights develop as history develops and so do human rights. As a result of the development of history, changes in the economic and political situation, the emergence of new political forces and the development of various struggles in the international community, the concept of human rights has become higher in content than what was defined by the Western bourgeoisie in the 17th and 18th centuries. As far as the concept of human rights defined by the United Nations is concerned, there have been two major developments.

1. Over a long period of time, the bourgeoisie regarded possession of private property as its most important human right. Therefore, it ruthlessly exploited workers and drove them to poverty. Since World War II, the working class' struggle for rights in capitalist countries has intensified, forcing the bourgeoisie to adopt some so-called welfare policies that gave certain benefits to the workers at their own expense.

Internationally, economic, social and cultural rights were embodied in the UN conventions on human rights. . . . The addition of economic, social and cultural rights make the concept of human rights richer in content.

2. Another major development in the concept of human rights is the addition of the notion that the people of colonies and dependencies have the right to self-determination and development....

The struggle to strive for and safeguard human rights is now being linked to the struggle against imperialism, colonialism and hegemonism.

Undue Emphasis on Individual

Some Western politicians and scholars reject the newest definitions of human rights. They place undue emphasis on personal human rights and advocate absolute individual freedom. They also claim these rights to be fundamentally necessary for economic development and ignore the reality of international politics.

One may ask: If a nation is deprived of the right to self-determination, a country is occupied by alien aggressors and the whole nation and people are enslaved and if a country is deprived of sovereignty over its wealth and natural resources and comes under control of colonialism, how can there be individual rights and freedoms? How can the basic conditions for economic development exist?

Immediate Democracy Impractical

The per-capita annual GNP in China is only US$400 and is lower than 100 other countries. In 1982 China had 237.9 million illiterates and semi-literates over 12 years old. The greatest concerns of many citizens are improving their living standards but not state or political affairs. Some farmers know little of things outside their own village and so find it hard to express their opinions about the election of deputies to the county people's congress. Under these circumstances, it is impractical to attempt to turn China overnight into a society with a high level of democracy, on the contrary, it will slow the democratization process.

Lu Yun, *The Beijing Review,* April 20, 1987.

The fact is that today some countries and nations are in such conditions due to the control and enslavement by hegemonism, imperialism and colonialism. In such cases, defence of national rights becomes a precondition for respecting personal human rights....

The bourgeoisie and some unscrupulous people attack the socialist system by taking advantage of human rights. Imperialists and the Western bourgeoisie have never ceased to use human rights to attack and slander China, nor have they reduced their efforts to engage in ideological infiltration of China. Western propaganda machines have consistently distorted coverage of China's human rights activities and social conditions. They claim that the socialist democratic system violates the so-called "human rights." Some have even provided support for people in China engaged in illegal activities under the pretext of promoting human rights. . . .

China's Stand on Human Rights

China's attitude is clear-cut with regard to the purposes and principles of the Charter of the United Nations, including respect for fundamental human rights.

Human rights are not an abstract slogan or an isolated question. They are closely related to international politics. The primary sources of the intense and chaotic international situation, the threat to human security and large-scale violations of fundamental human rights are hegemonism, imperialism, colonialism, especially the contention for hegemony between the two superpowers, the Soviet Union and the United States. The struggle to guarantee fundamental human rights can only be meaningful and succeed after it is combined with the struggle against hegemonism, imperialism and colonialism and becomes one of its components.

The most important task of the international community is to oppose the hegemonists' large-scale violation of fundamental human rights by their aggression against other countries. The Soviet Union's armed occupation of Afghanistan, which has resulted in millions of Afghan refugees living abroad, seriously violates the fundamental human rights of the Afghan people. With the support of the Soviet Union, the Vietnamese hegemonists have invaded Kampuchea and are slaughtering the patriotic Kampuchean soldiers and civilians, thus depriving the Kampuchean people of their fundamental human rights. The aggression of the Soviet and Vietnamese hegemonists runs counter to the purposes and principles of the UN Charter and the international charter of human rights. The United States supports Israel's serious violations of the Palestinian people's fundamental human rights and helps the South African racists who are systematically violating the fundamental human rights of people in southern Africa. Such violations of other people's fundamental human rights have been repeatedly denounced by the just international public opinion and the Chinese Government and people.

Duties of International Community

Another important task of the international community in promoting and guaranteeing fundamental human rights is for the third world countries to strive for the right to economic development. Because the rich countries exploit the poor countries, the people of many third world countries live in poverty and the people of the least developed countries are in still worse conditions. Therefore, the international activities of human rights should show special concern for safeguarding the right of the third world countries to develop their national economies and changing their people's state of poverty. These are also an unshirkable duty of the United Nations, other international organizations and countries, especially the developed countries.

The human rights goals advocated by the United Nations and other international organizations in social and cultural areas such as the elimination of discrimination against women, the protection of children, taking care of the old and the handicapped, the elimination of illiteracy and the promotion of science and technology are also concerns of the international community. China will continue to make its contribution in these fields.

Human Rights and Chinese Culture

Chinese culture appreciates the importance of individuals but places greater emphasis on how a person functions within the context of a larger group. The Chinese language provides insights into both the historical past and the modes of thinking for the present. There is no Chinese word for "privacy." Pause on that point for a few moments. What would be other key attributes of a culture that lacks a term for privacy? How much importance might a contemporary Chinese attach to privacy, or, indeed, how would he think about such a concept? More relevant to our inquiry, how can universal standards be drawn when the Chinese lack a word for one of the West's most important values? . . .

Nor was there a clear sense of a concept of "rights" as that term is used in the West. On the contrary, the emphasis was on the idea of duty. Phrasing obligations in this manner affected the means of enforcement. The principal remedy was subjective, in the sense that a person was made to feel through social pressure that he must perform his duty. The general community was involved by showing disapproval through methods such as gossip or ostracism. There was far less emphasis on giving an aggrieved party a "right" that could be formally enforced in a court or elsewhere against the person failing to perform. . . .

Victor Li, *The China Difference*, 1979.

Using the slogan of human rights to interfere in other countries' essentially international affairs is intolerable in international activities. China follows the Five Principles of Peaceful Coexistence and never interferes in other countries' internal affairs. It also holds that using alleged charges of human rights violations to vilify and attack China and to interfere in China's judicial and administrative affairs is an act unfriendly to China and the Chinese people and a violation of China's sovereignty. China has to refute and oppose it.

The human rights advocated by the bourgeoisie played a progressive role in history. Limited in concept, they primarily meet the needs of the bourgeoisie and are very deceptive to the working class and other working people. Class exploitation is the greatest social inequality. The system of exploitation is the major cause of various forms of social inequality. Under the system of exploitation of man by man, it is impossible to really satisfy people's demands for rights. Marxists hold that only when the system of exploitation is eliminated and social productive forces are fully developed can the broad masses of people fully enjoy political, economic, social and cultural rights and can the rights genuinely become universal.

China's socialist practice has proved that only the socialist system can guarantee the full implementation of the people's rights. By making revolution, China overthrew the rule of imperialism and feudalism, transformed the political system of dictatorship of big landlords and the big bourgeoisie, established the people's democratic political power, eliminated the system of exploitation and enabled social productive forces, science, education and cultural undertakings to develop rapidly. This has brought about a fundamental change in the political and economic positions of the Chinese people.

All the revolutionary achievements and all the rights the Chinese people gained are recorded in the Chinese Constitution. Its stipulations on citizens' freedom of person, political rights, as well as economic, social and cultural rights, and on equality of all nationalities, guarantee of the national minorities' legal rights and interests and prohibition of discrimination and oppression against any nationalities are specific manifestations of practising fundamental human rights. The stipulations on the inviolability of socialist public property, prohibitions against exploitation and guarantees of each individual's labour gains constitute a solid foundation for guaranteeing fundamental human rights.

Chinese System Superior

These principles were reiterated in the recently promulgated draft of the revised Chinese Constitution, which clearly stipulates that the freedom of person of citizens, the personal dignity of citizens and the homes of citizens are inviolable, and that the freedom and privacy of correspondence of citizens are protected by law. This shows that socialist democracy is in essence far superior to bourgeois democracy.

Anyone free of prejudice can see that the Chinese citizens' rights stipulated in the Constitution are superior to Western bourgeoisie's concepts of individual human rights. . . .

Along with the gradual improvement of our socialist democracy and legal system and the development of the four modernizations, our people's rights will surely be expanded and raised to a new height. Further evidence will prove that the socialist system is a reliable guarantee for fully implementing human rights.

"The concept of law, democracy, and human rights... is still alien to the Chinese Communists."

China Violates Human Rights

Franz Michael and Yuan-li Wu

Franz Michael is professor emeritus at George Washington University in Washington, DC, where he directed the Institute for Sino-Soviet Studies. Yuan-li Wu is a professor of economics at the University of San Francisco, and has written thirty-five books on China and Asia. In the following viewpoint, the authors criticize Communist China's human rights record. They argue that China's Marxist-Leninist leadership has uprooted the rights of many people because its totalitarian policies aimed at furthering the Communist revolution have denied individual freedom.

As you read, consider the following questions:

1. What traditional Chinese ideas do the authors believe support human rights?
2. What communist ideas preclude human rights, according to the authors?
3. According to Michael and Wu, how have human rights been violated in China?

Franz Michael and Yuan-li Wu, *Human Rights in the People's Republic of China.* Boulder, CO: Westview Press, 1988. Reprinted with permission.

Communism appears to be at a crossroads everywhere; China under communism is in a more uncertain state, thanks to Mao Zedong (Mao Tse-tung). Communist societies in general are looking for more viable solutions to their economic and social problems. This search is more urgent and critical in China. . . . The future of human rights in China is inextricably intertwined with whatever may emerge from the present flux.

In order to appreciate what the Chinese Communists have done, we must realize that, contrary to what some in the West might believe, modern concepts of human rights were deeply imbedded in certain ethical tenets fundamental to the Chinese creed. The ancient and traditional Chinese belief in a moral universe—"Heaven" in Chinese terminology—that is reflected in a "moral human order" goes back to the thirteenth century before Christ. The ruler was responsible to Heaven to maintain this bond: In order to fulfill this task he was given the Mandate of Heaven, which was bestowed upon him and his family only on condition that he possessed and retained the necessary moral quality—"virtue." When he lost the mandate, his dynasty could be overthrown. Virtue guaranteed ethically correct actions by the ruler and supplied the basis for the acknowledgment of the ruler's supreme authority by the people. The people's happiness, on the other hand, was to be his chief concern. Thus, virtue was the fountainhead of correct policy; correct policy legitimized the sovereign's rule. Finally, policy was correct when it promoted harmony among persons and between persons and nature.

Chinese Ethics

The substance of this Chinese traditional concept of morality was expounded by Confucius (551-479 B.C.), who prescribed moral standards for the family, society, and the ruler and which he claimed to have derived from the sages of the past. The most intrinsic of these Confucian and still traditional Chinese concepts are the principles of *jen*—compassion for others, often translated as "humanism" or "humanity"—and *i*—"integrity," a consciousness of the moral obligation of one's own right behavior. When Confucianism became the prevailing school of thought in the second century B.C., these and other Confucian ethical concepts came to constitute a moral code that was enforced by social pressure, which, although supplemented by legal sanctions, performed by itself the essential functions of law in the West. . . .

Throughout the recorded history of China there have been, of course, many incidences of cruelty, barbarism, and inhumanity. But these violated the ethical ideals set forth in Chinese political philosophy and constantly upheld by the political leaders steeped in the Confucian tradition. The humanist tradition of China, in fact, provided a hospitable climate for human rights. Chinese political history and political thought do not lack a well-developed, ever-refined concept of human relations that embodies human rights concepts. When the Chinese empire crumbled, traditional ethical principles provided the foundation for a new legal order, complete with due process of law, like that imported from European continental law. The new system was a synthesis of the two compatible systems that were promulgated by the Nationalist government after the abdication of the last Manchu emperor in 1911. Most students of Chinese history would argue that one can readily see how precommunist, traditional Chinese humanism would be at home with human rights in the Western tradition and how a new legal system introduced after the 1911 revolution eventually could become the nexus for a new national social order.

The Chinese Context

"Human rights are a Western concept, and thus have no relevance in the Chinese context." The inherent logic of this line of thought, though seldom expressed with such frankness, amounts to saying: "Human rights are one of those luxuries that befit us wealthy and advanced Westerners; it is preposterous to imagine that mere natives of exotic countries could qualify for a similar privilege, or would even be interested in it." Or, more simply: "Human rights do not apply to the Chinese, because the Chinese are not really human."

Simon Leys, *The Burning Forest*, 1986.

To us, the concept of human rights in the West is built on the fundamental principles of (1) protection under law; (2) genuine popular participation in government, that is, democracy; (3) economic freedom of choice, which provides the material base for personal and political freedom; and (4) freedom of the mind, spirit, or will. These concepts, which lead to limited government, are rooted in Western history, from ancient philosophies and legal codifications to major events in relatively modern times, such as the Declaration of Independence, the Bill of Rights, the United Nations Universal Declaration of Human Rights of December 10, 1948, to name a few. These same ideals are found in Chinese history.

Communism and the Chinese Tradition

By contrast, the Communist party that came into power in 1949 forsook the Chinese tradition. The party drew inspiration from the Marxist-Leninist theory of society while rejecting the ideals of Western political thought cited in the previous paragraph. Therefore, conditions in China changed radically after 1949. The Marxist-Leninist theory that the Chinese Communists made their own views society as composed of mutually antagonistic classes. This explains class struggle, which in turn explains the existence of a Communist party. This state of affairs precludes, by definition, the protection of the human rights of the individual. Furthermore, because the state, its institutions, and its legal norms are nothing but instruments used by the ruling class to suppress the other classes, these instruments remain in the hands of the revolutionary class only as instruments of suppression of opponent classes and as tools for the forcible transformation of society. This reasoning underlies the Marxist-Leninist concept of the "dictatorship of the proletariat," which is clearly incompatible with the idea of the protection of the individual's human rights. Class struggle replaces harmony; "historical necessity" and the laws of "historical development" govern human relations, truth, and justice. To make this conclusion, which is based on the original assumption of antagonistic classes, more convincing, the term *scientific socialism* then is employed.

V. I. Lenin spoke of the need for a group of professional revolutionaries, which he called "the vanguard of the proletariat." Such a vanguard is needed to articulate and carry out the will of the revolutionary class. Class differentiation and class struggle add to the inequality of status among citizens and justify the violation of human rights in the name of the goals of socialist revolution. . . . Since 1949, China, no less than the Soviet Union, has been an apostle of Lenin in all these aspects.

When the Chinese Communists established the People's Republic, their policies followed communist doctrine as a matter of course. The Communists abandoned traditional humanism because it was "feudalistic"; they discarded Western ideas that the Nationalist government had tried to introduce because they were "capitalistic," "bourgeois," and "imperialistic." The concept of human rights, because it was "bourgeois," had to be replaced by collective rights that serve and are served by the transformation of society to socialism through class struggle. The revolutionary class is justified, under "scientific socialism," in doing whatever is necessary for the purpose of building and sustaining a socialist system and supporting the Communist party and the "dictatorship of the proletariat" within the framework of Marxist-Leninist doctrine, to which has been added the Thought of Mao. Under Mao Zedong this policy reached an extreme form.

Three Developments

First, the whole legal order introduced by the Nationalist government, including civil codes, criminal law, the court system, and legal procedure, was abrogated in toto. But this order was not replaced by any formal legal structure, not even the kind of law that by then had been accepted in the Soviet Union. Mao, who regarded all forms of law as an unwanted restraint on the latitude of his violent actions, refused during the years to admit any legal norms that would

Mike Lukavich for the New Orleans Times-Picayune. Reprinted with permission.

have introduced an element of stability into his perpetual revolution.

Second, in their intention to carry out the violent class struggle and transformation of society, Mao and the Communist party as a whole employed instead another instrument of political force: the organization of mass movements of fanaticized followers in "campaigns" or "drives" against designated targets. These campaigns were turned on and off according to changing policy decisions; the campaigns were a weapon of terror that was stronger, more brutal, and more destructive of human nature and the social fabric than a normative tool for social transformation could have been. The campaigns were accompanied and partly preceded by the careful construction of a comprehensive network of controls over all aspects of the people's lives. Use of these tools and the arbitrary exercise of controls brought abuse and humiliations, imprisonment and forced labor camps, torture, brutalization, and death to tens of millions of people. The regulations employed by the authorities, such as the Statute for the Punishment of Counterrevolutionary Activities, first issued on February 20, 1951, and reissued as recently as 1979, three years after Mao's death, were vague in defining alleged crimes, retroactive and inordinately harsh, and undeserving of the term "law," in the Western sense.

Third, given the total absence of domestic and external restraints, with the tools of control and a messianic zeal the Communist party proceeded to make over Chinese society in the party's image. The means by which the goals of social transformation and economic development were pursued varied according to changing priorities.

The impact of these developments on human rights has been disastrous. The devastating consequences of early policies often have been compounded by new efforts to undo the effects of failed policies. The Great Proletarian Cultural Revolution of 1966-1976, launched by Mao Zedong, was the most recent of the movements. After the death of Mao in 1976, the communist leadership under Deng Xiaoping (Teng Hsiaop'ing) began to look for alternatives. It turned haltingly to the introduction of law, as had the Soviet Union. Laws are needed to deal with rampant crimes in a consistent manner and, more importantly, to provide legal guarantees for foreign business, which now is invited to enter the Chinese market in order to spur economic development and thus to help sustain the Communist party's rule. The PRC's new leaders began to experiment with reforms in order to rehabilitate the economy and thereby retreated from the original goal of social transformation. These leaders also once more began to try coopting China's intellectuals, whose assistance the leaders now realized they still needed. Consistent laws also would help, but the leaders can move in this direction only haltingly; having possessed total power for so long, they hate to risk losing it. In fact, the leaders considered loosening political controls extremely dangerous because it could release pent up desires for freedom and rights in China's millions that would jeopardize the party and the system. But these same leaders had to rebuild the public's confidence in the ability, truthfulness, and goodwill of the Chinese Communist party and its leaders.

US Lip Service

Amid all the deliberate, as well as aimless, thrashings of change, human rights have been given only inconsistent lip service. When President Jimmy Carter extended diplomatic recognition to the PRC in December 1978, he gave the Chinese Communists a much-needed boost and respite. However, when he declared that concern with human rights was "the soul" of U.S. foreign policy, Chinese leaders characterized this U.S. emphasis as "hypocritical farce."

When President Ronald Reagan visited Beijing in 1984 and spoke of personal security and the people's freedom "to think, speak, worship, choose their own way and reach for the stars" as the best conditions for economic development, his PRC hosts tried hard to restrict the public circulation in China of his message. The concept of law, democracy, and human rights, as well as their integral relationship to continual economic progress, is still alien to the Chinese Communists.

As late as March 1985, a ranking cadre challenged a court of law on the right to summon one of his lieutenants. When told that the court was acting in accordance with the law, he retorted: "Law is

114

meant for the foreigners to look at and to placate the democratic elements." On the other hand, Chinese Communist leaders always are ready to applaud when the United States admits its own faults in human rights....

The four fundamental or cardinal principles upon whose adherence Deng Xiaoping has insisted in his reform efforts—the leadership of the Chinese Communist party, the socialist road, the dictatorship of the proletariat, and Marxism-Leninism-Mao Zedong Thought—make clear that Communist party control continues and that the totalitarian framework and methods remain intact.

"No post-Mao campaign has involved more violations of elemental human rights than population control."

China's Population Policy Violates Human Rights

Steven W. Mosher

China's population stood at 548 million in 1949, 696 million in 1964, and over one billion in 1982. To limit further population growth, China began a policy in 1979 of limiting couples to one child. In the following viewpoint, Steven W. Mosher argues that this policy destroys human rights. He states that women have been coerced and forced to have unwanted abortions, and that because sons are traditionally prized more than daughters, the policy has led to female infanticide. Mosher directs the Asian Studies Center at The Claremont Institute. In 1979 he became one of the first anthropologists granted permission to conduct research in a rural area in China. He was later charged with spying and expelled by the Chinese government after publishing several articles that criticized China's population policy.

As you read, consider the following questions:

1. What examples of human rights abuses does Mosher describe?
2. Why do many Chinese prefer boys to girls, according to the author? Does he believe their reasons are justifiable?
3. Why does the author believe China might respond to US criticism of its programs?

Steven W. Mosher, "Human Rights in the New China." Published by permission of Transaction Publishers from *Society* vol. 23, no. 2. Copyright © 1986 by Transaction Publishers.

The People's Republic of China presents the world's most serious long-term human rights problem, not only in the number of violations but in their severity as well. The direction that post-Mao reform has taken in recent years—especially the return to family farming, the reopening of the rural markets, and the legalization of privately owned shops—has widened freedom of choice in the economic sphere. The carry-over of this liberalization into the political and cultural spheres has been minimal. The People's Republic of China (PRC) remains a one-party, Marxist state determined to maintain close control over how its populace thinks and behaves.

The Maoist tactic of the mass mobilization campaign—an all-out push for some party-identified objective—continues to be one of the primary means by which control is exerted. Since the normal rules of society are suspended for the duration, campaigns are very costly in terms of human rights. . . .

Population Control

No post-Mao campaign has involved more violations of elemental human rights than population control. The current campaign can be said to have begun in 1979 when Peking adopted a long-term plan to severely restrict population growth. As originally drawn up, the natural population increase rate (births minus deaths) was to be reduced from the then 1.4 percent to 0.5 percent by 1985, and to zero population growth by the end of the century. A decision the following year to hold the population under 1.2 billion by the turn of the century marked a retrenchment from these earlier goals, but still virtually mandated a limit of one child per family for the next twenty years. In February 1980 Chen Muhua, the vice-premier then in charge of population control, made this limit explicit: "We will try to attain the goal that 95 percent of married couples in the cities and 90 percent in the countryside will have only one child in due course."

In theory one child per family was to be achieved by a system of economic rewards and penalties. Couples could still choose to have a second or third child but would be taxed for doing so. In practice these penalties were so heavy—amounting in some areas to a year's income or more—that their imposition would have devastated a family's economy. Soon the one-child limit had become compulsory, and second and third pregnancies were to be aborted whenever they occurred. If there were any doubts that coerced abortion and sterilization was de facto state policy, they were dispelled by Wang Pingshan, the vice governor of Canton province and member of the Central Committee of the Chinese Communist party, who stated:

> Those women who have already given birth to one child must be fitted with IUDs, and couples who already have two children must undergo sterilization of either the husband or the wife.

Women with unplanned pregnancies must adopt remedial measures [i.e., abortion] as soon as possible. This is based on the directives of the Chinese Communist Party Central Committee and the State Council and on the summation of family planning practices of many years. . . . To put [the policy on childbirth] precisely, all state cadres, workers and employees, and urban residents, except for special cases which must be approved, may have only one child per couple. One child per couple is promoted universally in the rural areas. . . . Birth plan targets must be strictly set according to the policy on childbirth.

Vice governor Wang's references to "unplanned pregnancies" and "birth plan targets" were not made casually. By 1981 a nationwide quota system for births was in place. . . .

Changes Not Relaxation

"Attempts by Chinese officials and by foreign apologists to represent recent changes in China's family planning policies as a major relaxation of program requirements do not accord with the facts. . . . The Chinese program remains highly coercive."

John Aird, quoted in *National Right to Life News*, December 3, 1987.

Once annual provincial target figures for births are set, they are broken down proportionately by prefecture, county, town, and district. Each unit—a village, a factory, or government bureau—receives a yearly allotment of allowable births. Although it is the one-child-per-family limitation that has captured the attention of the media, the population control program actually goes well beyond the proscription of second and subsequent births. Couples are not only prevented from giving birth to more than one child, they are allowed to conceive that one child only after they have received written permission from their unit.

Officials Control Quotas

The quotas given to the basic units are very small. In the South China commune in which I lived during 1979-80, a typical neighborhood has been given a quota of only seven babies a year since 1981. Since newborns previously numbered fifteen to twenty in any given year, this has meant a substantial reduction in the number of live births permitted. As a result, there are far more couples anxiously awaiting parenthood than there are conception certificates available, and the competition is intense. Many newly married couples must remain childless for several years before they are awarded quotas.

Deciding who gets a quota is the prerogative of local officials, who often set additional conditions—such as eventual sterilization—for the anxious applicants. How this licensing of first births worked in one commune in South China was described to me by a population control worker. "Every village will be given an annual quota of babies," she explained. "Newlyweds who wish to have a child must apply to the commune birth control office for a birth quota. To receive this, they must meet two conditions: They must fall within their brigade's yearly quota. And they must agree to have only one child." Couples who conceive a child without first obtaining a permit are ordered to attend birth control meetings, at which they are pressured to accept the one-child limit and sterilization. "After all, sterilization is better than abortion," this official concluded.

Such a rigorous quota system could not be enforced if Chinese society were not already highly regimented by the Communist party. Every Chinese belongs from birth to a unit, and every unit is headed by party officials. These men (for they are almost invariably male) wield enormous power over the lives of their subordinates, deciding who earns bonuses, who gets housing space, who gets good land, who grows cash crops, who gets married, and now who has a child.

Local party chiefs have been told in no uncertain terms that they must "grasp fertility planning work firmly" and meet the quotas. 'Although the task is difficult, the birth targets can be attained with strong leadership," they are exhorted by higher-ups. To further strengthen the resolve of local officials, they have been increasingly subject to various rewards and sanctions. From the early eighties on, local leaders have been required to take the lead in family planning. They are expected to be the first in their units to sign a single-child pledge, to abort a child who does not have a quota, and to accept sterilization. Cadres who have been forced to severely limit their own fertility in this fashion will presumably be more zealous in limiting that of others in their domain....

Pregnancy a Crime

As in other campaigns there have been excesses. The most well-known may have occurred in Huiyang prefecture, a dozen counties in Canton province lying adjacent to Hong Kong. In the spring of 1981, orders went out that all unborn children over the quota were to be aborted. Force was to be used when necessary. Making a house-to-house sweep of each village in the prefecture, local authorities rounded up expectant mothers, including many in their last months of pregnancy. The public security bureau of one county even issued arrest warrants for pregnant women on which the word *pregnant* was entered as the offense for which they were charged. Women were often bound hand and foot, thrown into hog cages, and delivered by the truckload to rural abortion clinics. There they were strapped down on operating tables and aborted. For fifty days this local campaign lasted. The number of victims—mothers and infants—in one county alone reached 38,000.

For the most part, other techniques are used in China in preference to brute force. Pregnant women are often arrested, taken from their homes and families, locked up some miles away, and subjected to grueling propaganda sessions. The woman and her family are fined, harassed, and threatened over the course of these sessions. In the eyes of the government these measures are not coercive. Before the abortion itself is performed the woman must have ceased her resistance. She must walk to the abortion clinic under her own power. As long as she does, the party considers the abortion or infanticide that follows to be voluntary.

Coercion Exists

Planned Parenthood and the rest of the population establishment assert that the Chinese program is voluntary. They should think again. To the Chinese, the word "voluntary" includes pressuring someone until she or he agrees to use contraception or abortion. In the U.S. we call that arm-twisting.

This is supported by official Chinese sources. Indeed, although Chinese authorities repudiate particular events—such as coerced seven-month abortions—as unrepresentative excesses, the presence of government coercion in Chinese family affairs cannot be denied.

Julian L. Simon, *The Wall Street Journal*, February 29, 1988.

How much coercion is there? In a survey of peasant preferences as to size of family and sex of offspring I found that the official norm of one child per couple was unacceptable to the villagers I interviewed. All of the women I interviewed stated a preference for two or more children; none were willing to stop at just one. Official surveys from widely dispersed parts of China have produced similar results. Based on the results of these studies, I estimate that roughly 90 percent, or 47,000,000 of the 53,000,000 abortions performed in the last five years have been involuntary.

Evading the Ban

No campaign which is so contrary to the wishes of the Chinese people could achieve perfect compliance. Some women do manage to become pregnant outside of the plan, often by having their state-inserted IUDs removed by so-called black, or illegal, doctors for a small fee. They keep their pregnancies secret, telling only their families; they avoid prenatal physicals because the clinic midwives would report their condition to the authorities. They continue to work in the fields as usual, binding up their abdomens under their baggy pants and blouses from the fourth month on so that their pregnancy will not show. Many avoid detection until they are only two or three months from term. Others practice what is called "childbirth on the run," leaving their home villages and going away to live in the hills or in the homes of relatives in distant villages and towns. Because of the prevalence of these forms of passive resistance to the quota system, abortion in the second and third trimesters of pregnancy remains common. Although abortion is said to be illegal in China after the first trimester of pregnancy, this law is violated with impunity by officials under pressure to meet their quotas.

Those women who manage to carry their children to term face another challenge. In many areas a woman brought into a delivery room must prove to the satisfaction of hospital officials that she has a quota for the child she is in the process of birthing. Those who cannot produce a government-issued birth certificate are given an involuntary abortion. This is infanticide, for it results in the death of a full-term, healthy infant. In South China, where I was, the child is killed by means of a poison shot into the womb or by strangling as it emerges. In one area of North China, according to Michael Weisskopf in the *Washington Post,* the usual method was an injection of formaldehyde into the soft spot of the infant's head or the actual crushing of its skull by forceps. That this infanticide is carried out at the insistence of the party and government is indisputable. These operations are performed in government hospitals and clinics by government doctors acting under the orders of party officials.

Killing Baby Girls

Government-endorsed infanticide is the violent response of officials caught between the quota system and parents' desires for more children. Female infanticide is the desperate act of parents caught between those same pressures. In the killing of newborn baby girls, peasant resistance to one-child controls finds its most tragic expression.

The wave of female infanticide sweeping China is a direct consequence of a population control policy that restricts families to one child, ignores the realities of old-age economics in the countryside, and systematically denigrates the value of human life. While the arrival of a son has always been a more important event in a family than the birth of a daughter, Peking's one-child-per-family campaign has raised the stakes. For the peasantry, birth has become a kind of Russian roulette; the arrival of a son heralds a relaxed and secure old age; the coming of a daughter portends poverty and slow starvation during one's declining years. It is not feudal nonsense, as the government would have it, but economic reality that moves the parents to hope for a son.

If the child is not a male, then the choice is a stark one: either kill or abandon the newborn female infant, reserving your one-child quota for the birth of a boy, or face a harrowing old age. It is no surprise that many peasants decide in favor of their own security and trade the infant's life for their own. Were parents in America forced to choose between their social security pensions and their newborn child, surely we should find cases of infanticide occurring here as well. . . .

With quotas imposed on a reluctant population by powerful local officials—themselves pressured by their party superiors to curb births—widespread coerced abortion, government infanticide, and female infanticide have been the inevitable result. The human costs of the birth control campaign are staggering. Deaths from female infanticide to date, based on calculations from official statistics, have probably reached 1,300,000. Higher mortality rates among women of childbearing age, a result of government denial of prenatal care to women pregnant with overquota children and of the dangers of late-term abortions, suggest several hundred thousand more persons must be added to this casualty list.

The main cost of the program must be counted in infants' lives. Between 1971 and 1984, China's state-run abortion clinics performed over 114,000,000 abortions, a number greater than the population of Japan. . . .

The US Response

In considering possible United States responses to the human rights abuses associated with the several continuing PRC mass campaigns, especially the birth control campaign, two interrelated questions must be answered. Is it in the interest of the United States to attempt to improve the human rights situation in China? What action by the United States, if any, would achieve a worthwhile amelioration of conditions in the PRC?

As a nation founded specifically to preserve human rights, such concerns have always been central to America's conceptualization of itself and a primary focus of our foreign policy. Unless there is reasonable cause to think that any action taken toward the PRC would be counterproductive, either because it would exacerbate the human rights situation over the short term or because it would reduce the attractiveness of our democratic traditions as a model over the long term, we are obliged to make an effort.

The human rights policy of recent administrations has two sides, the positive and the negative. The positive side is embodied in the way we seek over the long run to promote democracy, the surest safeguard of human rights. The negative side refers to the way in which we oppose through actions or words specific human rights violations in the short term. Long-term prospects for the gradual democratization of the PRC must be rated pessimistically. The Communist party appears determined not to allow the spread of liberalization from economics to other areas of China's polity, nor even to permit significant deviation from its own ideological and social norms. Under these circumstances, there is little we can do on the positive side to contribute to the reestablishment of democracy in China. At the same time, we need not be concerned that by asserting the importance of human rights we would create an internal backlash in the PRC that would jeopardize a nonexistent ideological and political liberalization.

We can ameliorate the worst violations of human rights committed in the heat of coercive campaigns. The PRC, to a greater extent than the Soviet Union and many other countries, is concerned about its image overseas because of traditional Chinese considerations of saving face. While the Chinese authorities are remarkably insensitive to public opinion at home—except when it is viewed as a threat to their control—they are remarkably sensitive to international criticism. This sensitivity—the exaggerated Chinese response to praise or criticism—should not be made an excuse for inaction, as it sometimes is, but used as a basis for affirmative action in human rights.

"In China there is no alternative but to put the One-Child Policy into practice so as to benefit the whole society."

China's Population Policy Is Necessary

Sun Yuesheng and Wei Zhangling

In recent years the Chinese government has acknowledged problems with its policy of limiting couples to one child. However, China still maintains that overpopulation is a major problem, and that efforts to control population growth are needed. In the following viewpoint, Sun Yuesheng and Wei Zhangling list positive and negative results of China's One-Child Policy. They conclude that population control is essential for China's future development. Sun and Wei are members of the Chinese Academy of Social Sciences in Beijing, China.

As you read, consider the following questions:

1. What traditional attitudes towards population and families do the authors describe? How do they affect population planning in China?
2. What problems stemming from the One-Child Policy do the authors describe? How do they respond to them?
3. What differences do the authors describe between Chinese and Western societies? Do you think this makes foreign criticism of China less valid?

Sun Yuesheng and Wei Zhangling, "The One-Child Policy in China Today," *Journal of Comparative Family Studies*, Summer 1987. Reprinted with permission.

When we talk about the One-Child Policy in contemporary China, it is necessary to point out the following three facts:

1. Population theories, policies, and adjustments depend on, as well as direct and impel, human social practice.
2. Throughout history, societies have shared some common theories and practices regarding population growth and control. However, each society has also developed its own unique theories and practices, in light of its unique socio-economic situation and experience. This is especially true in the area of direct population adjustment.
3. Conscious adjustments by particular societies to control the growth of their populations will center around family planning and will be based on the situation faced by individual societies. As the world becomes smaller, however, the destinies of human beings become more closely intertwined. Therefore, it is necessary to evaluate the population policies of different societies, and to view the world as one community rather than for each society to act in isolation. . . .

In regard to different population policies of the Chinese government, we can divide the 37 years since the Liberation of 1949 into three periods: (1) From 1949 to 1963 (except 1958-1960) there was a high rate of marriages and a high rate of fertility in general. At the same time the mortality rate decreased quickly and the natural growth rate of the population was rising rather quickly; (2) From 1964 to 1977 the government advocated that young people should marry at a later age and began to control fertility; (3) From 1978 up to the present the policy of the government first encouraged and then required couples to bear only one child.

China's Policies

In general, the One-Child Policy in contemporary China is the required and expected approach to the stresses of unrestrained growth. There is no alternative but to deal firmly with the urgent population problem. In 1949, China's population was already rather large, at 548 million. The average natural growth of the population each year since 1949 has been above 20%. Since then, there have been two periods of very high birthrates: 1954-1957 and 1962-1971. During these years, an average of 20 million children were born each year. Expressed another way, each year China reproduced a population analogous to the populations of Holland and Belgium. In world history, it is unusual to find such an extreme population explosion. As the life of the Chinese people improved and became more stable, the pattern of high birthrate, high mortality and low natural growth before 1949 was replaced by a pattern of high birthrate, low mortality and high natural growth after 1949. Of the one billion Chinese people today, half of them were born after 1949. . . .

It is well-known that China is mainly an agricultural country. The following basic factors have forced the government to carry out the One-Child Policy in present-day China.

1. The extent of cultivated area in China is very small, and is currently estimated at 1.4-1.8 billion Chinese mou [1 acre=0.15 Chinese mou]. The amount of cultivated land is decreasing because of the development of industry and transportation. In the countryside the average cultivated area per capita has declined from 3 mou in 1949 to 1.5 mou at present. This represents a sharp reduction of 50%. It is a heavy burden to feed a large population with a limited amount of cultivated land.

2. The population distribution of China is not proportionate. The west part, between Mohe in Heilongjiang Province to Ruili in Yunan Province, comprises about half the area of China yet accounts for only 6% of the Chinese population. Moreover, the population density in the west is 10.7 people per square kilometre, compared with 590 in the Jiangsu Province in the east.

The small and middle-sized cities are not so developed. In 1983 the total urban population was 241.26 million, constituting 23.5% of the whole population. Among the urban population, the population of towns constitutes 27.6%, while cities account for 72.4%. The metropolitan population has become a heavy burden to the country. There is no alternative but to carry out the One-Child Policy so as to alleviate the problem.

Posters throughout China encourage families to have only one child.

3. The standard of living in China is still very low, as China is a developing country. In the cities, the problems of housing, shopping, child care, education, medicine, sanitation, communication, and transportation have become extremely pressing and must be solved. In 1982 the National Statistics Bureau of China investigated the living facilities of 232 cities. The results reveal a low standard of living and inadequate living facilities.

In China there is no alternative but to put the One-Child Policy into practice so as to benefit the whole society. Even if there was only one child born for each couple beginning in 1980, it would still take 30 years, i.e., until 2010, to reach the goal of zero population growth for the whole country. Since the fertility of Chinese women is rather high, this goal is not easily reached. . . .

From the above facts we can draw the following three conclusions:
1. The One-Child Policy in China today is a product of Chinese historical development;
2. The One-Child Policy in China today is a product of the changing population policies formulated by the Chinese government since 1949; and
3. The One-Child Policy in China today has developed as a result of urgent social and economic circumstances. It is designed to relax population pressure in this historical period, and it is destined to change in the future.

Achievements of the One-Child Policy

Any society is complex. A policy such as China's One-Child Policy is bound to be met with resistance and achievement of this policy's objectives will certainly exact a sacrifice from the people. Nevertheless, provided this sacrifice is beneficial to later generations in that this kind of sacrifice will not be necessary in the future, and provided that this sacrifice is beneficial to the world community generally by preventing the serious consequences arising from a population explosion, then the sacrifice is worthwhile. Meanwhile, though, the Chinese people must deal with the negative effects of the One-Child Policy.

Since 1978 the Chinese government has concentrated on controlling fertility. The new Marriage Law promulgated on September 10, 1980 (taking effect on January 1, 1981) stipulates that the minimum legal marriage age for women is 20 years and for men is 22 years. The twelfth article of the Law especially stipulates: Both the husband and wife in a family have the obligation to practice family planning. As early as 1978, the government began to encourage young couples to bear only one child. At that time, the slogan was: "One child is best." In recent years the rules and regulations of birth control have been perfected. Now, the regulations are as follows:

Among the national cadres, workers and urbanites, one cou-

127

ple is only allowed to bear one child, except those people who are approved by the authorities as exceptional cases... In the countryside we advocate that one couple only bear one child in general. For some masses, if they really have practical difficulties and require to bear the second child, it could be arranged into plan after examination and approval. In any case, it is unallowable to bear the third child. As regards national minorities, the demand could be properly relaxed.

Since the One-Child Policy has been carried out, it has been marked by considerable achievements. During the 30 years from 1949 to 1979, the average natural population growth was about 25%. According to 1985 statistics, the national fertility rate is now 16.97%, the national mortality rate is 6.16%, and the national natural population growth rate is 10.81%. This achievment indicates the success of the One-Child Policy as well as the great sacrifice made by the ordinary people in China.

No Evidence of Human Rights Violations

Public opinion in the United States was greatly influenced by dramatic reports from 1981 to 1983 of widespread female infanticide and coercive abortions. But since that time, intensive research has failed to find evidence of coercive practices. The U.S. Embassy in Beijing reported that [in 1986] it found no evidence of human-rights violations....

When the one-child policy started in 1979, China was still recovering from the severe social trauma of the Cultural Revolution. Based on my field work in all parts of China, I believe that more unwanted babies are now being killed or abandoned in the United States than die from infanticide in China.

Carl E. Taylor, Minneapolis *Star Tribune*, September 2, 1987.

It is well-known that the One-Child Policy has had both positive and negative effects from Chinese society and families. The positive effects are:

1. *Higher Standard of Living.*
   The policy has helped to develop the national economy, and to raise the national income and living standard. From 1979 to 1982, the average annual growth rate of national income was 6.3%. The gross industrial and agricultural output increased by 7.3% per year, while population grew an average of 1.3% per year. The ratio of these three indicators was: 4.8:5.6:1.0. Although these figures provide some grounds for optimism, we cannot be satisfied with this performance. Because of the long-term high growth rate of the population and the difficulties in economic development, China still has a long way to go in dealing with the dilemma.

2. *Social Development.*

The policy provides the opportunity to clear away the old and backward family ideas, customs and habits, such as the patriarchal-feudal clan system, the inferior position of women, patriarchal behavior, superstitious belief, and tedious family etiquette. Thus, it will contribute a lot to women's liberation and contribute to the trend from large families to small ones, and from extended families to nuclear ones.

3. *Increased Quality of Life.*

The policy serves to raise the quality of the nation. Since only one child is allowed per family, the whole society and all families are inclined to pay greater attention to the birth, nurture, care and education of the children. In this sense, eugenics will develop in our country. The system for physical examination before marriage has been reinforced. Sex education among adolescents and adults has been encouraged, and yet just a few years ago, this was a forbidden topic.

4. *Increased Social Assistance.*

The policy renders support to enlarge social welfare and security and employs this as an effective measure to relieve the fear of the old people. Since liberation, many homes for the elderly have been set up, and the whole society has shown solicitude for the old people. More and more articles on this topic have been published in newspapers and magazines. As a result, this policy will lead more and more old people to become independent of their offspring, although the official propaganda and public opinion have appealed to the younger generations to take good care of the elders. This tendency will gradually result in substantial changes to family structures.

Negative Effects

The negative effects of the policy are:

1. *Social and Psychological Maladjustment and Pressure.*

The policy has already caused many problems for the one-child families. The parents and grandparents tend to spoil an only son or daughter. From the sociological and psychological perspectives, the only child is inclined to be wilful, arrogant, unsociable and eccentric. He lacks peers to play with, and has no brothers and sisters to assist the socialization process. He will be overloaded with family responsibilities when he grows up. We must pay attention to these problems now; otherwise, the only-child problems will become more serious in the future and last for a long time.

2. *Unbalanced Sex Ratio.*

The policy will make the sex ratio somewhat inappropriate. That is because the one-child policy will lead some people fond of boys to kill or injure the baby girls, or use some secret recipe (handed down from generation to generation) to control sex selection of babies. The ratio of males to females in China has always been rather high in most parts of the country (except Shanghai and Tibet). This phenomenon has something to do with the traditional idea that sons are superior to daughters. How long will this last? It is a complicated problem.

3. *Increased Incidence of Divorce.*

The policy may cause the divorce rate to rise. Reasons for a higher divorce rate would probably include: changes in social and family values; the wilfulness of the only-child; a decreased burden associated with child-raising; and, the inappropriate sex ratio.

4. *Older Population.*

The policy will alter the demographic composition of the population. There will be a tendency towards larger numbers of old people as mortality and fertility decrease. . . .

Resistance to the One-Child Policy

It goes without saying that there is great resistance to promoting the One-Child Policy in China. The resistance mainly stems from the following two factors:

1. *Ideology.*

The feudalistic and patriarchal family ideas have been lingering in the minds of the Chinese people for several thousand years. The core of the feudalistic and patriarchal family ideas is that in any family, be it an ordinary family or the family of an emperor, there must be sons to inherit the family career and property. Ethical norms such as this seem more powerful than laws. . . .

Infanticide Illegal

Infanticide is illegal, and violators face prison. Chinese officials readily admitted that some overzealous local officers went off the deep end and practiced coercion when the one child policy was first implemented. . . . But they say, and Western observers agree, that such instances are increasingly infrequent and that the uproar in the Western media focused Government attention on the problem.

James H. Scheuer, *The New York Times*, January 24, 1987.

The One-Child Policy is a direct challenge to this deep-rooted prejudice. It means that in the forthcoming decades, millions of new couples who have girls must break with this traditional ideology and sacrifice their preference. This kind of deep sorrow in people's minds can be hardly understood by couples of Western societies who neither like to have more children nor prefer to have boys over girls.

2. *Practical Considerations.*

The One-Child Policy has created many practical problems. Especially in the present-day countryside of China, the peasants need

130

more hands to do manual labor, and they prefer to have more boys. In general, the peasants' attitudes to child-bearing are determined by the following considerations:

1. More children mean more laborers.
2. If a family has no sons, then its heritage will be handed down to daughters. When the daughters get married, the heritage will fall to other families with different surnames.
3. After the marriages of the daughters, the parents without a son will feel lonely and be afraid that a careless funeral ceremony will be carried out by strangers when they die.
4. If there is any dispute with the neighbors, the families without sons will feel unsafe, for the old parents and the weak girls may be easily bullied by the neighbors.
5. The only-child will feel lonely, and the only-child families may fear losing him or her in an accident.

In the cities, among the young workers and especially among the young intellectuals, the attitude towards child-bearing has changed significantly for a variety of reasons, including: low salaries; the tense housing problem; the busy life of work and study; the severe shortage of nurseries and kindergartens; and, the rapid changes in family and cultural values. Hence, there is less resistance toward the One-Child Policy in the cities than in the countryside. Still, even in the cities, some resistance towards the policy remains.

Collectivism over Individualism

In order to overcome this resistance, government at various levels has tried every means to persuade the masses, especially young couples, to abide by the regulations of family planning. The mass organizations of the Trade Unions, the Youth League and the Women's Federations at various levels have carried on active propaganda for the One-Child Policy. Local governments have been issuing certificates to the one-child families and providing them with rich and varied rewards. . . .

In evaluating the One-Child Policy in China today, we must bear this fundamental fact in mind: China is a state with centralized authority, and the prevailing philosophy and ideology have emphasized collectivism instead of individualism. Indeed, the ideology of collectivism is advocated by Confucius, Sun Zhongshan and Mao Zedong, though the specific content of their philosophies varies. This consistent philosophy has served to unite the centralized state with the families in China. In general, the Chinese people attach more importance to the relationship between the father and the son, and between the country and the family than the peoples of Western societies. Thus, if the One-Child Policy were transplanted to Western societies where the people attach more importance to individualism than collectivism, it may meet even more resistance than it has in China.

It is a dilemma that the new generations must sacrifice their own interests to remedy the defects of the older generations. This kind of great sacrifice is both solemn and stirring, moving and tragic. This sacrifice is not only for the prosperity of China, but also for the stability of the whole world. Just like the people of the upper reaches are willing to have flood-diversion for weakening the flood of the lower reaches when the river is in flood, the new generations of China sacrifice their own interests to alleviate the stress of their later generations. This reflects the collectivist outlook. Just as the younger generations of a family take the responsibility to repay the debt incurred by the older generations, even if it means cutting back their own budgets, the sacrifice of the Chinese people shows that China is a responsible and conscientious neighbor worthy of respect by the international community. This sacrifice could only be made by the valiant and industrious Chinese people who have lived in the abyss of misery for centuries. It is really a moving and tragic sacrifice.

Warning Signs

Unless China's leaders slow the birth rate, the task of feeding, clothing and housing millions of new people will put impossible demands on the economy.

The warning signs are plentiful. In 1987, for the second straight year, the population grew by 15 million people, 3.5 million more than the official target. Population experts predict that China will continue to grow at this fast clip until 1995, by which time the baby boom that began in the Cultural Revolution might finally taper off.

Aprodicio Laquian, *The New York Times*, May 27, 1988.

In closing this article, we draw the following three conclusions:
1. The One-Child Policy of China today is a compelled adjustment by the Chinese government and it represents a great sacrifice by the Chinese people for the peace, stability and prosperity of China and the world.
2. The One-Child Policy of China today has been marked by many achievements. The natural population growth rate has been reduced and is projected to become zero in about 2010. This policy will certainly create problems for Chinese society. To overcome its negative effects it must eventually be ended. In other words, just as it appeared historically, it will eventually disappear.
3. The duration of the One-Child Policy of China will depend upon the effect and speed of national economic development and cultural change throughout the country. Of course, these factors are closely interrelated but in the final analysis, the most important factor is national economic development.

"The prevalence of serious human rights abuses in Tibet is beyond dispute."

China Denies Human Rights in Tibet

Asia Watch

Many outside observers have accused China of violating human rights in Tibet. In the following viewpoint, the organization Asia Watch argues that Chinese policies deny Tibetans freedom of religion and expression, and that many Tibetans are tortured and made political prisoners. The US-based Asia Watch was established in 1986 to monitor human rights abuses in China and other Asian countries.

As you read, consider the following questions:

1. Why does Asia Watch disagree with the assertion that the Tibetan situation is an internal Chinese affair?
2. What is China's policy toward religion in Tibet, according to Asia Watch?
3. What political freedoms do the authors argue are often violated in Tibet?

Human Rights in Tibet published by the Asia Watch Committee. Washington, DC, February 1988.

133

Although documented contact between China and Tibet goes back at least to the sixth century, the modern-day debate about the historical status of Tibet takes the thirteenth century as its starting point, for it was at that time, so the present Chinese argument goes, that Tibet was drawn into the map of China. The basis for the Chinese argument is the conquest of both realms by the Mongols, even though Mongol domination of Tibet and China began and ended at different times. The extent to which Tibet was made specifically subordinate to the Yuan dynasty (1270-1368), the dynastic apparatus through which the Mongols ruled China, seems vague at best. The Mongol empire was a world empire, and though there is no doubt that Mongol domination extended into Tibet, there seems little basis for maintaining that the Mongols appended Tibet to China.

The succeeding dynasty, the ethnically Chinese Ming dynasty (1368-1644), clearly recognized that Tibet was quite distinct and separate from China. In an early document the first Ming emperor referred to Tibet as a foreign state, in language that was unequivocal. There were no serious attempts during the Ming dynasty to make Tibet a part of China. . . .

The Qing Dynasty

The question of Tibet's relationship to the Qing dynasty (1644-1911) is more problematic. The Qing, like the Yuan, was a conquest dynasty. Its Manchu rulers established an empire that had clear lines separating the administration of Tibetans, Mongols and Chinese; and governing their relations to the throne. What complicated the situation was the intense Sinicization of the Manchus in China during the eighteenth and nineteenth centuries, ultimately resulting in a people who considered themselves distinct from their Chinese subjects but who nevertheless had largely lost the most telling of distinctions: their own language. This metamorphosis was visible enough in China, but ironically did not really affect the administrative structure binding Tibet to the throne in a Manchu empire.

Tibet was incorporated into the Manchu dominions by various stages in the eighteenth century; at century's end Tibet was clearly under the control of the Manchu throne. The administrative arrangements under which this control existed were, however, quite separate from those pertaining to China. Chinese officials and Chinese provinces had no part in the governing of Tibet, save when in the eighteenth century large portions of eastern Tibet were detached from the jurisdiction of the Dalai Lama's government and placed under that of provincial and court officials. Today those portions of eastern Tibet still remain outside the modern Tibet Autonomous Region (TAR) although the cultural, religious and ethnic links between the Tibetan populations remain. . . .

In the years following the Qing collapse, the Chinese republic was able to lay claim to all of the Qing dominions without the issue ever coming to a head. To some extent this was surely because the Republic of China could do little more than claim these areas. The territory of the present TAR was wholly under the rule of the Dalai Lama's government, with no regard shown for Republican claims. The Mongolian People's Republic, under Soviet protection, was likewise beyond China's reach, as was much of Xinjiang for a good part of the pre-1949 period.

The Number of Political Prisoners

It is extremely difficult to obtain an exact figure on the prison population of Tibet. The best estimate, however, reveals that in the autonomous region's 75 district and five divisional prisons alone, there may well be between 10,000 and 20,000 Tibetan inmates. How many of these are political prisoners? Given prevailing conditions in Tibet, one could make a case for all of them. Those arrested for anti-state activity, though frequently labeled as common criminals to obscure their status, number roughly 3,000-4,000.

John F. Avedon, *Cultural Survival Quarterly*, volume 12, no. 1, 1988.

The establishment of the People's Republic of China (PRC) in 1949, and the flight of the Guomindang Republican government to Taiwan, marked the eventual end of Tibet's independence. It should be understood that when Tibetans raise this issue they are conscious of a time in the recent past—i.e., prior to 1951—when the territory of the present Tibet Autonomous Region was in fact independent of any Chinese rule. Moreover, whatever one may think about the justice or viability of Tibetan claims to independence, it ought to be acknowledged that the Chinese historical view of the situation is not necessarily accepted by Tibetans; it is surely not the point of view that Tibetan activists bring with them to the political dialogue.

Tibet After 1949

The history of Tibet as part of the PRC is likewise controversial. By 1949 the PRC was in control of most of those areas of the Tibetan Plateau that had been detached by the Manchus from the government of the Dalai Lamas. On October 7, 1950, troops of the People's Liberation Army crossed the *de facto* line of control of the Dalai Lama's government and, shortly thereafter, defeated the small and ill-equipped Tibetan Army. The Dalai Lama's government was forced to negotiate with the Chinese central government and to accede to the Agreement on Measures for the Peaceful Liberation of Tibet, which was signed on May 23, 1951.

This did not put an end to tension between Tibet and China.

Tibetan areas inside and outside the territory of the present TAR were treated quite differently. In the latter regions, which were placed under Chinese provincial administration, social and political policies rooted in the Chinese experience were followed that precipitated an armed rebellion in the early 1950s....

The rebellion began in the eastern areas of the Tibetan Plateau, outside the bounds of the present TAR, but it eventually spilled over into that area, culminating in an uprising in Lhasa in 1959. The Dalai Lama fled to India along with many other Tibetans, ultimately creating an exile community that presently numbers over 100,000. For a short time the Chinese government made use of the Panchen Lama, another important Buddhist hierarch, but he fell into disfavor and disappeared until the late 1970s (since which time he has actively cooperated with the Chinese government). The crushing of the rebellion led to the application in Central Tibet (the area of the present TAR) of the social and economic policies that had been applied in the east. It also led to a massive number of imprisonments. It is said that most of those sent off to prison in the wake of the 1959 uprising in Lhasa never returned. Those who did return seem to have spent close to twenty years in prison; most were released only in the late 1970s....

Human Rights in Tibet

Against this background there remains an obvious reserve of resentment against China on the part of many Tibetans. Unfortunately this is exacerbated by what Asia Watch considers the systematic violation of certain basic human rights. It has become clear that despite liberalization in some areas, political imprisonment, torture, and discrimination are also characteristic of the current situation in Tibet, specifically in various towns and cities on the Tibetan Plateau. This disregard for human rights is very close to the surface of political, social and religious life in Tibet. Although the government of the PRC maintains that this is wholly an internal affair, Asia Watch strongly believes that human rights are a universal issue, and that the human rights situation in Tibet is an extremely serious one and warrants international attention....

Limits to Freedom

The moderation that may be said to characterize some of the policies implemented in the TAR during the present decade does not extend into the realms of free political discourse or full religious freedom, in spite of governmental insistence to the contrary.

Religion in Tibet may be considered a private affair only to the extent that believers keep their faith within carefully prescribed limits. Those limits can only be intended to hamper the propagation and unbounded reinvigoration of religion in Tibet....

Tibetans in Tibet state that there are clear limits on their right to practice Buddhism. They say that generally they are only accorded the freedom to perform certain rituals and to make public displays of some aspects of religious faith. Thus they may perform prostrations in the vicinity of various sacred objects or sites. Many Tibetans believe that this, like the reconstruction of monasteries, is linked to tourism. The sight of Tibetans prostrating themselves in streets and in temples is not simply picturesque, however; it also creates the impression that the PRC grants full religious freedom to Tibetans and that, to all appearances, religious practice in Tibet is little more than the performance of bizarre acts of abasement rooted in superstition. Official tolerance of such activities is intended to be seen by tourists and visitors who are otherwise unfamiliar with Tibetan culture as a manifestation of religious freedom in Tibet.

Tibetan Prisons

Life in Tibet's prisons is characterized by unremittant labor, regular interrogation sessions during which the prisoner is beaten, ineffective medical care, borderline rations of black tea and barley and an ongoing death toll resulting from the harsh conditions. Prisoners sleep on the floor, are chained at night and only have bedding if family members donate it. Informants keep inmates wary of one another; even when a prisoner's term expires, he will often not be freed. Instead, he'll become a *lemi-ruka,* a part-time prisoner. He lives in a compound outside the prison proper and is permitted to go home one day a week; for the rest of the week, he continues in hard labor on whatever project is assigned to him. He has a permanent "black hat," as the Chinese call it, on his head.

John F. Avedon, *Cultural Survival Quarterly,* volume 12, no. 1, 1988.

Nevertheless, it is obvious that limits on religious practice are stringently maintained by the authorities. As one would expect, it is forbidden to offer prayers publicly for the Dalai Lama. Monks do this privately, however. . . .

Propagation of the Buddhist faith is another area in which Tibetans feel they are denied religious freedom. There is a prohibition on religious teachings, it appears, in most of Tibet. . . .

Freedom of Expression

Freedom of written and spoken expression is another area in which there are restrictions that warrant concern. At present the suppression of free speech via harsh measures in Tibet appears to relate largely to political issues, particularly those issues surrounding the status of Tibet, the return of the Dalai Lama, and the presence of large numbers of Chinese in Tibet. The authorities control book, magazine and newspaper publication and thus there is no free access to the media. Nevertheless, the present variety and diversity of publications in the Tibetan regions of the PRC is quite remarkable when compared with the situation prior to 1979/1980. . . .

Restrictions on freedom of expression and freedom of assembly in Tibet are stringently applied to all political utterances and actions. Tibetans emphatically state that the influx of Chinese into Tibet now affords the PSB [Public Security Bureau] in Tibet and its local branches the opportunity to maintain more effective surveillance over the populace. . . .

Political opinion that runs counter to China's official stand on the Tibetan question is expressed publicly in leaflets and wall posters. The PSB is vigilant with regard to such expressions of dissident sentiments. According to Tibetan sources, when written tracts or posters calling for Tibetan independence appear, the PSB acts quickly to uncover their source. . . . Penalties for being implicated in such activity may be imprisonment and brutal treatment, as will be discussed below.

It is not simply leaflets or tracts originating in Tibet that put one in danger of arrest. Mere possession of the flag of the traditional Tibetan government is also a serious offense. Even more serious is possession of political materials originating among the Tibetan exiles in India. It is maintained by Tibetans in Tibet that possession of such materials automatically implicates one as a spy for the Dalai Lama. . . .

Political Arrests

As already mentioned, the PSB maintains effective surveillance over the Tibetan population in most major towns and cities. When an individual is suspected of speaking out against Chinese rule in Tibet or in favor of Tibetan independence he or she is watched ever more carefully. Note is taken of where the person lives, what he or she looks like, and a special surveillance is set up. The person's residence is also likely to be searched. If leaflets or other materials calling for Tibet's freedom or independence are found, an arrest is made immediately. . . .

The interrogation at the PSB branch is carried out by the People's Procuratorate of the local municipality or district, while the court proceedings are held under the auspices of the People's Criminal Court of the same area. According to Tibetans the rights of the accused extend no further than being allowed to acknowledge the crimes with which he or she is charged. It is forbidden for the prisoner to speak up and dispute the charges.

Torture

Torture is not spared in the interrogation of political prisoners, according to informed and credible observers in Tibet. It is a means for obtaining information and for dealing with recalcitrant prisoners.

As one person described it:

> If one speaks forcefully, if one gives an account of Tibet as be-
> ing independent, they apply cattle prods [in Tibetan, *gloggi rgyug-*
> *pa;* literally "electric batons"]. One's feet are shackled, one's arms
> are shackled. The whole body trembles and one can't speak.

The use of cattle prods in Tibet unfortunately corresponds to other
descriptions concerning the use of these instruments on prisoners
elsewhere in the PRC. During the most recent clashes in Lhasa, the
PSB use of cattle prods also figures in accounts of violence against
protesters.

Political Prisoners

It is generally believed that in recent years (i.e., since approximately
1980) sentences for political crimes have become lighter. Whereas
previously the possession of leaflets or the pasting up of posters asserting Tibet's right to independence and professing antipathy to the
Chinese presence in Tibet might bring a sentence of twenty years
(or death), sentences now generally amount to three to five years.
Nevertheless, the authorities reserve the right to increase such
sentences later on if it is believed that the prisoner is being obstinate
in holding to counter-revolutionary ideas. . . .

The mistreatment of political prisoners does not end with interrogation and sentencing. Such prisoners are subjected to various
forms of abuse and torture during their imprisonment. Geshe Lob-
sang Wangchuk, probably the most well-known example, was left
with little use of his hands as a result of this sort of mistreatment.
Beatings in prison can take on a regular, routine air. . . .

It is distressing, but no longer surprising to find that torture is
part of the prison routine in Tibet. Torture and violence against
prisoners in China proper has even received attention in Chinese
publications. Unfortunately, the sensitive nature of the Tibetan issue
has caused the Chinese authorities to maintain a strict refusal to
acknowledge improprieties against prisoners in Tibet. . . .

Conclusions

Asia Watch believes that the prevalence of serious human rights
abuses in Tibet is beyond dispute. The various matters that have
been detailed in this report—restrictions on freedom of expression
and assembly, political imprisonment, secret trials, the mistreatment
of political prisoners—all are part of a system of repression in Tibet
that violates accepted international norms of respect for human
rights.

It does not do to assert that such abuses are beyond the bounds
of discussion for those outside China's borders; the world we live
in today makes that an antiquated argument. Nor does it do for PRC
spokesmen to hark back to the alleged evils of pre-1950 Tibet as
justification for present practices. We live in the 1980s and we deal

with problems and questions of the 1980s; no one seriously suggests that the only alternative to present practices in Tibet is the institution of arbitrary eye-gouging and amputations. The alternative must lie in the cessation of secret trials, political imprisonment, torture, discriminatory practices, and other violations of basic human rights.

"Liberation lifted the veil of dire poverty and extreme backwardness which had darkened Tibet for ages past."

China Does Not Deny Human Rights in Tibet

The National Minorities Questions Editorial Panel

Many people argue that Tibet was an independent country that was invaded by the Chinese Communists in 1950 and again in 1959, when China drove Tibet's Buddhist ruler, the Dalai Lama, into exile in India. The Chinese government has maintained that Tibet is an historical part of China. The following viewpoint is excerpted from *Questions and Answers About China's National Minorities*, a book that was written by a Chinese editorial panel of scholars. Using a question-and-answer format, the panel argues that Tibetans were treated as slaves in the traditional Tibetan society, and that their human rights have improved greatly under Chinese socialism.

As you read, consider the following questions:

1. How do the authors describe Tibet's traditional society?
2. What evidence do the authors provide to show Tibet is a part of China?
3. Is there religious freedom in Tibet, according to the panel?

The National Minorities Questions Editorial Panel, *Questions and Answers About China's Minority Nationalities*. Beijing, China: New World Press, 1985.

Q.: What's the population of Tibet?

A.: Tibet's population has now grown to 1.8 million, of whom more than 90 per cent are Tibetans and other minority people. There are no more than 100,000 Han workers and staff.

The rapid growth of Tibet's population is a great change which is the direct consequence of the reform of its social system. Before liberation Tibet was a serf society under the rule of feudal manorial lords which combined elements of both a theocracy and a secular dictatorship. In those days production was backward and the economy stagnated. The people lived in dire poverty. There was an utter lack of the most basic medical and health services, let alone maternity and child care. Under such conditions the mortality rate of adults was high and the survival rate of infants low. The population steadily declined until 1950, at which time it stood at merely about one million. The 1959 democratic reform overthrew feudal serfdom and liberated productive forces in the region. Production developed fast. The resultant improvement in living standards as well as the improved medical and health services made possible with the Chinese government's aid has led to rapid growth of the Tibetan population.

The Hans in Tibet are for the most part administrative personnel and trained professionals sent in by the government to work in culture, education, medical services, transport and communications. . . .

Tibet's History

Q.: Will you please outline Tibet's history and its present conditions?

A.: The Tibetans are a nationality with an ancient and complex history. According to historical records, Tibet first entered the period of the slave society during the sixth century when the Yarlung tribe of the Shannan area assumed leadership of an alliance of the local tribes and selected a leader whom they called *btsan-po* (king). Meanwhile, they came into contact with Hans and various ethnic groups in northwest China. . . .

Following its establishment the Yuan dynasty (1279-1368) unified all of China's nationalities under its powerful central government. Consequently, Tibet was formally incorporated into China's domain as an adminstrative area. . . .

After the fall of the Yuan dynasty in 1368, the Ming court in effect preserved the Yuan system of administration in Tibet, taking over its government organs and institutions. Relations between the Ming central government and the Phag-mo-gru-pa court became stronger and contacts between Hans and Tibetans broadened. The Phag-mo-gru-pa dynasty was followed by the Karma dynasty. Feudal serfdom was gradually superseded by slavery; the struggle between the various groupings of serf-owners, which superficially appeared

142

to be a conflict between different religious sects, became ever more acute. The Yellow Sect, founded by Tsong Khapa (1357-1419), became increasingly powerful as it had most of the serf-owner groupings behind it. Finally, backed by the armed strength of Gushri Khan, chieftain of the Hoshod Mongols, the Yellow Sect toppled the Karma dynasty and put the Fifth Dalai Lama at the head of the newly established regime . . . .

Later Developments

In modern times, while aggressively making inroads into China's coastal areas and hinterland, the forces of world imperialism extended their claws of incursion into the Tibetan region. The most glaring instances were the two armed inroads carried out by British imperialism in 1888 and 1904 respectively.

Human Rights and the Law

As for "human rights," they are indeed very precious to the Tibetans. As one of the biggest serf owners in the past, I know very well just how many "human rights" my serfs enjoyed. Today, as one of the vice-chairmen of the National People's Congress, I am familiar with the rights of the Chinese people as guaranteed by the Constitution. Tibetans enjoy one more right than the Han people, that of autonomy. However, any country that ensures "human rights" also has its laws, and it is impermissible to break them.

The Constitution of China clearly stipulates that "Tibet is an integral part of China." Any attempt at "Tibetan independence" is an attempt to split the country and therefore unconstitutional.

The Panchen Lama, *China Reconstructs*, January 1988.

From the founding of the Republic of China in 1912, all the successive central governments have had a body charged with administering Mongolia and Tibet, namely, the Commission for Mongolian and Tibetan Affairs. In 1933, the Tibetan local government reported the death of the 13th Dalai Lama to the Chinese central government. On receiving the report, the central government posthumously granted the title "Grand Master of Patriotism, Magnanimity, Benevolence and Sagacity" to the late Dalai and dispatched an official named Huang Musong to Tibet to pay homage to his memory. In 1934, the central government established a regional office of the Commission for Mongolian and Tibetan Affairs in Lhasa to act as the representative of the central authorities in Tibet. Then in 1940 the central government sent Wu Zhongxin, Minister of the Commission for Mongolian and Tibetan Affairs, to Tibet to preside over the ceremony of the installation of the 14th Dalai Lama, Bstan-'dzin rgya-mtsho. All these historical facts show that Tibet is an inalienable part of China.

With the founding of new China, the Tibetans entered the great community of the Chinese nationalities on an equal footing with all other members. The signing in 1951 of a 17-article agreement between the Central People's Government and the Tibetan local government brought about the peaceful liberation of Tibet.

Communist Liberation

Liberation lifted the veil of dire poverty and extreme backwardness which had darkened Tibet for ages past. The democratic reform of 1959, in particular, led to the abolition of the feudal system that had shackled the Tibetan people for centuries, reducing the great mass of them to the status of serfs or slaves, and emancipated them in the truest sense of the term.

Like the rest of China, Tibet was thrown into a state of turmoil during the years of the "cultural revolution", seriously damaging nearly all sectors of its society. Nevertheless, following the overthrow of the Gang of Four, especially after the Third Plenary Session of the Eleventh Central Committee of the Chinese Communist Party held in 1979, at which new and flexible policies were adopted, agriculture, livestock breeding and all other undertakings in Tibet have picked up with renewed vigour. . . .

China's Position on Tibet

Q.: What are the striking features of the Tibet Autonomous Region?

A.: Tibet, an inalienable portion of Chinese territory, stands out in a number of aspects as an autonomous region of special significance.

With regard to its natural conditions, Tibet is a vast area with a sparce population. It has serried chains of mountains and numerous lakes and rivers. It is high in elevation, has a cold climate, rarefied atmosphere, capricious weather, and is rich in natural resources. Geographically, it is of strategic importance due to its location in China's southwestern frontier. However, communications and transport are very difficult because of the region's rugged terrain and its vast distance from the hinterland. In one respect, Tibet differs from all the other autonomous regions, in that the native Tibetans comprise the vast majority of the local population and thus are virtually self-governing. As for religious belief, since Buddhism was introduced from India and interior China at the beginning of the seventh century, the religion has prevailed and gradually become the faith of the entire nationality. It has exerted profound influence on the minds of the people. In political history, it lived under feudal serfdom characterized by a merging of clerical and secular rule for centuries before liberation. The three categories of manorial lords (the high clergy, aristocrats and local government officials) held sway over the life and property of the serfs and slaves. Furthermore, they made use of religion to poison the minds of the enslaved people, so as to consolidate their rule. All this accounted for conditions of extreme poverty and backwardness which long characterized Tibet.

A Serf's Perspective

Southeast of Lhasa, there is a county called Doilungdeqen. The village of Zuzhan here was a feudal estate belonging to the Dalai Lama's mother prior to the democratic reforms of 1959. Some 80 families live here today. Most of them were former serfs.

The ex-serf Chosdol, now in his 70s, had this to say, "I came here as a serf at the age of 17. I had to get permission from my master to speak and to pray. I had to kneel in his presence and, if he was dissatisfied with me, he had me whipped and beaten. You see my bent back? That was the result of a beating by my master. There are more than 40 people like me in our village today, all with incurable injuries caused by this brutal treatment. . . .

"In the democratic reforms of 1959, the people's government gave me land, houses, draft animals and seed. I began to live like a human being. Today we have nine in my family. Some work the land, others are in Lhasa doing other jobs. We make a total of 5,000 yuan a year. Life is really free and happy. Talk about the past to us old people and it's like speaking of death."

Qiogya, *China Reconstructs*, February 1988.

The peaceful liberation of Tibet in 1951 gave the region a new lease on life. The 1959 democratic reforms, in particular, put an end to the long-standing feudal system and emancipated all the serfs and slaves. Since then the once downtrodden masses have led a free, happy life and adhered to the road of socialism.

Religion in Tibet

Q.: How about religious belief in Tibet?

A.: Due to certain historical and social factors, almost all the people in pre-liberation Tibet believed in Buddhism. Buddhist influence penetrated every sphere of social life, including ways and customs. As the doctrines of Buddhism are markedly fatalistic, the people under the sway of such conceptions can be easily controlled and manipulated by their religious leaders. Turning the people's religious devoutness to their advantage, the monasteries and high clergy managed to amass large amounts of livestock and land and keep a great many serfs. The democratic reforms which were carried out in 1959 led to the abolition of exploitation of the masses by the monasteries and high clergy. Although this more or less raised the people's political consciousness, the influence of religion nevertheless remains deep-rooted in their thought.

Q.: What's the government policy concerning religious belief?. . .

A.: After liberation, the Chinese government formulated a policy for political unification, for the separation of religion from civil administration and freedom of religious belief. This policy is applicable to Tibet as well as to all other parts of the country. By freedom of religious belief we mean freedom to believe in, or not to believe in, any religion, freedom to believe in this or that religion. All such freedom is protected by law, and nobody may compel anyone else to believe in, or not to believe in, any religion. This government policy is supported by the broad masses of people, religious or non-religious. Nevertheless, while protecting the people's normal religious activities, the government will crack down on any counter-revolutionary sabotage perpetrated in the name of religion. . . .

Education in Tibet

Q.: Could you please talk about the current situation in Tibetan education?

A.: Well, in old Tibet the manorial lords paid no attention to promoting education and culture, but rather pursued an obscurantist policy so as to keep the masses in a state of benighted ignorance. The few private schools which existed in Tibet were run for the sole purpose of training clerical and temporal officials or the sons of aristocratic families. Education for the benefit of the ordinary people was simply unheard of.

It was only after liberation that headway began to be made in establishing educational undertakings devoted to the interests of the people. The first post-liberation school in Tibet, a primary school, was opened in Qamdo in the early fifties, followed by the setting up of a number of others in Lhasa, Xigaze, Gyangze, Nyingchi, Yadong and Dengqen. Meanwhile, the government put up a large fund as grant-in-aid for poor pupils. After the 1959 democratic reforms the government adopted the policy of "Lay stress on the running of schools by the people with state aid, supplemented by that by the state". As a result, Tibet's education forged ahead. At the time of the establishment of the autonomous region in 1965, Tibet had over 1,800 primary schools with a total enrollment of 66,700 pupils, four middle schools with an enrollment of over 1,000, and one institution of higher learning with an enrollment of over 2,200 students.

Tibet's educational system was thrown into utter disarray during the decade-long "cultural revolution". However, after the fall of the Gang of Four in 1976 the government stepped up financial assistance and soon Tibet's educational system was restored and revitalized. . . .

In recent years, a certain number of Tibetan middle school graduates have been annually enrolled by institutions of higher learning in the hinterland.

At present, further steps are being taken to improve the Tibetan educational system, and specifically to increase and broaden the use of Tibetan as a language of instruction in the region's schools.

Health Services

Q.: Will you please give me some information concerning Tibet's medical and health services?

A.: A striking feature of Tibet's medical and health services is the free medical care system which has been in existence throughout the region for the past three decades or more.

By any estimate, progress in these services has been quite fast. The region now has more than 800 clinics and hospitals, or 19 times the 1958 figure; over the same period of time the ranks of its medical personnel have swelled to over 6,000, a 13-fold increase, and the number of sick beds has increased 23-fold to 4,000.

From time to time, mobile medical teams are dispatched to the agricultural and pastoral districts to dispense medical treatment and prophylactic services.

Encouraging advances have been made in sanitation and anti-epidemic work, research in altitude physiology and mountain sickness, and the systematization of traditional Tibetan medicine and pharmacology.

The Chinese government sets great store by traditional Tibetan medicine and pharmacology and gives it every support, which has considerably contributed to its impressive development. A well-run hospital of Tibetan medicine with an affiliated research institute has been established in Lhasa. Its pharmaceutical works turns out an increasing amount of Tibetan drugs in ever-greater variety. In 1979, for instance, it produced 60,000 kilogrammes of some 300 different kinds of drugs, as against some 250 kilogrammes of 19 kinds in 1959.

Supporting Tibetan Culture

Q.: Will you please say something about Tibetan culture?

A.: Tibetan culture has a long history and rich contents. For one thing, there is a vast amount of literary heritage. Tibet, southern Gansu and Sichuan are now known to have kept hundreds of thousands of volumes of complete works by writers of Tibet, biographies, historical and religious writings, poems, folk rhymes, maxims, fables, folk stories, writings on grammar and orthography, dramas as well as works on astronomy, medicine, Buddhist treatises and other subjects in more than 25,000 titles.

In the initial years after liberation, the Chinese government did much to preserve and sort out Tibetan culture. After the disruption caused by the "cultural revolution", it continued its efforts with renewed vigour. A dozen or so classical Tibetan works. . .have been collated and published. Large numbers of folk rhymes, maxims and folk tales have been collected and re-edited. A number of Tibetan plays have been refined and re-staged to win mass appeal.

The Chinese government, moreover, has appropriated a special fund to finance the renovation of the historic monuments in Tibet. Since their renovation, the well-known ancient monasteries, the Potala Palace, Drepung, Sera, Trashilumpo, Jokhang and Sakya, have begun to attract even more visitors and pilgrims. . . .

Tibetans Abroad

Q.: What's the Chinese government's policy towards Tibetans residing abroad?

A.: You see, those Tibetans who left Tibet for foreign lands following the 1959 armed rebellion staged by the reactionary upper strata of Tibetan society have been abroad for more than two decades. Naturally most of them have become homesick and are seriously considering returning home. Towards such people the Chinese government adopts the following policy: Those who wish to return to the motherland are welcome to do so; proper arrangements will be made for their life and work when they come back; if they wish to leave again after coming back, their departure shall be facilitated; if they wish to make a brief visit just to see their friends and relatives, they are likewise welcome to do so. . . .

We hold that Tibet is an inalienable part of Chinese territory and that the 1959 rebellion should not have been carried out. Today, however, after a lapse of more than 20 years since that time, China has entered a new historical stage during which lasting political stability is possible, the economy is continuing to flourish and all nationalities have become more united. To further enhance unity between the Han and Tibetan nationalities and to facilitate the realization of the modernization programme, the Chinese government welcomes the Dalai Lama and his followers back home. The government's policy towards them may be summarized in the following terms: All patriots belong to one big family, whether they rally to the common cause early or late; let bygones be bygones; freedom to come and go is guaranteed; those who return and settle down shall be given political consideration and be properly cared for; those who return just to have a look with no intention to settle down are also welcome.

We would like to point out here that the plot to create an "independent Tibetan state" came to nothing long ago. Our advice to them can be aptly summed up in the Buddhist saying: "The bitter sea has no bounds, only repent and the shore is at hand". Well, they will do better to return early. The motherland's door is always kept open to them.

Distinguishing Bias from Reason

When dealing with controversial issues, many people allow their feelings to dominate their powers of reason. Thus, one of the most important critical thinking skills is the ability to distinguish between statements based upon emotion or bias and conclusions based upon a rational consideration of the facts.

The following statements are taken from the viewpoints in this chapter. Consider each statement carefully. *Mark R for any statement you believe is based on reason or a rational consideration of the facts. Mark B for any statement you believe is based on bias, prejudice, or emotion. Mark I for any statement you think is impossible to judge.*

If you are doing this activity as a member of a class or group, compare your answers with those of other class or group members. Be able to defend your answers. You may discover that others come to different conclusions than you do. Listening to the reasons others present for their answers may give you valuable insights in distinguishing between bias and reason.

> R = *a statement based upon reason*
> B = *a statement based upon bias*
> I = *a statement impossible to judge*

149

1. Some unscrupulous people attack the socialist system by taking advantage of the human rights issue to slander China.

2. I found that the official norm of one child per couple was unacceptable to the villagers I interviewed. Official surveys from other parts of China have produced similar results. Based on these studies, I estimate that 90 percent of the abortions performed in the last five years have been involuntary.

3. The basis for the Chinese argument that Tibet is a part of China is the conquest of both realms by the Mongols in the thirteenth century. But the Mongol empire was a world empire, and there seems little basis for maintaining that the Mongols appended Tibet to China.

4. The Chinese liberation of Tibet has freed the serfs from bondage and enabled them to build a happy life under socialism.

5. There is harsh suppression of freedom of speech and expression in Tibet. Mere possession of the flag of the traditional Tibetan government can lead to arrest. Brutal treatment of prisoners has been recorded.

6. The Tibetan Buddhist rulers made use of religion to poison the minds of the enslaved people, so as to consolidate their rule. This accounted for the conditions of extreme poverty and backwardness which long characterized Tibet.

7. The Constitution of China clearly stipulates that "Tibet is an integral part of China." Any attempt to promote "Tibetan independence" is therefore unconstitutional.

8. The One-Child policy of China today represents a great sacrifice by the Chinese people for the peace, stability, and prosperity of China and the world.

9. Among the Chinese people, the most severe verbal insult is "May he die without sons." The One-Child policy is a direct challenge to this deep-rooted prejudice.

10. There is no way universal standards on human rights can be drawn when Chinese lacks a word for "privacy," one of our most important values.

Periodical Bibliography

The following articles have been selected to supplement the diverse views presented in this chapter.

David H. Adeney — "Growth and Restraints: Today's Church in China," *Eternity*, October 1987.

Don Browning — "The Protestant Church in the People's Republic of China," *The Christian Century*, March 4, 1987.

Vern L. Bullough and Fang-Fu Ruan — "China's Children," *The Nation*, June 18, 1988.

Maria Hsia Chang — "Totalitarianism and China: The Limits of Reform," *Global Affairs*, Fall 1987.

China Reconstructs — "A Reader's Questions on Tibet and Some Answers," February 1988.

Zijiang Ding — "A Historical Look at China's Constitutional Framework," *In These Times*, December 16-22, 1987.

Ron Dorfman — "Let a Hundred Flowers Wilt," *The Progressive*, March 1987.

William Gasperini — "China's Lost Horizon," *In These Times*, November 4-10, 1987.

Marie Gottschalk — "Political Reform in China," *The Nation*, May 23, 1987.

Elizabeth Hall — "China's Only Child," *Psychology Today*, July 1987.

Liu Fong Da and John Creger — "Execution Day in Zhengzhou," *The American Spectator*, December 1986.

Steven W. Mosher — "A Mother's Ordeal," *Readers Digest*, February 1987.

Susan Ruel — "Dissident China," *Reason*, February 1988.

Orville Schell — "China's Andrei Sakharov," *The Atlantic Monthly*, May 1988.

Benjamin I. Schwartz — "The China Syndrome," *The New Republic*, February 9, 1987.

Lesley Wischmann — "Turmoil in Tibet," *The Christian Century*, December 9, 1987.

Is China a World Power?

Chapter Preface

Is China a world power?

In some ways, China falls under the superpower rubric. It is second in geographic size only to the Soviet Union. It has a population of over one billion people. China's People's Liberation Army is the largest standing army in the world. China is the only Asian country that possesses nuclear weapons. It has also become the world's fourth largest exporter of arms.

Paradoxically, China shares some of the characteristics of less industrialized nations. Its high population, widespread poverty, and limited industrialization seem to contradict a superpower image. In addition, China adamantly refuses any formal tie to either superpower. Instead, the People's Republic acts as an ally of Third World countries in the United Nations.

These facts reveal that China's world identity remains ambiguous. The authors of the following viewpoints debate which perspective is accurate.

"China is seen as a powerful and legitimate force in international affairs."

China Is Becoming a World Power

Harry Harding

Harry Harding, a senior fellow in the Brookings Foreign Policy Studies program, argues that China's world influence continues to increase. The longevity and stability of the current government combined with successful internal economic reforms allows China to focus more on the Asian region as well as the rest of the world.

As you read, consider the following questions:

1. How has China's relationship with the two superpowers changed in the post-Mao era?
2. According to Harding, what changes has China made that have affected its place in the world?
3. What criteria does Harding use to determine that China is a world power?

Harry Harding, *China's Second Revolution*. Washington, DC: The Brookings Institution, 1987. Reprinted with permission.

For at least one hundred and fifty years, the world has awaited the modernization of China with both anticipation and apprehension. When compared with the advanced nations of Europe, and even with the Japan of the Meiji era, the China of the nineteenth and early twentieth centuries was technologically backward, economically stagnant, and politically divided. Nonetheless, Western strategists recognized early on that China's size, resources, and culture gave it enormous, and worrisome, potential. Napoleon is credited with the admonition that China should be allowed to sleep on, undisturbed. "When she wakes," he allegedly said, "she will shake the world." Franklin D. Roosevelt also foresaw the growing power of China, but he depicted it in more benevolent terms. Throughout World War II, Roosevelt insisted that China should eventually join the United States, Great Britain, and the Soviet Union as one of the four great powers that would guarantee the peace in a postwar world.

The awakening of China anticipated by Napoleon and Roosevelt does not date simply from the death of Mao Zedong in 1976. Ever since the Chinese Communist Revolution of 1949—some would say since the May Fourth movement of the late 1910s, or even since the self-strengthening movement of the late nineteenth century— China has been stirring. Even in the late Maoist period, before the reforms initiated by Deng Xiaoping, China was already widely considered an important force in international affairs. In the early 1970s, Henry Kissinger spoke of a five-sided international system, composed not only of the United States and the Soviet Union, but also of Japan, Europe, and China. Other analysts, in both the Soviet Union and the United States, talked about a "strategic triangle," in which Peking, Moscow, and Washington determined the balance of power in world politics. As they had for more than a century, Western merchants saw China as perhaps the greatest untapped economic market in history, with a billion eager consumers and a nearly insatiable demand for modern technology. . . .

China's Growing Influence

But China's size, strategic location, and independence from the two superpowers allowed it to occupy a "swing" role in international affairs that no other nation could match. No other major actor in global politics—not Japan, not Western Europe, and not Eastern Europe—could plausibly threaten to shift sides in the world strategic balance, moving from alignment with one superpower to tacit cooperation with another. No other large developing country—not Indonesia, not Nigeria, not Brazil—had its natural resources so magnified by a strategic location. And no other nation, not even India, could offer to Western commerce an untapped market of the scale of China's.

Furthermore, China had deployed limited material resources with special flair. In the mid-1950s, Peking started a surprisingly large and successful foreign aid program, sometimes providing technical and economic assistance to countries whose per capita income was larger than that of China. Through the clarity and self-assurance of its foreign policy doctrine, and through the skill and poise of its diplomats, China became a principal commentator on world developments. In its support of national liberation movements and communist insurgencies on three continents, Peking threatened the internal stability of those governments that had displeased it. And on numerous occasions, in Korea, in the Taiwan Strait, along the Sino-Indian and Sino-Soviet frontiers, as well as more recently in Vietnam, China showed a willingness to use its modest military resources in support of foreign policy objectives, even against more powerful adversaries.

China's Material Resources

In the post-Mao era, China's material resources are growing even more rapidly, enabling the country to realize even more of its potential. China's second revolution seems to have reversed the slow decline in economic growth rates that had plagued the late Maoist period. The revival of scientific research, the development of academic exchange with foreign countries, and the import of foreign equipment are helping to raise China's technological level. China's economic and political reforms are again capturing the attention of much of the world, particularly in the socialist camp and among the developing nations, although those who are attracted by the Chinese model of today are often very different from those whose imagination was captured by the revolutionary Maoism of the late 1960s and early 1970s. China is committed to a long-term program of military modernization, with preliminary results already evident in better organization, improved training, updated tactics, and more sophisticated equipment.

Influential Role

China is a very large and very distinct political and cultural entity capable of an increasingly influential role in world affairs, particularly as a stabilizing element in both the regional and global correlation of forces—not as a client of the United States or of the Soviet Union but as a secure and independent power in its own right.

The Atlantic Council, *China Policy for the Next Decade*, 1984.

Moreover, the arenas in which China is deploying resources are also expanding. China is now a member of almost all the major international organizations. It has vastly increased the level of foreign trade, broadened its range of trading partners, and expanded the scope of commodities that it buys and sells. It is not only welcoming foreigners to invest in China but is also beginning to make investments overseas. Its cultural, educational, scientific, and tourist exchanges have increased dramatically since the death of Mao Zedong little more than ten years ago. And although its influence remains limited, China's diplomatic reach now extends far beyond Asia, into Africa, Europe, the Middle East, and even Latin America.

From a broad historical perspective, these recent developments mean an unprecedented awakening for China on at least two dimensions. For the first time in history, the mainland of China is ruled by an effective government, with firm control over its territory, that is committed to sustained economic modernization as its highest priority. None of the previous regimes interested in reform and modernization, such as the government of the Kuang-hsü Emperor in 1898, or the government of Chiang Kai-shek in the late 1920s and early 1930s, were able to consolidate their power. Conversely, all the earlier Chinese governments that had established firm control over the country's vast population had been committed to other goals, be they the order and stability of the traditional imperial order or the continuing revolution of Mao Zedong. The combination of effective government and sustained modernization is unique to post-Mao China.

Second, for the first time since the late nineteenth century, China is seen as a powerful and legitimate force in international affairs. No longer is China viewed as the "sick man of Asia," or as a "derelict hulk" adrift in the seas of world politics. No longer is China regarded as the satellite of a foreign power, as it was widely, if inaccurately, believed to be in the mid-1950s; or as a nation committed to the undermining and destruction of the international system, as it was generally, and perhaps somewhat more justly, considered in the mid-1960s. . . .

China's Emergence Positive

If the first half of Napoleon's prophecy is rapidly being fulfilled, the second half is more problematic. Will the growth of China's political, economic, and military power shake the world, or shore it up? Thus far, China's emergence in the last decade has been a fairly positive and stabilizing development. Nonetheless, a few disturbing undertones give many of China's neighbors pause as they look toward the future. . . .

China has adopted what can well be described as a policy of omnidirectional peaceful coexistence. With the exception of Vietnam, the People's Republic has tried to improve relations with its traditional rivals and adversaries, including India, Indonesia, and the Soviet Union. In contrast to the mid-1970s, when Peking encouraged the United States to undertake more forceful and effective resistance to Soviet expansion in the third world, and when it warned that arms control agreements between the two superpowers could only ratify and institutionalize the superior military position of the Soviet Union, China has more recently encouraged a reduction of tensions between Moscow and Washington and tentatively endorsed the arms control negotiations between them.

Peking's emphasis on economic development also implies China's acceptance of the legitimacy of the current international economic and political system. In the late Maoist period, China seemed bent on overthrowing the international order or at least making revolutionary changes in it. It called at various times for widespread "people's war" against the two superpowers, disparaged the United Nations and other international organizations, gave moral and material support to radical movements overseas, and proposed the creation of a "new international economic order." Today, such rhetoric has almost disappeared from Chinese commentary on international affairs. Peking has reduced, if not eliminated, even moral support for revolutionary movements in the third world. It has joined almost every significant international organization and has taken an active and constructive role in their work. Although China continues to advocate changes in the international economic system that would benefit the developing countries, its proposals for reform are less radical, less comprehensive, and less prominent than they were in the mid-1970s; and Peking advocates that they be adopted through negotiation and compromise, rather than through confrontation, between North and South.

On the Global Stage

One cannot formulate policy toward China without considering its impact upon other countries in the region such as the Soviet Union, Japan, Korea, Southeast Asian nations, and the world at large. China has long been a major factor in East Asia. In recent years, it has become a much more active player on the global stage, and its views and policies increasingly make a difference in international fora.

Gaston J. Sigur Jr., Speech given before the World Affairs Council of Northern California, in San Francisco, December 11, 1986.

Finally, growing flexibility and pragmatism have characterized China's foreign relations in recent years. Although the repudiation of the doctrines of the past has not been as thoroughgoing in foreign affairs as in domestic matters, the Chinese have quietly abandoned the ideological framework that once provided both consistency and rigidity to its conduct of foreign affairs. Thus the "theory of the three worlds," announced by Mao Zedong and Deng Xiaoping in 1974, fully elaborated in 1977, and noted favorably in the resolution on

Party history of 1981 as one of the few worthy theoretical innovations of the late Maoist period, is now rarely mentioned in discussions of the conceptual underpinnings of Chinese foreign policy. Nor are analyses of international affairs constructed around the same ideological categories as in the past. Neither the United States nor the Soviet Union is frequently described as an imperialist power, although many of their policies are still called examples of superpower "hegemonism." China still claims that the attempts of Moscow and Washington to establish global and regional dominance are resisted by smaller countries, but it no longer depicts this process as an international "united front" or as a "people's war" on a global scale.

A Case-by-Case Basis

Instead, China now deals with international issues on a pragmatic, case-by-case basis, finding common ground with each superpower on some issues while opposing it on others. As Premier Zhao Ziyang said in 1986, Peking will determine its position on international questions "on the merits of each case" and will not base "closeness with or estrangement from other countries on the basis of their social systems and ideologies." Thus China is usually supportive of American policy in Asia, particularly toward Indochina and Afghanistan, indicates its general approval of American military deployments in the region, and is more willing privately to acknowledge common interests with the United States even on sensitive issues like Korea and Taiwan. Peking remains, however, critical of American positions in the Middle East, South Africa, and Latin America. Similarly, China sharply opposes the Soviet military buildup in East Asia and its interventions in Afghanistan and Indochina. But Chinese views on some aspects of strategic arms control—for example, the Strategic Defense Initiative and nuclear free zones— parallel those of the Soviet Union.

China's new pragmatism has enabled Peking to be more flexible in dealing with sensitive issues than it was in the past, exemplified by Peking's acceptance of a range of economic relationships once regarded as ideologically proscribed. Similarly, in negotiations with Great Britain over the future of Hong Kong, Peking entered into a joint declaration that was more generous, more explicit, and more binding than most observers had believed would be possible. On other issues affecting the sensitive question of national sovereignty— from the nuclear cooperation agreement with the United States to the procedures for obtaining standby credit from the International Monetary Fund—Peking has also proved relatively supple and forthcoming. These developments reflect not only the openmindedness of China's current leadership but also a more professional and institutionalized process of foreign policymaking in Peking.

However, the rise of China's economic power and diplomatic clout

159

in recent years has also been accompanied by a growing nationalism in Chinese foreign policy. It is true that China denies any intention of becoming a superpower and insists that it remains a developing country sharing a common lot with the rest of the third world. As Deng Xiaoping assured a visiting foreign dignitary in May 1984, "China will always belong to the Third World . . . [and] will remain there even when it becomes prosperous and powerful, because China will never seek hegemony or bully others." But Chinese leaders increasingly qualify this familiar assertion by adding that China, as a major power, occupies a status that sets it apart from other developing countries. One purpose of modernization and reform, officials say, is to build a successful and powerful China that will become more influential in international affairs. By the year 2000, Deng Xiaoping has pointed out, China could have an annual military budget of about $50 billion simply by allocating 5 percent of its gross national product to national defense. By the turn of the century, Deng continued, "China will be truly powerful, exerting a much greater influence in the world."

"It is a virtual truism that China remains a regional rather than world power."

China Remains a Regional Power

Jonathan D. Pollack

Jonathan D. Pollack is a researcher at the Rand Corporation, an institution in California that studies issues of national security and public welfare. In the following viewpoint, he argues that because China is the largest and strongest power in the Asia-Pacific region, smaller countries like Korea and Vietnam perceive it as a threat. This misperception combined with the facts of China's limited trade, outmoded military technology, and unstable government all prevent China from becoming more than a regional power, Pollack concludes.

As you read, consider the following questions:

1. What reasons does Pollack cite that keep China a regional power and prevent it from taking a prominent place in the world?
2. How does China's relationship with other Asian countries affect its status in the world, according to the author?
3. Does Pollack believe that China is solely responsible for its inability to become more than a regional power? If so, why?

Jonathan D. Pollack, "China in the Evolving International System," in *China: The 80s Era*, Norton Ginsburg and Bernard A. Lalor, eds. Boulder, CO: Westview Press, 1984.

It is a virtual truism that China remains a regional rather than world power. China's strategic, economic, and technological relations with the West may be justified on the basis of global imperatives, but these relations are rooted in China's immediate political and military environment. The exercise of Chinese power (as distinct from Peking's broader international strategies) is regional rather than global in scope. The consequences of growth in Chinese economic and military capacities will continue to be felt along China's periphery, not elsewhere. By virtue of its size, geographic position, historic role, and the absolute dimensions of its military effort, China's centrality in Asia overrides the endless examples of Chinese backwardness and vulnerability.

The smaller states of Asia will always live in the shadow of Chinese power, but the terms of this relationship remain problematic and uncertain. In previous decades, with the People's Republic of China convulsed by internal turmoil and largely isolated from the outside world, calculations about China were more short-term than long-term. The pervasiveness of the United States' political and military presence throughout East Asia further eased anxieties about Chinese power. The same assumptions no longer hold. The retrenchment in the American military presence in Asia after the Vietnam conflict, while potentially reversible, is unlikely to be altered dramatically in the near future. At the same time, the Soviet Union's political and military presence in Asia has increased enormously, as indicated by the growth of Soviet forces deployed in the region and Moscow's alliance obligations to Hanoi. The erosion of America's dominance in economic terms has been even more pronounced. The remarkable economic growth in various neo-Confucian cultures—felt initially in Japan, but now extending to South Korea, Taiwan, Hong Kong, and Singapore, to name the more prominent examples—has transformed the face of Asia. These societies, long on entrepreneurial and management skills but woefully short of natural resources, must rely on continued access to foreign capital, markets, and resources to sustain their export-oriented economies. It is little wonder that Japan and the East Asian "four tigers" place such importance on the unhampered movement of goods and resources.

China Pursues Trade

Unburdened of the dogmatic self-reliance of the Maoist era, China in the late 1970s undertook far-reaching political and economic changes of its own. In political terms, China normalized ties with virtually all the noncommunist states of East Asia, and even began limited economic relations with Taiwan and South Korea. Total foreign trade grew from 27.25 billion *yuan* in 1977 to 73.5 billion *yuan* in 1981, a nearly threefold increase in only four years. China also initiated new commercial practices previously unthinkable for

From *China's Foreign Relations in the 1980s*, Harry Harding, ed. Copyright © 1984 by Yale University.

any Chinese government, including the establishment of export processing zones and joint venture arrangements, as well as the solicitation of foreign capital and technology for the development of China's offshore oil reserves. The success of the modernization program depends critically on these endeavors, in particular generating substantial earnings of foreign exchange through export of energy resources.

Leaders in Peking are also trying to come to terms with the consequences of well over a decade of political turmoil and societal upheaval. The human and material costs of the Cultural Revolution and its aftermath—a generation of ill-trained or untrained students, a severe retrogression in scientific and technological capabilities, and stagnation or damage to the industrial, transportation, and communications infrastructure—may be unparalleled for a society not involved in major armed conflict. In a March 1982 conversation with American physicist Li Zhengdao, Party Chairman Hu Yaobang bluntly conveyed a "never again" mentality: "In the past 142 years since the Opium War, the Chinese people have suffered inordinate hardship and suffering...to build a strong and prosperous China. The Cultural Revolution was the last time we shall endure such suffering; the ten years of internal chaos made China even poorer. The people today will no longer accept such poverty. This is a very profound lesson. We can no longer pursue stupid and divisive policies which only bring about poverty." The People's Republic of China nonetheless remains severely disadvantaged in relation to its more developed noncommunist neighbors, all of whom built, trained, and prospered while China burned. Except for textiles, certain light industrial goods, and surplus labor for international construction projects, China still cannot compete seriously with its more advanced neighbors.

China and Its Neighbors

Given the disparities in industrial and technological development and China's acute shortages of trained manpower and managerial expertise, there will continue to be striking discontinuities between China's developmental prospects and needs and those in noncommunist Asia. China will remain a largely agrarian society well beyond the end of this century.... The awesome tasks of feeding, clothing, and housing China's billion people will continue to set limits on Chinese economic interactions with the outside world. Except for industrial and urban development in China's coastal regions, comparisons between China's economic needs and those of its noncommunist neighbors seem overly facile.

The degree of technological, institutional, and managerial innovation permitted in relation to the outside world constitutes a critical issue for the Chinese leadership. Peking has openly sought Asian as well as Western entrepreneurial involvement in its modernization program. Mutual and complementary interests exist, provided that satisfactory arrangements can be implemented for the involvement of foreign capitalists in China's development. Yet, has China fully considered the political and economic transformation underway within Asia? Is Peking prepared to break unequivocally with

164

the rigidities of a highly centralized, overly bureaucratic planning process? Will the Chinese be willing to accept diversity and inequality between and among regions and economic sectors? To what degree will leaders in Peking accommodate to the economic and commercial practices of the newly industrializing societies of Asia, even if such accommodation puts Marxist values at risk?. . .

A Military Power

Assertions of Peking's vulnerability and weakness ignore China's role as Asia's strongest and largest indigenous military power, a role underscored by the People's Republic of China's repeated willingness to employ force when its leaders have judged key security interests at risk. The prospect of China strengthening its defense industrial base through Western assistance fuels lingering suspicions in Asia that the United States ultimately wants China to supplant American power in East Asia, enabling the United States to concentrate its defense resources elsewhere.

Security Focus

China's security concerns focus on Asia, and its military power does not extend beyond the region. Its political and cultural influence have been strongest in Asia, and the largest proportion of its foreign trade is conducted with its Asian neighbors.

Steven I. Levine, *China's Foreign Relations in the 1980s*, 1984.

Since the extent of American involvement in China's defense modernization remains highly uncertain, leaders in Peking continue to plan on the basis of their own capabilities and doctrines. Through an incremental but steady effort, China's strategic planners and military commanders have begun to devote increasing attention to the long-term directions of Chinese military power. For such a large and varied defense structure, the only meaningful long-term strategy is to maximize China's autonomy from external control— technologically, doctrinally, and organizationally. The gradual development of an externally oriented, independent defense structure (notably in both strategic weapons and in naval forces) will be far more pronounced by the end of the 1980s. Other Asian states as well as the superpowers will pay careful heed to such developments. Although Peking is very unlikely to embark on what Liddell Hart terms an "acquisitive approach" to grand strategy, China's military efforts will lend growing credibility to Chinese power and policy goals. . . .

The political and economic revolution of post-Mao China has also been unsettling to leaders in Pyongyang. Chinese attacks on one-man rule and the cult of personality, two issues with which Kim Il-song is intimately familiar, suggest how domestic developments can impinge upon foreign relations. Kim Il-song's greatest fear—that his political independence will be compromised by great powers pursuing their own interests at his expense—has no doubt been conveyed to Deng Xiaoping. Even if the People's Republic of China has good reasons for preserving the *status quo* in Korea, it cannot run an overly great risk of alienating the North Korean leadership. Deng has tried to steer a careful course, reassuring Japan and others of China's interest in stable, mutually beneficial relations with noncommunist Asia, while still paying heed to the concerns and sensitivities of a proud, nationalistic leadership in Pyongyang; but he can hardly incur the risks of doing more. To push the North towards genuine accommodation with the South would be anathema to Kim Il-song, since it would confirm Kim's worst suspicions of the willingness of various "dominating forces" to sacrifice his vital interests.

Independent of China

Like Vietnam's leaders, Kim Il-song has the capability to act independent of China. It remains extremely unlikely that Pyongyang would grow so alienated from China that it would rush into the embrace of Soviet power; nor does China face a moment of decision akin to its break with the Vietnamese in 1978. Indeed, Sino-North Korean relations appeared to improve significantly during 1982. Yet, a future deterioration cannot be excluded, especially with the likelihood of a succession to Kim Il-song before the end of the decade. If North Korea became another Vietnam for Peking, China's worst strategic nightmare might come to pass, with Moscow making major gains in its long-term effort to encircle and pressure China from an increasing number of geographic points.

Chinese leaders, yet again, may have to ask if they are prepared to live with a powerful, regional communist power on their borders that acts in defiance of Chinese interests and preferences. China in the 1980s will therefore need to confront the limits of its strategic vision in several respects. In both the communist and noncommunist world, the number of independent powers continues to grow. The time may not be too far distant when the Chinese will have to concede that the security of Asia derives from far more than the machinations of one or more hegemonic powers. The long-term prospects for peace and stability in Asia will increasingly depend on how China is prepared to interact with the outside world.

"The Chinese people will make unremitting efforts... to ease world tension, check the arms race and prevent a nuclear war."

China Promotes World Stability

Hu Yaobang and Zhao Ziyang

Part I of the following viewpoint is by Hu Yaobang, who was China's Communist Party general secretary from June 1981 until January 1987. Part II is by Zhao Ziyang, who is the premier and has replaced Hu as the party general secretary. The authors argue that China plays a continuing role in world arms control based on the Five Principles of Peaceful Coexistence. These are mutual respect for sovereignty and territorial integrity, mutual nonaggression, noninterference in each other's internal affairs, equality and mutual benefit, and peaceful coexistence.

As you read, consider the following questions:

1. How does China, according to the authors, contribute to arms control around the world?
2. What reasons do Hu and Zhao give as motivations for China's commitment to peace?
3. What role do the authors believe the superpowers, the United States and the Soviet Union, play in China's motivation to encourage arms control?

Hu Yaobang and Zhao Ziyang, "Two Statements on International Cooperation and Disarmament," in *China and the Bomb*, Ken Coates, ed. Nottingham, England: Spokesman, 1986. © 1986 Spokesman.

I

In recent years, our Party and the Chinese Government have solemnly stated on many occasions that the primary objective in China's foreign policy is to safeguard world peace. Though the danger of a world war still exists due to the rivalry of the superpowers for hegemony, we are confident that as long as the people of the world truly unite and wage resolute struggles against all expressions of hegemonism and expansionism, world peace can be maintained. The strong peace movement prevalent in various countries of the world today exactly reflects the world people's abhorrence of a world war and their strong desire for peace.

China is working and will continue to work for the cause of construction in order to gradually meet the increasing material and cultural needs of the Chinese people, and it thus genuinely wishes that world peace can be maintained and sincerely desires to develop relations with various countries of the world on the basis of the Five Principles of Peaceful Coexistence. We are opposed to hegemonism, but we have no intention of straining our relations with the superpowers, and we also wish that the strained relations between the superpowers could be eased. When the superpowers' rivalry is intensified, the people in countries caught in the middle are often the first to suffer the harmful consequences, which, at the same time, are also brought to bear on the people within the superpowers. The Chinese people will make unremitting efforts, along with the people of Europe and other countries, to ease world tension, check the arms race and prevent a nuclear war.

The rise of the third world in the post-war international arena is a very important event of our era and a powerful factor in defending world peace. China belongs to the third world, and shares with other third world nations a common desire and destiny. China considers it its international obligation to safeguard the rights and interests of the third world countries, and firmly supports them in their struggles to safeguard their national independence and state sovereignty, to develop their national economies, and to establish a new international economic order. . . .

Political Forces

The socialist, social democratic and labour parties in many countries are political forces that have broad mass support and strong influence. They have made positive efforts to safeguard world peace, promote social progress and strengthen friendship among the people of various countries. Since the founding of the People's Republic of China, we have kept up friendly exchanges with representatives of the socialist and social democratic parties of some countries. In recent years, the Communist Party of China has established friendly ties with the German Social Democratic Party as well as the socialist, social democratic and labour parties of a number of other countries. Our Party is ready to develop all forms of friendly exchanges with all those socialists, social democratic and labour parties that are willing to establish ties with us. And, in so doing, we will strictly abide by the principles of independence, complete equality, mutual respect and noninterference in each other's internal affairs. Our Party will not only refrain from interfering in the internal affairs of any foreign party, but will also refrain from making use of our relations with a foreign party to interfere in the internal affairs of any foreign country and from making use of these relations against any third parties or countries. In developing these relations, our intentions are genuine and sincere: we want to promote mutual understanding, develop friendly co-operation, safeguard world peace and advance the progress of mankind.

II

During the first half of the century, mankind went through two world wars with untold sufferings. In spite of the absence of a new world war in the past four decades since the end of World War II, the turbulent international situation indicates that the danger of war is yet to be removed. . . .

Progress in Disarmament

The Chinese Government and people have always stood for genuine disarmament and positive efforts towards progress in disarmament. Since the 1960s, the Chinese Government has put forward on a number of occasions its views and proposals on disarmament and on strengthening international security. We have always opposed the arms race and the threat or use of force in international relations, and we are against any country carrying out aggression or expansion by means of superior military strength.

Huang Hua, *China and the Bomb*, 1986.

China needs peace; the Chinese people love peace. In peace lie the fundamental interests of the Chinese people. As a developing socialist country, China can achieve prosperity only through peaceful development. It requires sustained efforts of several generations for a country like ours to achieve socialist modernization and to approach or catch up with the developed countries economically. We need peace not only in this century, but also in the next. As China is a big country in the East with a population accounting for nearly one quarter of the world's total, its position on the question of world peace and its efforts towards this end have a major worldwide impact now as well as in the future. Aware of this important mission entrusted by history, China is ready to make its due efforts and contributions for the sake of world peace and stability.

The Chinese Government pursues an independent foreign policy of peace. The basic objective of our foreign policy is to oppose hegemonism and maintain world peace. Firmly standing by the third world, we will steadily strengthen and increase our solidarity and co-operation with other third world countries. We are actively seeking to establish and develop normal relations and friendly co-operation with various countries in the world on the basis of the Five Principles of Peaceful Coexistence. We will never enter into alliance or establish strategic relations with any superpower. We are opposed to interference and aggression against any country and the use or threat of force in international relations. We are in favour of the settlement of international disputes by peaceful means and on a fair and reasonable basis. No matter how the world situation may evolve, we will steadfastly implement these foreign policies, which have been proved correct through practice.

Disarmament Through Deeds

At present, the ever-intensifying arms race between the superpowers has caused concern among the people of various countries. Although numerous disarmament proposals have been put forward, they have not brought people any sense of security, because disarmament can only be achieved through deeds, not words.

China opposes the arms race and will never take part in such a race. The level of our military expenditure and armament is far lower than that of other big powers, and yet we have taken repeated measures on our own to reduce our military forces and cut our defence expenditure. China's limited nuclear force is for the sole purpose of defence. . . .

As the question of disarmament concerns the security of all countries, it should not be monopolized by a few big powers. The disarmament agreement between them must not jeopardize the interests of other countries. All countries, big or small, militarily strong or weak, should enjoy equal rights to participate in the discussions and settlement of problems related to disarmament.

China Supports Disarmament

The above position and views of the Chinese Government on the question of disarmament have taken into account the desire of all the peoples in the world and the viewpoints of all the interested parties. We support all proposals truly conducive to disarmament and are ready to continue our efforts to promote genuine progress on disarmament together with other countries.

Of course, the question of disarmament is not the only issue affecting world peace and security. World peace and national security are closely inter-related. In this sense, encroaching upon a nation's independence and sovereignty means jeopardizing world peace.

The Chinese Government wishes to reiterate that in order to relax tension and eliminate regional conflicts, it is imperative to observe strictly the principle of equality among all countries, big or small, in international relations and to refrain from interfering in the internal affairs or encroaching upon the sovereignty of other countries in any form. Only thus will it be possible to contribute to the maintenance of world peace.

The maintenance of world peace is the dedicated goal and sacred duty of the people of all countries. Human destiny must be held in the hands of mankind itself. The factors making for peace are growing faster than those making for war. So long as the people of the world keep up their unremitting efforts, they will certainly win peace.

"Communist China's participation in long-term competition on the international arms market has a...detrimental influence on international security."

China Promotes World Instability

Ya-chün Chang

Ya-chün Chang contributes to *Issues & Studies*, a Taiwanese journal of China studies and international affairs. Ya-chün argues that China's arms export trade to fighting countries like Iran and Iraq, while providing much needed income to China, also promotes unacceptable arms proliferation.

As you read, consider the following questions:

1. What does Ya-chün cite as China's reasons for selling arms?
2. Does the author believe that China's arms sales are justified given China's clientele? Do you agree?
3. What are the results of China's arms sales, if any, according to the author?

Ya-chün Chang, "Communist China's Arms Export," *Issues & Studies*, September 1987.

Since Communist China adopted the open-door policy in the early 1980s, one of its key export items has been arms. In recent years, its arms have become increasingly competitive on the international market.

From 1979 to 1982, Communist China was the seventh largest arms-exporting country, next to the Soviet Union, the United States, France, Britain, West Germany and Italy. However, its arms export in 1984 suddenly increased to US$1.7 billion, making it the fifth among arms-exporting countries. In 1986, its total arms export further increased to US$2.5 billion.

It is widely believed that Communist China has been supplying arms to both Iran and Iraq, the two Middle East countries now in their seventh year of war. Therefore, the sudden increase in its arms export may have been caused by the escalation of the Iran-Iraq War.

In fact, Communist China has already become an active competitor on the international arms market. Since 1984, the North Industrial Corporation, which handles the export of Communist Chinese-made heavy industry and defense products, has put on sale various kinds of arms including armored vehicles, tanks, anti-tank weapons, machine guns, artillery shells, fighter planes and missiles. It is said that Communist China's aviation industry departments have already exported more than 10,000 pieces of military aircraft to some ten countries.

Arms Exhibitions

In recent years, Communist China has seized upon every chance to participate in international arms exhibitions. For instance, it sponsored an international arms exhibition in Peking in November 1986. At a meeting with the foreign delegations who came to take part in the Peking exhibition, Chao Tzu-yang asserted Communist China's intention to strengthen military exchanges and arms trade with foreign countries. This indicates that at the same time as Communist China is trying hard to introduce Western military technology, it is making vigorous efforts to promote the export of arms that it has developed by itself.

Communist China has good economic reasons to promote arms exports. By so doing, it may earn more foreign exchange to reduce the imbalance between its foreign exchange earnings and expenditures.

Since Communist China opened its door in the 1980s, it has never been able to achieve, through normal market regulation, a balance between its foreign exchange earnings and expenditures. The core of the problem is that Communist China must import many expensive machines and precision equipment from the West to enhance its modernization program. The quick drain of its foreign exchange reserve has already forced it to reduce the import of foreign technology and equipment through two economic readjustment

Far Eastern Economic Review, June 2, 1988.

drives in 1981 and 1985. However, if the reduction is allowed to go too far, it will affect the progress of its modernization plan. Therefore, the best way for Communist China to extricate itself from this difficult situation is to expand its arms export.

It is reported that Communist China has delivered arms to Iran in exchange for four million tons of petroleum. This is highly possible because a direct exchange of arms for important materials will entail no payment in foreign exchange.

In promoting arms export, Communist China also aimed at tapping new financial resources for the development of its defense industry. Since its arms lag behind the West for about fifteen to twenty years, Communist China wishes to boost its defense industry so that it may be able to stop buying large quantities of Western weapons and achieve self-reliance in national defense some day. Under these circumstances, Communist China's defense industry must accelerate the development of both advanced and conventional arms. However, the reduction of Communist China's defense expenditure would impair the research and development work in its defense industry. Although Teng Hsiao-p'ing has already reshuffled some military personnel, simplified military organizations and reduced the troops by one million, the People's Liberation Army remains bulky. After deducting from the defense budget the funds needed for maintaining such a big army, not much money can be saved to develop the defense industry. Therefore, Communist China intends to solve this problem by exporting arms. In fact, arms export may raise ample funds for research and development or for the purchase of Western military technology and equipment. At the same time, the expansion of arms export may lower the per-unit production costs of its arms. Thus, the development of Communist China's defense industry may not be hindered by the tightening of its national budget.

Promotion of Arms Export

Communist China's promotion of arms export also has political and strategic objectives. In the past, to "export revolution," Peking supplied free arms and ammunition to many Communist organizations, liberation movement groups and some Third World countries. At present, to ensure its own security and regional balance, it continues to supply arms to North Korea, Pakistan, Thailand, Afghan resistance forces, and Cambodian guerrillas. It also supplies arms to some Third World countries, including Egypt, for friendship considerations. Nevertheless, it has already abandoned its former policy of supplying free military aid. Except a few resistance or guerrilla groups, most countries now must pay for arms supplied by Communist China.

The international arms market has become increasingly pluralistic as more and more countries have joined in the competition for economic reasons. Communist China is one of the few countries that are able to compete as long-term sellers. Its gradually consolidated defense industry has enabled it to become a long-term supplier of arms. What is most important is that its arms are relatively inexpensive and easy to operate. Moreover, their exports are not subject to restrictions as in Western countries. Therefore, they are attractive to Third World countries that are engaging in wars or are faced with political instability and economic difficulty.

Communist China's advertisements in foreign military publications emphasize especially that its arms are inexpensive, durable and easy to operate. In general, Communist Chinese-made arms lag far behind their Western counterparts in precision. However, Communist China has added to some of its own products precision accessories from the West. For instance, the M-type light fighters manufactured in Chengtu are equipped with a precision electronic system, which has not only improved their performance, but has also made them more competitive on the international arms market.

Communist China's participation in long-term competition on the international arms market has a rather detrimental influence on international security. Of course, the arms sales by the United States and other Western countries and the Soviet Union and East European countries are also detrimental to international security. However, arms exports by Western countries are subject to appraisal by administrative organizations, supervision of public opinion and approval by friendly nations. Arms exports by East European countries must gain tacit consent of the Soviet Union. Communist China alone is under no restrictions at all. Moreover, it has a unique logic about foreign policy and international peace and security, which is quite different from that of the West. It always tries hard to bypass international intervention. For instance, it has so far refrained from giving the United States the assurance not to transfer nuclear technology to third countries. When the United States expressed concern over its arms supplies to Iran and Iraq, it flatly denied the deals, saying that Iran had obtained those arms from the open market.

Without any restrictions, Communist China's increasing arms export may speed up the flow of Western advanced technology to the Third World and enable more Third World nations to become arms suppliers. Then, regional disorders and confrontations will be much more difficult to solve, and international peace and security will be harder to achieve.

"The two sides of the Taiwan Straits must be reunified, as this is the common aspiration of the Chinese people of both sides."

Taiwan and Mainland China Should Be United

Li Jiaquan

Taiwan is ruled by the Kuomintang [KMT] or Nationalist Party which ruled mainland China from 1928 to 1949. KMT members fled the mainland in 1949 when the Communist Party took over China. Beginning in 1986 and 1987 the Taiwanese government began to relax military law and decrease Kuomintang party domination. In the following viewpoint, the deputy director and research fellow of the Taiwan Research Institute under the Chinese Academy of Social Sciences, Li Jiaquan, proposes that the Taiwanese people push for reunification with their motherland, mainland China.

As you read, consider the following questions:

1. Why does the author favor the "one country, two systems" plan for reunifying Taiwan with China?
2. What anti-unification arguments does Li cite? How does he refute them?
3. What methods does Li propose to begin the reunification process? In your opinion, are they necessary? If so, why?

Li Jiaquan, "Again on Formula for China's Reunification," *Beijing Review*, March 28/April 3, 1988. Reprinted with permission.

Some encouraging changes have taken place recently in Taiwan and in the mainland's relations with Taiwan. While conducting "political restructuring" on the island, the Kuomintang authorities have readjusted their mainland policies, which had been static for many years. The ban on Taiwanese making Hong Kong the first stop in their travels was lifted, and people have been allowed to visit the mainland to see relatives (excluding serving members of the army and government). More recently, the Kuomintang authorities extended this permission to KMT cadres and civil servants who had been excluded previously. In addition, the Taiwan authorities have also relaxed controls over indirect trade, and cultural and academic exchanges between the two sides of the Taiwan Straits, and over economic information and "non-political" books from the mainland. All these are decisions to be welcomed.

Thus, the 40-year-old freeze between the Chinese mainland and the island of Taiwan has begun to thaw and a new enthusiasm for the mainland is growing in Taiwan. Cigarettes, liquor, books and traditional herbal medicines from the mainland make people in Taiwan feel a sense of kinship.

Not long ago, a scholar from Taiwan told me that people on both sides of the Taiwan Straits are of one family. Over the last few decades, however, Taiwan has only cultivated its relations with the United States, Japan and West European countries. It seems that only recently the island has discovered, just across a strip of water, a "new, vast continent" with abundant resources, whose people bear kindred feelings for it.

The "mainland craze" in Taiwan also inspires a "Taiwan craze" on the mainland. For many years, the sense of kinship the mainland's government and people have had for Taiwan was mocked as "unrequited love." At last there is some response. Over the last few months, people on the mainland have joyfully played hosts to Taiwan visitors.

Opposition Articles

However, not all the news from the other side of the Taiwan Straits is heartening. The newspapers in Taiwan often seem to be striking a note at variance with the general atmosphere. Since the beginning of [1987] influential newspapers in Taiwan have published a few dozen signed articles on the reunification of Taiwan with the motherland, many of which were written by noted scholars, both in Taiwan and overseas. A few papers have written editorials or commentaries. They all express identical views. Whether this is a mere reflection of the official view or there is more to it, this author is not willing to guess. Some of their ideas, including the cessation of all hostilities, encouraging friendship between the people and holding cultural and economic exchanges, and allowing people on both sides to have mutual visits, are all positive and should be encouraged. But other

178

opinions are less acceptable. . . .

What is more surprising is that some of the writers link the "one country, two systems" concept to the four cardinal principles (the socialist road, the people's democratic dictatorship, the leadership of the Communist Party, and Marxism-Leninism and Mao Zedong Thought) upheld by the Communist Party in the mainland, and conclude that the "one country, two systems" formula is a non-starter.

In fact, the formula of "one country, two systems" as proposed by the Chinese Communist Party is an answer to all these questions. The concept of "one country" is established on the basis of acknowledging the differences and keeping the "two systems." At the same time, the Chinese Communist Party stresses that neither side should seek to swallow up the other, and that both must learn from each other's strong points to offset their own weaknesses in long-term peaceful coexistence. The formula does not require the application of the four cardinal principles in Taiwan and the replacement of Taiwan's Three People's Principles (nationalism, democracy and people's livelihood) with the socialist system of the mainland. Therefore, it is absurd that the Taiwan authorities demand that the mainland give up the four cardinal principles and replace its socialist system with Taiwan's Three People's Principles.

Seductive Proposal

Concrete and seductive proposals have been made to Taibei. The present economic and political system would continue on the island for at least 50 years after reunification, and no troops or administrative personnel would be sent from mainland China to Taiwan.

The attractiveness of these proposals is increased by the current reforms aimed at doing away with administrative methods of economic management and encouraging contacts with foreign private business. Taiwan businessmen already have the opportunity to establish close cooperation with their compatriots on the mainland.

Evgeny Sevastyanov, *New Times*, February 1988.

The solutions which have been worked out for Hong Kong and Macao with Britain and Portugal prove that the "one country, two systems" formula is practical. Although the Taiwan question is not identical to either of the two, the formula's basic principles and spirit are applicable. The theory that China is still in the primary stage of socialism, which was put forward at the recent CPC [Communist Party of China] 13th National Congress, indicates that two systems and various economic elements will coexist in China for a long time to come. In both theory and practice, it provides an answer to all the questions about the "one country, two systems" formula. In this sense, the theory is the most reliable guarantee for the "one country, two systems" concept. . . .

The "one country, two systems" concept is the only reasonable and practical one. It allows the two sides to cultivate their common ground while reserving their differences, conforms to the principle of "one China," safeguards the unity of the country, fulfils the wishes of the whole nation, takes into account the history of both sides and their current conditions and conforms to reality and the traditions of China as a whole. It is also conducive to Taiwan's stability and prosperity and to the great cause of rejuvenating the Chinese nation.

Later, some articles were published in overseas Chinese newspapers, including those in Taiwan, criticizing the "one country, two systems" concept and putting forward some so-called new formulas which are said to be better than the "one country, two systems" method. In fact, most of these proposed formulas differ only in form and presentation; their substance is the same. . . .

"One country under a fine system." The so-called "fine system" is the Three People's Principles. It suggests bringing all of China under the Three People's Principles. (Taiwan's *Central Daily News*, editorial, April 16, 1987)

"Two systems, one country." This suggests allowing the two systems now in operation to develop until conditions are ripe. Reunification should be undertaken at this point. (Professor Chen Qing, in Taiwan's *China Times News*, June 7, 1987)

"Two countries, two systems." It recommends "peaceful coexistence, co-operation and mutual help" between the two sides for another hundred years "when all the people will be rich" and then "the time will be ripe and the goal of 'one country, one system' will be reached." (Tao Baichuan, in Taiwan's *United News Daily*, October 3, 1987)

The Cultural Approach

"The cultural approach." This view suggests that China's reunification be undertaken in two stages—first cultural and only then political. (Li Dayi, in *Taiwan Daily News* on October 15, 1987)

"One country, under separate administrations." It suggests the mainland and Taiwan enjoy sovereign rights jointly, to administer separately and compete with one another peacefully. This was proposed by Shen Junshan in an article published in *China Times News* on September 1, 1987. It is similar to the "one country, two bodies" he proposed before.

"One country, two seats" advocated by Winston L.Y. Yang suggests that before China achieves reunification, there should be an interim stage of "one China, two seats." Yang has published articles in Hong Kong's *90s* and other journals, elaborating on this idea, which is very similar to Shen Junshan's notion of "one country under separate administrations."

Other formulas such as the federal idea, the confederation model, the multiple systems model, the Korean model, the German model and the so-called Taiwan model are still being discussed in some publications. As they contain nothing new, this article will not dwell on them.

Shared Notions

All the models mentioned above share four notions: 1) that reunification is a matter for the future, and the time is not yet ripe; 2) that to achieve reunification the Communist Party must give up its four cardinal principles (which is tantamount to insisting that China be reunified on the "Taiwan model"); 3) that for the present, Taiwan and the mainland must be two equal political entities, each with the status of an independent "international legal person"; and 4) that use of arms must be ruled out.

Where is the concept of reunification in them? They seem to regard it as a chimera. Put bluntly, all these propositions are simply designed to keep the status of "one China, two governments" while not endangering the "legally constituted authority" of the Kuomintang. They are in fact disguised products of the "two Chinas" camp and are slipping down the road of "Taiwan independence" whether they know it or not. . . .

For Reunification

In China, whoever dares to go against the desire of the Chinese nation for reunification and, under the support of some foreign countries, plots independence of Taiwan will be looked upon as a traitor to China and will be denounced by all Chinese. Any political leader who vacillates or shrinks from the mission of reunification will surely be cast aside by the Chinese people. In the same way, any nation that plots permanent separation between Taiwan and the mainland will be resolutely opposed by a billion Chinese people.

Chen Qimao, *Asian Survey*, November 1987.

At the end of [1987], a Chinese newspaper in Thailand published a signed article on relations between Taiwan and the mainland. It says, "The two sides of the Taiwan Straits must be reunified, as this is the common aspiration of the Chinese people of both sides and is also the desire of all descendants of the Yellow Emperor (Chinese people) residing abroad. In all fairness, it is unrealistic for either the mainland or Taiwan to unify by imposing on the other side its own doctrine. The mainland authorities have put forward the 'one country, two systems' idea. It does not call for reunifying China through socialism and should be regarded as realistic."

Ignoring the realistic nature of the suggestion, some people have unfortunately hastily rejected this idea, which cannot but set one thinking. The problem is not in the proposition of "one country, two systems" itself, but in the psychological and practical obstacles to the proposal.

In Taiwan it is first the attitude of the Kuomintang authorities. Sun Yun-hsuan, former president of the Executive Yuan, once said, "We can hardly protect ourselves if we are content to retain sovereignty over only a part of the country, while separatism will eventually lead to our extinction." Many other high-ranking officials of the Kuomintang are also very clear about this. However, their chief concern is their fear of being relegated to the status of a local government. In fact, Taiwan has always been a province of China and never a state. The Kuomintang authorities should have the courage to face this historical reality. If they continue to hold out for a "country," or if in the future they are replaced by authorities who adopt the title "country," they will certainly bring calamity to the nation and be condemned by history.

A Special Administrative Region

If reunification is accomplished early on, a different picture emerges. As a special administrative region of China, this author believes with good reason that Taiwan's political status can be still higher than other provinces and special administrative regions. Some Kuomintang officials can take posts in the central government. Co-operation between political parties and groups and between people of all nationalities on both sides of the Taiwan Straits must be based on co-operation between the Communist Party and the Kuomintang. Nobody can deny this.

The second problem lies in the attitude of all the non-KMT political forces in Taiwan. Currently their main preoccupation is to force the Kuomintang to grant them democracy and redistribute power. They are afraid that the introduction of "one country, two systems" and the promise involved in it that certain things will be unchanged, will "fix" the current political power of the Kuomintang. They worry that the Kuomintang, joining hands with the Communist Party, will render prospects for freedom in Taiwan more remote.

In fact, the "one country, two systems" notion will not affect the Taiwan people's struggle for freedom. The elimination of antagonism between the two sides of the Straits and their reconciliation will help the opposition's struggle for freedom. Besides, the mainland is carrying out reform, making efforts to open its door wider, and going all out to develop its social productive forces. Talent is badly needed everywhere on the mainland, and there are many able people in the political, industrial, commercial and scientific circles in Taiwan. The policy of letting certain things remain unchanged means that the central government will never use arms or pressure to compel the Taiwan authorities to change the existing political and social systems. This is all quite separate from the issue of the Taiwan people's democratic movement.

The Taiwan issue has always been a thorn in the side of Sino-US relations. Soon after the two countries resumed diplomatic relations, the United States passed its "Taiwan Relations Act" to continue to interfere in China's internal affairs. Although sometimes US government officials have made remarks meant to help improve relations between the mainland and Taiwan, in general, the US government has never given up its so-called "double track" policy of straddling two boats. When the Taiwan authorities and some local newspapers attacked the Communist Party's "one country, two systems" policy, some people in the United States enthusiastically advocated improving US-Taiwan relations, saying it was a perfect combination, like mingling milk with water. It is natural for people to link the two issues, for right up to the present, without the support of the United States, the Taiwan authorities could not hold such a stiff position. This author believes that the US government will come to understand that to continue to interfere in China's internal affairs will help neither the United States nor the people on both sides of the Taiwan Straits....

Helpful to Development

The problem will not be difficult to solve if the process of reunification goes forward and the future of Taiwan gradually becomes clear and bright. Only a narrow strip of water separates Taiwan and the mainland, and the two economies are complementary to each other.... The effect of reunification will not only be helpful to the development of the whole country, but also beneficial to the further economic growth of Taiwan and the raising of its standard of living. In addition, the export-oriented economy of Taiwan requires broad relations with other countries in the world, and these could be handled better after reunification.

Chen Qimao, *Asian Survey*, November 1987.

"One country, two systems" is the best model for resolving the issue between Taiwan and the mainland. Given the current international and domestic situation, no other model is better. Although it is not understood and accepted by the Taiwan authorities and some prominent people in Taiwan, it will be accepted sooner or later because it is scientific, fair and practicable. Historical trends are irresistible. Those who move against the tide of history will eventually be overwhelmed by it.

"The long-term interest of Taiwan to carry out democracy on the island is far more urgent and important than unification with China."

Taiwan Should Remain Independent of China

Trong R. Chai

According to Trong R. Chai, mainland China cannot legally claim Taiwan as its territory. China spent decades after World War II completely closed off from the Western world. During this time Taiwan developed a strong economy and equally strong trade and diplomatic relationships with many countries. As a result, Taiwan is now far more developed than mainland China, the author argues, and reunification with the mainland is unappealing. Chai contends that Taiwan's independence is established indisputably and the Taiwanese people have a guaranteed right to determine the future of their country. Chai is a political science professor at New York's City University.

As you read, consider the following questions:

1. How does Taiwan's economy affect the desire for Taiwan's continued independence, according to the author? Why?
2. What legal grounds does Chai give for establishing Taiwan's independence and how to they relate to the reunification with China?
3. What plan does the author propose to determine the wishes of the Taiwanese people in terms of their country's government?

Excerpted from "The Future of Taiwan," by Trong R. Chai in *Asian Survey*, Vol. XXVI, No. 12, December 1986, pp. 1309-1310, 1317-1323. © 1986 by The Regents of the University of California.

On December 15, 1978, in his remarks on the establishment of diplomatic relations between the United States and China, President Carter said that "normalization between our country and the People's Republic will not jeopardize the well-being of the people of Taiwan" and that "we will continue to have interest in the peaceful resolution of the Taiwan issue." On the same day, China stated that: "As for the way of bringing Taiwan back to the embrace of the motherland and reunifying the country, it is entirely China's internal affair.". . .

Taiwan has achieved one of the world's highest economic growths over the past quarter of a century. With the exception of 1974 and 1975, the island's GNP grew at an annual rate of more than 10% in real terms in the period 1961-81. In spite of the recent world recession, Taiwan's GNP has continued to grow, in real terms, by 3.9% in 1982, 7.3% in 1983, and 10.6% (the highest in Asia) in 1984. At the same time, the unemployment rate has rarely risen above 2%.

Because of this economic boom, Taiwan has rapidly developed from an agricultural into an industrial society. This is evidenced by the fact that in 1982 only 8.7% of goods and services originated from agriculture, as against 43.9% produced by manufacturing. Concomitant figures in 1952 were 35% from agriculture, and 18% from manufacturing. To create sufficient capacity in this burgeoning economic growth, the KMT [Kuomintang] has spent tens of billions of dollars to complete 22 major construction projects in the past decade. . . .

Now the Taiwanese people fear that China will eventually take over the island. This fear has precipitated a growing flow of wealth from Taiwan. In testimony before the Senate Foreign Relations Committee in November 1983, Fu-chen Lo, a visiting professor of economics at the University of Pennsylvania, stated: "Already a so-called Hong Kong phenomenon is experienced in Taiwan. Based on a banker's estimates, some $3 billion in capital, equivalent to 7% of the GNP of Taiwan, has flown into Los Angeles alone.". . .

China's Unification Policy

Believing that Taiwan is its territory, China has recently redoubled its efforts to take over the island. At the end of September 1981, Ye Jiangying, Chairman of the National People's Congress, issued a nine-point policy for "reunification" with Taiwan. Two years later, in his talk with Professor Winston L.Y. Yang, Deng Xiaoping, the country's leader, made a six-point offer to Taiwan. These proposals are similar to the Hong Kong agreement between China and Great Britain, which was initialed in September 1984 and ratified in May 1985. That agreement states that after the Chinese takeover of Hong Kong in 1997 "the socialist system and socialist policies shall not be practiced in the Hong Kong Special Administrative Region and

© Bac/Rothco.

that Hong Kong's previous capitalist systems and life style shall remain unchanged for 50 years."...

This agreement provides a Chinese guarantee for a capitalist system to remain in Hong Kong under the sovereignty of communist rule. The Chinese want to make this British colony a model that might lure Taiwan back under a similar formula. This is evidenced by the fact that a few days after the agreement was initialed, Premier Zhao Ziyang, asserting that the formula of "one country, two systems after unification is most reasonable," said "we are ready to start joint consultation with the Taiwan authorities and personages of all circles in Taiwan for the early realization of a way of peaceful reunification acceptable to both sides."

Will China keep its promise and allow Taiwan to maintain a different system if it takes over the island? The experience of the Tibetans might provide an answer. In its 1951 agreement with Tibet, China made arrangements similar to those contained in the Hong Kong document, whereby Tibet could maintain its own cultural, political, and religious systems.... Tibet could keep its traditional systems for an indefinite period of time—which, of course, could be longer than 50 years as stipulated in the Hong Kong agreement—unless the Tibetans initialed and brought about changes by themselves.

Less than eight years later, in March 1959, China invaded Tibet and drove the Dalai Lama, the Tibetans' leader, out of his country.

In Lhasa alone "almost 10,000 people had died in three days of fighting," according to John F. Avedon. In 1965, China made Tibet one of five autonomous regions of China and in 1967 the Chinese army took control of the mass media, banks, and the security bureau. Though autonomous in name, Tibet remains under strict Chinese control. In August 1985, the Dalai Lama charged that as a result of 30 years of Chinese rule, "our religion and culture has been destroyed. The people of Tibet have suffered tremendous physical and economic deprivation, and at least 1.2 million have died as a direct result of the occupation." The case of Tibet clearly demonstrates that China has failed to translate its words into deeds. The Hong Kong formula should thus be seen as nothing more than an empty promise.

Taiwan and China Differ

Taiwan has been separated from China for nearly a century. Consequently, the island differs from the mainland in several significant ways. Taiwan's economic development is far ahead of that of China. The island has larger foreign trade than the mainland, and Taiwan's per capita income ($3,200) is the fourth highest in East Asia and is ten times that of China. In Asia, Taiwan is second only to Japan in educational quality and achievement. The Taiwanese illiteracy rate is less than 10%, compared with more than 30% for China. The percentage of college graduates in Taiwan is 10 times higher than in China: 6% as compared to .6%.

Individualism is widespread in Taiwan; collectivism prevails in China. The Taiwanese advocate liberalism and human rights; the Chinese regard liberalism as "spiritual pollution." China has been successful in creating a mass society and compelling its citizens to accept communism as an absolute truth. But Taiwan has gradually moved toward a pluralist society, and the Taiwanese have begun to question the values promoted by the KMT.

The Taiwanese oppose any form of dictatorship, right or left, and fear that the KMT's rule may pass and be replaced by the far greater dictatorship of China. Their favorable attitude toward democracy is reflected in the following joint statement, issued in September 1982 by four leading Taiwanese politicians from their prison cells after imprisonment for their political beliefs by the KMT: "For more than 300 years, our courageous ancestors have come to settle in Taiwan, in order to gain freedom. With their new thinking and new way of life, they developed a spirit of self-reliance and laid the foundation for a democratic society." Consequently they maintained that "in the long-term interest of Taiwan, to carry out democracy on the island is far more urgent and important than unification with China."

The Taiwanese seem to have developed their own identity, and long to shape their own destiny. In 1971, on the eve of President Nixon's historic visit to China, the Presbyterian Church in Taiwan, the only voluntary association free from KMT dominance, issued a statement to "oppose any powerful nation disregarding the rights and wishes of 15 million people and making [a] unilateral decision to their own advantage, because God has ordained and the United Nations Charter has affirmed that every people has the right to determine its own destiny."

Today a great number of Taiwanese both within and outside the island demand self-determination. In November 1983, more than 50 overseas Taiwanese associations issued a joint statement stressing that "self-determination is a sacred, inalienable right of the people on Taiwan." Similarly, the joint platform of opposition candidates in the 1985 local election in Taiwan stated that "the future of Taiwan should be determined by the people on Taiwan."...

Dashed PRC Expectations

Taiwanese want no association with the PRC as it is currently constituted. Thirty-nine years of separation has left a gulf between Taiwan and the PRC in living standards and economic freedoms; Taiwan's democratization will deepen the political schism, too.

Thomas Omestad, *Foreign Policy,* Summer 1988.

However, China does not respect the Taiwanese right to self-determination on the ground that "the signboard of the so-called 'self-determination' of the people on Taiwan" is employed to "perpetuate the separation of Taiwan from China" and that "it is entirely China's internal affair as to how the Taiwan question should be resolved." Here arise several legal questions: Are the Taiwan question and its solution China's internal affair? And particularly, can China invoke domestic jurisdiction as a justification to oppose the application of the principle of self-determination to the solution of the Taiwan problem? The answers to these questions appear to be negative.

First, the legal status of Taiwan involves the interpretation of the San Francisco Peace Treaty with Japan and many other international treaties and agreements, and is thus not a matter of China's domestic jurisdiction. In the Right of Passage case, in rejecting India's claim of domestic jurisdiction, because Portugal invoked a treaty which India controverted, the International Court of Justice held that "to invoke, whether rightly or wrongly, such principles is to place oneself on the plane of international law....to decide upon the validity of those principles does not fall exclusively within the jurisdiction of India."

Second, a territorial dispute, such as the Chinese claim to Taiwan, is a matter of international concern. China cannot invoke domestic jurisdiction until it has affirmatively established that Taiwan is a part of China. Therefore, the Taiwan question—the question as to whether Taiwan is Chinese territory—is not China's internal affair.

Third, the solution to the Taiwan question is not always a matter of China's domestic jurisdiction. Aureliu Cristescu states that "the violation of the principle of equal rights and self-determination of peoples, on the other hand, constitutes a danger to the very existence of those peoples; it is an offence against international legality and a threat to world peace," a situation "likely to endanger the maintenance of international peace and security" under Article 33 of the Charter. This kind of solution would be a matter of international concern. It follows naturally from what has been said that, whether or not Taiwan is a part of China, unless the future of Taiwan is determined with the consent of the people on Taiwan, free of coercion, the solution to the Taiwan question is not China's internal affair.

Fourth, according to current practice in the U.N., the application of the principle of self-determination is not a matter of domestic jurisdiction. After an intensive study of the question of self-determination in that world body, James Crawford found that "matters of self-determination cannot be within the domestic jurisdiction of the metropolitan State." Crawford points out that "colonial enclaves constitute in effect an exception to the self-determination rule, and that the only option is for the administering authority to transfer the enclave to the enclaving State. The wishes of the enclave are not regarded as relevant." Crawford defines a colonial enclave as "small territory claimed by a neighbouring State." By any definition Taiwan is not a colonial enclave. The island is 110 miles off the Chinese coast, and, with a population of 19 million, has more people than 123 of the 159 members of the U.N. Its GNP exceeds $60 billion, which is larger than that of any U.N. member in the Middle East and Africa. Thus, on the basis of international law and practice, China cannot invoke domestic jurisdiction to deny the Taiwanese the right to self-determination....

A New Political Entity

To support the Taiwanese right to self-determination, the U.S. should urge the KMT to hold a plebiscite in the island. If its outcome favors Taiwan's independence, the KMT should then declare Taiwan a new political entity, separate and independent from China.

In practical terms, there are three possible solutions to the Taiwan question: (1) to continue the KMT's one-China policy, (2) China's annexation of Taiwan on the basis of the Hong Kong formula, and (3) to proclaim Taiwan's independence.

The current KMT rule has encountered great difficulties as the international community cannot continue to accept the KMT's claim that it represents China. Nor can the people on Taiwan continue to tolerate the KMT's measures. Moreover, both the Taiwanese people and the KMT leadership cannot live incessantly under constant

189

and growing fear of a Chinese Communist takeover.

The Hong Kong formula of "one nation, two systems" is not quite applicable to Taiwan. In the first place, Taiwan and China do not belong to "one nation": Taiwan is not Chinese territory and the legal status of the island remains unsettled. In addition, it would be difficult, if not impossible, for China to maintain "two systems": Tibet's experience illustrates that China appears to be unable to keep its promise to protect the freedom and existing socioeconomic system in Taiwan.

Separate from China

The majority of Taiwanese want a Taiwan separate from China. They think all Chinese are Communists.... They want self-determination....

Beijing's view is ridiculous. They want us to join their Chinese family. "Keep your security forces," they tell us. "Just use our name." That is like entering into a marriage that is not supposed to be consummated—where the name, not love, is the object.

Antonio Chiang, *World Press Review*, November 1987.

Taiwan is significantly different from China in economy, education, culture, and polity. Consequently, the Taiwanese seem to have developed their own identity and demand to shape their own political future. Their right to self-determination is enshrined in contemporary international law and should be respected. Just as the Republican Party in the U.S. pledged in its 1984 platform to "fully support self-determination for the people of Hong Kong," Americans should uphold the principle of self-determination—not the Hong Kong formula—for the solution of the Taiwan problem.

Thus, the U.S. should urge the KMT to hold a plebiscite and to declare Taiwan a new nation if that is the wish of the Taiwanese. Unless the future of Taiwan is determined by the people on Taiwan, there will be no just solution to the Taiwan problem.

Understanding Words in Context

Readers occasionally come across words which they do not recognize. And frequently, because they do not know a word or words, they will not fully understand the passage being read. Obviously, the reader can look up an unfamiliar word in a dictionary. However, by carefully examining the word in the context in which it is used, the word's meaning can often be determined. A careful reader may find clues to the meaning of the word in surrounding words, ideas, and attitudes.

Below are sentences adapted from the viewpoints in this chapter. In each excerpt a word is printed in italics. Try to determine the meaning of each word by reading the excerpt. Under each excerpt you will find four definitions for the italicized word. Choose the one that is closest to your understanding of the word.

Finally, use a dictionary to see how well you have understood the words in context. It will be helpful to discuss with others the clues which helped you decide on each word's meaning.

1. In spite of the recent world economic *RECESSION*, Taiwan's GNP has continued to grow, in real terms by 3.9% in 1982, 7.3% in 1983, and 10.6% (the highest in Asia) in 1984.

   RECESSION means:
   a) regression   c) repression
   b) approach   d) relation

2. The fear has *PRECIPITATED* a growing flow of wealth from Taiwan. Based on a banker's estimates, some $3 billion in capital has flown to Los Angeles.

   PRECIPITATED means:
   a) rained   c) precluded
   b) hastened   d) eased

3. Some of their ideas, including the *CESSATION* of all hostilities, encouraging friendship between the people and holding cultural and economic exchanges, and allowing people on both sides to have mutual visits, are all positive and should be encouraged.

CESSATION means:
a) ending
b) sensation
c) continuation
d) death

4. Western merchants saw China as perhaps the greatest untapped economic market in history, with a billion eager consumers and a nearly *INSATIABLE* demand for modern technology.

INSATIABLE means:
a) satisfiable
b) sufficient
c) improbable
d) unquenchable

5. China has adopted what can well be described as a policy of *OMNIDIRECTIONAL* peaceful coexistence. With the exception of Vietnam, the People's Republic has tried to improve relations with its traditional rivals and neighboring countries.

OMNIDIRECTIONAL means:
a) centered
b) hostile
c) all directions
d) all powerful

6. Neither the United States nor the Soviet Union is frequently described as an imperialist power, although many of their oppressive policies are examples of superpower *HEGEMONISM*.

HEGEMONISM means:
a) decency
b) dominance
c) exploitation
d) ineptitude

7. China considers it its international obligation to safeguard the rights and interests of the third world countries and firmly supports them in their struggles to safeguard their national independence and *SOVEREIGNTY.*

SOVEREIGNTY means:
a) subjection
b) ruler
c) supreme authority
d) souvenir

Periodical Bibliography

The following articles have been selected to supplement the diverse views presented in this chapter.

Evgeny Bazhanov	"Who Is Against Reunification?" *New Times*, August 10, 1987.
C. Fred Bergsten	"The New Era in Economic Relations," *Vital Speeches of the Day*, January 15, 1988.
Fredrick F. Chien	"The Taiwan Experience," *Vital Speeches of the Day*," December 1, 1986.
Marc J. Cohen	"One China or Two?" *World Policy Journal*, Fall 1987.
Han Xu	"China-US Relations," *Vital Speeches of the Day*, January 15, 1988.
Pamela C. Harriman	"In China, Kremlin Watching," *The New York Times*, August 19, 1987.
Selig S. Harrison	"Taiwan After Chiang Ching-Kuo," *Foreign Affairs*, Spring 1988.
Kim R. Holmes	"US-Soviet-China Relations and Strategic Defense," *The Heritage Lectures*, No. 76, 1986. Available from The Heritage Foundation, 214 Massachusetts Ave. NE, Washington, DC 20002.
Thomas Omestad	"Dateline Taiwan: A Dynasty Ends," *Foreign Policy*, Summer 1988.
James A. Robinson	"Taiwan's Generation-Long Political Evolution," *Vital Speeches of the Day*, August 1, 1987.
Gerald Segal	"As China Grows Strong," *International Affairs*, Spring 1988.
Tai Ming Cheung	"China's Bargain Sale: Bangs for a Buck," *Far Eastern Economic Review*, June 2, 1988.
Russell Watson and Melinda Liu	"Why China Sells Arms," *Newsweek*, July 4, 1988.
Donald S. Zagoria	"China and the Superpowers," *The World & I*, November 1987.

What Should US Policy Be Toward China?

Chapter Preface

China has reportedly sold arms to North Korea, Pakistan, Egypt, and other, smaller countries. In total, China has become the fourth largest arms seller to the Third World, grossing $5.3 billion between 1983 and 1986. China has also sold arms to Iraq and Iran, volatile countries that have expressed hostility toward the US. These sales and China's willingness to ally with US enemies raise questions about China's trustworthiness as a US trading partner and ally.

While the US and China have maintained cordial relations since 1979, their relationship has been fraught with caution and distrust. Some argue that because China is a communist country, with hidden internal policies, it has the potential for harming the US far more than helping it. These people point to China's sale of its Silkworm missiles to Iran as a good example. Iran, an extremely unstable nation that has pledged eternal enmity toward the US, could conspire to use the missiles to aid another equally noxious opponent.

Others believe that remaining close allies with China can only help the US. China's traditional hostility toward the Soviet Union, these people argue, should be a major reason to maintain good relations. China's periodic alliances with countries unfriendly to the US are insignificant in comparison. In addition, if the US is allowed to fully participate in China's trade market, it could mean an economic boon for US industry. They would be able to establish profitable businesses and sell much needed manufactured goods to one billion new consumers.

What the nature of the US-China relationship should be is the subject debated in this chapter.

"It is in America's hard headed self-interest to help China modernize and relate to the world."

The US Should Support China

Winston Lord

Winston Lord is the US Ambassador to the People's Republic of China. He is also the former president of the Council of Foreign Relations in New York City. In the following viewpoint, Lord argues that the US will benefit from increased trade and business relations with China and from a strategic alliance with China that would promote stability in the Pacific region. For these reasons, the US should support China.

As you read, consider the following questions:

1. What does the United States gain from Sino-American relations, according to Lord?
2. What changes have occurred in China to inspire Lord's argument for such close involvement?
3. According to Lord, in what fundamental ways have Sino-American relations improved? How will closer relations with China benefit the US?

Winston Lord, "Sino-American Relations: No Time for Complacency," *Department of State Bulletin*, September 1986.

Kipling argued that between East and West the twain shall never meet. But—as his ballad itself depicts—they do meet sometimes when people with courage seize fate. Fifteen years ago, I was privileged to be present at the creation, when farsighted leaders in Beijing and Washington began opening doors and tearing down walls, indeed, even walking on them. As one who has worked ever since for better relations, I can speak with the candor of commitment.

We have made great strides since that opening.... Success is a process, not a fixed condition. Many problems remain. Many opportunities beckon. And just as bad relations—indeed, no relations—were not immutable in the past, so good relations are not inevitable in the future.

My basic message is this: Let us—China and America—use this relatively quiet phase of sound relations not to cheer ourselves on what we have done but to chart a course on where we should go.... Whereas geopolitics brought us together in the 1970s, economics is now a major force driving us forward. The growth of our bilateral links is one of the astounding success stories in international relations. But this very progress has spawned new problems, even as it holds out vast potential.

The Bilateral Relationship

This is hardly surprising. Time and space divide us. We have totally different histories and cultures. For a generation, we peered across an ocean of antagonism. There are sharp contrasts in our politics, societies, and values. China is gradually shedding a long period of estrangement from Western countries. We are still learning about the real China, trying to steer between our historical poles of romance and hostility.

Since China emerged from the holocaust of the Cultural Revolution, its national preoccupation has been modernization. Under Chairman Deng Xiaoping, the Chinese have opened up to the rest of the world and have unleashed a titanic wave of change.

• They have successfully boosted agricultural production. China now feeds its 1 billion people, with some left over for export.

• They have restructured their economy to lift living standards even as they tackle severe bottlenecks in transportation and communications and shortfalls in energy and management.

• They have created special economic and development zones along the Chinese coast to drive economic development and relay foreign technology to the less developed interior.

• They have begun enacting legislation to provide a framework for foreign trade investment.

• They have taken a more active role in global economic institutions, including the International Monetary Fund (IMF), the World Bank, and the Asian Development Bank, and they eye the General Agreement on Tariffs and Trade (GATT).

• Finally, and most ambitiously, they have embarked on an unprecedented course in urban reform. The goal effectively is to transform the industrial system which China modeled on the Soviet Union in the 1950s. They seek to replace it with one more flexible, more responsive to the market, more efficient in production and distribution—although, as they say, basically socialist in character.

China's New Direction

China's new direction is one of the boldest domestic ventures in modern history. No wonder serious problems arise. It has not been clear sailing since 1978. [In 1985] initial moves to abandon the cumbersome, irrational system of regulated prices helped fuel the highest rate of inflation in 30 years. Decentralization spurred excessive growth in the supply of money and credit. . . .

As a result, the Chinese are consolidating. They are slowing urban reforms, holding down prices, conserving foreign exchange, lifting grain production, and fighting corruption. The leaders stress that the reforms and the openings are irreversible, that the momentum will resume in 1987.

Contacts Should Be Strengthened

Contacts between the leaders and the peoples of the two countries should be strengthened. For the past few years, the exchange of visits by high-ranking officials of China and the United States have been increasing. Communications in the scientific and cultural fields are growing. There are more Chinese students studying in the United States than in any other foreign country. Mutual understanding and friendship between peoples significantly influence the futher development of bilateral relations. Contacts, both official and unofficial, should be encouraged, since the improvement of Sino-American relations will not only benefit the two peoples, but will contribute to peace and stability in Asia and the world.

Jia-Lin Zhang, *Current History*, September 1985.

Where does the United States fit into China's modernization? Here again, the progress has been remarkable. Fifteen years ago, trade was negligible. There was no investment, no science and technology cooperation, no military ties, no students or teachers at each other's universities, no tourism, no cultural relations. In short, the two societies had been sealed off from each other for over 20 years. Indeed, China had been isolated from most of the globe.

Contrast that landscape with today. Our bilateral trade exceeded $8 billion in 1985, up 25% in 1 year. American business has invested roughly $1.4 billion in China, second only to Hong Kong. About 250 U.S. companies now have offices in China. We have the largest

bilateral science and technology exchange program in the world—
[in May 1986] we signed our 27th protocol. Our military relations
are being pursued on three fronts—high-level visits, working-level
exchanges, and limited defensive arms sales.

An Historic Development

In a historic development, American campuses have become home
to over 15,000 Chinese students, almost half of all those abroad. More
than 100 American universities have shaped over 200 exchange
agreements with Chinese counterparts. Hundreds of Chinese and
American cultural and professional groups criss-cross the Pacific each
month. Over 200,000 American tourists and throngs of businessmen
flock annually to China. Almost 1,000 Americans now teach there.

The Chinese people have growing access to Western books,
periodicals, movies, radio and television programs. China is now
receiving a much more balanced view of the outside world. This
is in China's interest, for a major nation in today's complex world
must have accurate knowledge of global trends to make rational
decisions.

The merit of certain advances depends on your point of view.
Some Chinese are trading in baggy blues and traditional opera for
skin-tight jeans and disco. Others can sample *Rambo* and *Amadeus*,
Kentucky Fried Chicken and Elizabeth Arden, even the barbarian
Super Bowl. There will be a Holiday Inn in Tibet.

In any event, the general flow of goods, people, and ideas promotes China's modernization. It yields opportunities for American
business. It enriches the cultural life of both nations. And it builds
American and Chinese constituencies for the overall relationship.
In times of future stress, more people on both sides will work to
preserve ties. By helping China to help itself, we make it less
vulnerable to outside pressures and more integrated with the world
economy.

Today's International Environment

In today's international environment, China has many potential
foreign partners.... China will become stronger with or without
U.S. assistance. It is more apt to be receptive to American ideas if
we have thickened our cooperation. It is more apt to be responsible
in the region and the world if it is an active participant in the global
economy.

Today China's doors are open again, voluntarily and wider than
at any time in our memory. If they remain open, the viewpoints
of the leadership and people over the coming decades will undergo
important changes. We should be part of this process.

In sum it is in America's hardheaded self-interest to help China
modernize and relate to the world.

The course will not be easy. Two completely different societies are interacting after a long period of mutual isolation. For Americans many practices in China clash with our concepts of human rights. For Chinese the growing web of foreign contacts resurrects a riddle faced by earlier reformers: how to capture the magic of Western technology without forfeiting China's essence.

China's Modernization

The United States has an obvious interest in the success of China's modernization efforts. An economically progressing Chinese nation with a stable government in control of its own population is eminently desirable. The alternatives—failure to make progress toward modernization and political stability or the rebirth of regionalism and the catastrophic breakup of China into warring units and factions—would bring serious instability to Asia and to the world. Although there is a limit to what the United States can do to support current economic trends in China, those few things that can be done should be done. Specifically, the provision of technology for peaceful purposes in energy, light and heavy industry, and agriculture—technology suited to the conditions of an underdeveloped economy and technology specifically requested by the Chinese—should be made available whenever possible. Educational opportunities and vocational training, where sought by the Chinese, should be offered. Advances in science, medicine, and agricultural technology, where helpful and applicable, should be made available to them on the same basis as to other friendly, nonaligned, developing countries.

The Atlantic Council, *China Policy for the Next Decade*, 1984.

There are, moreover, many misperceptions on both sides. In my experience, even educated Chinese still do not comprehend the American system. As for Americans, our understanding of China is still cramped by the formal, restricted nature of our access, whether it be our journalists, academics, or government officials. . . .

Exciting Process

None of this detracts from the positive momentum in our ties. The process is exciting, diverse, and far beyond what was predicted just a few years ago. But hard work lies ahead—both to solve prickly issues and to insulate them from the overall relationship.

Let me suggest how Americans and Chinese might address some of these issues. First on our side. Protectionism must be resisted. Access to foreign markets and technology is crucial to China's development and reform. The President [Ronald Reagan] devotes enormous effort to blunting domestic pressures. As a late entrant, especially in textiles, China is clearly at a disadvantage, which we have sought to recognize. The Administration, congressional leaders, and American business must lead public opinion. . . .

We must continuously monitor our performance on technology transfer. In recent years, the Administration has worked hard to ease exports in the U.S. and in COCOM member countries [Coordinating Committee for Multilateral Security Export Controls]. There are limits set by national security concerns and some sensitive technology even we and our allies do not share. Within this context, we must ensure that what we said would happen happens. This, too, boosts American exports as well as overall relations.

American Business

American business should carefully prepare for China. Neither U.S. interests nor U.S.-China ties are served by encouraging ill-prepared firms to jump into the Chinese market. It takes a great deal of knowledge, skill, patience, and—let's face it—money to be able to compete effectively there. And it takes precise written agreements to prevent subsequent disputes. We should encourage American investment in China. . . .

In turn, there is much China can do.

The Chinese have pushed hard to attract foreign business. But they are hobbled by inexperience, misunderstanding of foreign needs, and the tension between foreign and domestic regulations. Thanks to the efforts of both the U.S. Government and business, there is a growing awareness among concerned Chinese officials that they have a long way to go. They are beginning to recognize that China must compete with scores of countries to entice foreign investment.

The Chinese often ask what they can do to improve the commercial environment. It reminds me of the visit Alexander the Great made to Diogenes, who lived in a barrel. Standing before the entrance the young king boomed, "I am Alexander, conqueror of the largest empire on Earth. Name your gift and it shall be yours." The philosopher replied simply, "Get out of the light." Getting out of the light would be a good first step. While the choices are for the Chinese to make, they will have to improve the overall climate. Several areas need priority attention.

China must bridle those bureaucratic elements who seek to get rich quickly by charging foreigners exorbitant prices for housing, services, and office space. It must resist the urge to tax heavily the imported equipment needed by foreign businessmen. . . .

The International Context

Fifteen years ago, the international scene first drove our two countries together. Now the global elements of our relationship are more muted, but no less important. They need nurturing, because our relationship cannot thrive on economics alone. . . .

In the late 1970s, Soviet and proxy advances spurred the process of normalization between Beijing and Washington. Since then, with some pauses, the bilateral results have been truly impressive on many fronts—visits and agreements, trade and investment, science and technology, culture and education.

Meanwhile, the Asian region has shown dramatic progress, thanks in large part to the easing, then growth, of Sino-American relations. As we carved out a new relationship with Beijing, we removed the elements of instability inherent in U.S.-Chinese antagonism. The fall of Vietnam in 1975 had sowed major doubts in the United States, and even more in Southeast Asia, about America's staying power. Yet now, years later, the Asian scene is generally one of achievement and hope. With the tragic exception of Indochina, the dominos did not drop. Asia boasts the world's most dynamic economies. It is America's largest regional trading partner. Our influence and stakes have never been greater. . . .

A Broader Base

Today, therefore, the base for our relations with China is much broader than parallel concerns about security. This is healthy. The Asian context has developed positively as we and China have moved from confrontation to convergence. This is encouraging. . . .

We would like to ease relations with the Soviet Union. We cannot do so without Soviet reciprocity. We will not do so at the expense of allies or friends. But if we do so, it would serve not only global stability but our dealings with China itself.

So let us be clear on this point. We are strengthening the relationship with China for its own sake, not to play triangles or to play cards. Our policies toward Beijing and Moscow clearly are interrelated, but they are pursued on different tracks. . . .

First, China depends on a stable balance of power. The Chinese realize that a strong United States is essential for its own security.

Second, China knows we pose no threat to it. We, in turn, have demonstrated in both word and deed that we are willing to contribute to its historic drive to modernize. . . .

The quality—and results—of our dialogue will depend largely on the attitudes we each bring to it. Let us understand each other's perspectives and purposes. Where we disagree, let us debate each other's methods, not motives. Let us strengthen cooperation where it already exists. And let us seek fresh areas of collaboration.

In this way we can, over time, shore up the international foundations for our growing bilateral links. . . .

China *is* on the move. But the very speed of its pace and rigors of its course will require it to apply the brakes often.

"The national and revolutionary interests of the People's Republic of China are not... compatible with the national and foreign policy interests of the United States."

The US Should Not Support China

A. James Gregor

In the following viewpoint, A. James Gregor argues that the United States should be involved with China only on a limited basis. The US should not help strengthen a communist country by economic, military, or political means. He further argues that scholars and the media have presented an exaggerated view of China's importance to the United States.

As you read, consider the following questions:

1. What are some of the reasons the author gives for his argument that China is unimportant to the US?
2. Ideologically, why should the US remain distant from China, according to Gregor? Does he consider the practical reasons more or less important than the ideological?

Reprinted from *The China Connection: US Policy and the People's Republic of China* by A. James Gregor with permission of Hoover Institution Press. © 1986 by the Board of Trustees of the Leland Stanford Jr. University.

Since the inception of the Chinese Communist Party, "imperialism" has been the touchstone of its domestic and foreign policy. During the revolutionary struggle, their presumed relationship to "imperialism" determined the lot of the Chinese population. Beijing's official foreign policy has always been "anti-imperialist." Nonetheless, the PRC [People's Republic of China] has, at various times, had relations with traditional monarchies, sheikhdoms, military juntas, and overtly anticommunist regimes. For the theoreticians in Beijing, such flexibility is part of historical and revolutionary "dialectics." Revolutionary struggle requires the flexibility that permits collaboration with those with whom one has a common interest, however temporary, in order to mobilize resistance against one's principal adversary. These tactical accommodations are dictated by the peculiarities of any given situation. As long as the United States was the principal adversary of "proletarian China," Beijing made common cause with a variety of political regimes—so long as those regimes were prepared to oppose U.S. imperialism.

When the Soviet Union became "social imperialist" and replaced the United States as the principal adversary of Communist China, the United States became a potential member of a prospective "united front" against Moscow's hegemonic intentions. Now that the Soviet Union appears prepared to negotiate some kind of settlement with the PRC, and the United States seems disposed to serve as a counterweight to Soviet military forces in East Asia, Beijing apparently has opted for foreign policy "independence." It seeks an alliance with the "progressive forces" in the Third World to accelerate the collapse of all forms of imperialism and hegemony and to facilitate the advent of world communism, anticipated by the philosophers of dynastic China as the "Great Harmony" of Confucius.

What all this seems to indicate is that Beijing's relations with imperialist and hegemonic powers will be cautious and manipulative. Many of the interests Beijing shares with such powers are transient. In judging where its interests lie, Beijing will, in the last analysis, keep its own counsel—which is not at all surprising. Sovereign nations have been doing just that since time immemorial.

Cautious Cost Accounting

It should be borne in mind, however, that the national and revolutionary interests of the People's Republic of China are not often compatible with the national and foreign policy interests of the United States. Consequently, relations between the two nations should be conducted on the basis of cautious cost accounting. A reasonable assessment should be made of both potential benefits and anticipated costs. Principles of strict reciprocity should govern bilateral trade, and the U.S. national interest should determine whether technology transfers to the PRC should continue. Unfortunately, such an assessment is not easy to make. There is considerable evidence that suggests that U.S. policymakers have been influenced by judgments of academics and media professionals that could most charitably be characterized as sinocentric.

Allen Whiting has identified as "unduly sinocentric" the notion that the PRC might either divert Soviet forces in East Asia from their anti-Western pursuits or free them for just such use. The PRC is incapable of accomplishing either. The People's Republic of China will remain a regional military power. Unlike Japan, it lacks virtually all the qualities necessary to enable it to serve as a swing-weight between the United States and the Soviet Union.

Commitment to Communism

I hope that our leaders will not be so bemused by the good things happening in Moscow and Peking as to forget the fundamental commitment to Communism of both major Communist powers.

Brian Crozier, *National Review*, December 18, 1987.

Americans tend to overlook the fact that Beijing has the potential for working considerable mischief among the East Asian allies of the United States. As we have seen, Beijing has used force in the South China Sea to secure what it considers the "sovereign territory of the motherland." It has threatened violence against the Japanese in the dispute over the Senkaku Islands in the Asian continental shelf. Its claims in the South China Sea also conflict with those of the Philippines, Indonesia, Malaysia, Brunei, and Vietnam, not to mention the Republic of China on Taiwan. Beijing's insistence that all the maritime territory of the region constitutes part of the PRC "may foreshadow military action there once the PLA [People's Liberation Army] acquires the capability. . . . Strengthening Beijing's ability to pursue its territorial claims . . . in the South China Sea is antithetical to [the United States'] larger interests, whatever [the] particular problems [of the U.S.] with Vietnam, Laos, and Kampuchea may be. . . . In short, the American judgment that a strong China will serve the cause of peace and stability in Asia is not shared by all [U.S.] allies and friends there."

A Critical Region

Beijing's insistence upon the "reunification" of Taiwan with the regime on the mainland threatens to destabilize a region critical to the defense of East Asia. Beijing's continued formal support of North Korea's demands on South Korea complicates the planning necessary for the strategic defense of Japan. Any nonpeaceful change on the Korean peninsula that would reduce the U.S. presence there would make the defense of the West Pacific far more difficult.

As for economic relations between the United States and the PRC, it appears that either nation will be vital to the other for the remainder of this century. Beijing has diversified its export markets and utilizes various suppliers; consequently, U.S. trade, technology, investments, and loans—although convenient and useful—are not essential to the PRC's ongoing development. United States trade with, and investment in, the People's Republic of China will remain marginal. A number of U.S.-based international corporations will probably enjoy substantial profit from their relations with the PRC, but it is doubtful whether Communist China will make any real contribution to the material well-being of Americans in general. In fact, Americans have underwritten, with their tax dollars, at least part of the economic and political reconstruction now going on in the People's Republic of China. U.S. government appropriations constitute about 25 percent of all capital loans made available to the PRC by the World Bank and the International Monetary Fund and about 25 percent of the grants and financial assistance made available to the PRC by the United Nations agencies. U.S. government guarantees for export-import transactions and relief from tariff duties—Washington's designation of the PRC as a most-favored nation, and the benefits that derive from the relaxation of restrictions on technology transfers to the PRC—have all contributed to Communist China's welfare and were made possible, directly or indirectly, by U.S. taxpayers.

A General Review

Relations between the United States and the People's Republic of China have probably reached a stage at which a general review of those relations would be salutary. How much is the United States prepared to invest in the rehabilitation of the neo-Stalinist political system that prevails in the People's Republic of China? What are the real benefits—strategic, economic, and political—that Washington can reasonably expect from its "China connection"? In order to obtain those benefits, will the United States have to mortgage the interests of the noncommunist nations of Asia?

It has become evident to a great many Americans that the United States does not have a principled China policy. Washington seems simply to have made ad hoc responses to issues and opportunities as they have arisen, and relations between Washington and Beijing have simply "developed." As relations between the two countries developed, constituencies formed in the United States, composed of individuals who benefited from those relations. Military men found themselves associating with their counterparts in the People's Liberation Army; academics became involved in exchange programs; businessmen became increasingly enthusiastic about the prospect of access to the "world's single largest market"; and farmers began to profit from the sale of wheat and soybeans.

What seems to have been lost in all this is the general interest. It is unlikely that "enhanced" strategic cooperation with the PRC—possibly to the detriment of long-standing U.S. relations with allies in East Asia—will serve the security interests of the United States, however much it might serve the interest of some constituency in the military. It is equally unlikely that most Americans will find it in their ultimate best interests to support the perpetuation of a Marxist-Leninist bureaucracy and agree to the rehabilitation of a neo-Stalinist China with capital and technology transfers, however much U.S. business interests might profit from such cooperation.

Dedicated to Reform

The United States has sought to foster the establishment and maintenance of pluralistic societies and open-market systems in East Asia and throughout the world. The People's Republic of China may seem dedicated to "reform," but it is most unlikely that the Chinese Communist Party will ever surrender its bureaucratic control of China—or abandon its legitimating commitment to "Marxism-Leninism-Mao Zedong Thought." The leadership in Beijing might modify its political creed, but it is not likely that the ensconced bureaucracy will surrender its privileges in the pursuit of "bourgeois democracy" or capitalism.

In the last analysis, the future of Asia and the best interests of the United States depend not on the cultivation of relations with the People's Republic of China, but on Washington's success in balancing its relations with the PRC and with those nations with which Americans share more in terms of political and economic modalities and security interests. Ultimately, Japan, the Republic of Korea, the Republic of China on Taiwan, the Republic of the Philippines, Malaysia, Singapore, Thailand, and Indonesia will have a more determinate influence on the future of East Asia than will the People's Republic of China. In that sense, maintenance of the "China connection" may ultimately prove to be of secondary importance to the West Pacific policy of the United States.

"Prudence dictates that the United States pursue a cautious policy in selling arms to China."

The US Should Limit Arms Sales to China

Martin L. Lasater

Martin L. Lasater is the former director of the Asian Studies Center at The Heritage Foundation and is now president of the Pacific Council, based in Columbia, Maryland. In the following viewpoint, Lasater contends that the United States government should reduce arms sales to the Chinese government. Because of improved Sino-Soviet relations, the Soviet threat to China has decreased, Lasater argues, thus diminishing the need for US military assistance.

As you read, consider the following questions:

1. What specific reasons does Lasater discuss as the basis for limiting arms sales to China?
2. What is the history behind US arms sales to China and what, according to the author, has changed since they began?
3. According to Lasater, which arms should the US continue to sell to China? How important does he believe the arms are?

Martin L. Lasater, "'Yellow Light' for US Arms Sales to China." This article appeared in the May 1988 issue and is reprinted with permission from *The World & I*, a publication of *The Washington Times Corporation*, copyright © 1988.

Prudence dictates that the United States pursue a cautious policy in selling arms to China. This is particularly true in an era of improving Sino-Soviet relations, when China's military arsenal may be focused less on the diminishing Soviet threat and more on achieving Chinese ambitions elsewhere in Asia. . . .

First, it is impossible for the United States to modernize the PLA [People's Liberation Army] through arms sales and other defense cooperation. It has been estimated that over $50 billion in U.S. weapons would have to be sold to the PRC [People's Republic of China] to enable that country to defeat a Soviet invasion. Congress would never approve $50 billion in military sales to China, nor would the Pentagon wish to deplete its stocks to the extent necessary to equip the PLA. Futhermore, the Chinese soldier lacks the education and training necessary to use and maintain the high-tech equipment used by the United States.

Second, China has very limited resources with which to purchase American arms and technology. Because of a lack of foreign exchange reserves, the PRC cannot afford to buy many foreign weapons systems. Due to the vast needs of the three-million-man PLA, China must build its own defense equipment whenever possible. Thus, the PRC wants American high-tech prototypes and technology rather than complete weapons systems. A further restraint on PLA purchases is the ranking of China's military modernization behind that of industry, agriculture, and science and technology.

Third, China will buy only limited amounts of weapons and technology from the United States because Beijing does not want to become dependent upon a foreign source for its military needs. During the 1950s, the PRC depended upon the Soviet Union for virtually all of its military equipment. When the Sino-Soviet split occurred in the 1960s, Moscow withdrew its military assistance and created enormous difficulties for the PLA. Beijing will not repeat that mistake by becoming dependent on the United States.

Arms Sales

Fourth, U.S. arms sales to the PRC are constrained by their unpopularity in Asia. None of China's neighbors wants to see the PRC become a strong military power. The historical memory of China's regional suzerainty remains very much in the minds of non-Chinese Asians. Beijing perceives Asia to be its "sphere of influence," and the Chinese openly proclaim their intention to play a more active role in regional affairs in the future. Washington's allies in Asia frequently caution the United States to go slow in its military sales to Beijing.

Fifth, there is the question of Taiwan to consider. The United States has close unofficial ties with the people of Taiwan, including legal commitments under the 1979 Taiwan Relations Act to help Taiwan defend itself. The PRC has never renounced the use of force to solve the Taiwan issue. In fact, it has said on many occasions that if Taipei refuses to negotiate reunification with Beijing, then China may have to use force against the island. There is concern on the part of many in the United States that the weapons the United States sells to the PRC someday may be used against Taiwan. This concern tends to restrict U.S. arms sales to China as well.

Security Ties

Several factors militate against further arms sales and the rapid development of security ties between the United States and China. Washington and Beijing believe that Moscow will view closer Sino-American security ties with alarm. Neither side sees an advantage in alienating the Soviet Union. Indeed, current Chinese foreign policy calls for the encouragement of a rapprochement between Beijing and Moscow. While insisting on the resolution of the "Three Obstacles" standing in the way of such a rapprochement, the Chinese nonetheless believe that improved relations with the Soviet Union will prove to be an advantage to China.

John Bryan Starr, *Current History*, September 1986.

The initial dialogue between the American and Chinese military establishments began in 1980. Since then, basic guidelines for the relationship have evolved. Essentially, these guidelines include high-level strategic dialogue between senior U.S. and Chinese military leaders; functional military exchanges between the two armed forces; and several military mission areas for U.S. arms sales and technology transfers to the PRC. During the first term of the Reagan administration, these mission areas were defined as antitank, artillery, air defense, and surface-ship antisubmarine warfare.

Restrictions

There have been restrictions placed on arms sales as well. In 1984, for example, the United States determined that it would deny the PRC advanced production technologies, state-of-the-art military technology and weapons systems, and certain highly sensitive technologies in mission areas of interest to the Chinese. These included nuclear weapons and their delivery systems; electronic warfare; antisubmarine warfare; intelligence-gathering; power projection; and air superiority. . . .

It appeared by mid-1987 that the United States and China were moving rapidly toward an expanded arms sales program. Negotiations were under way for coproduction of Improved TOW antitank guided missiles. The United States also had indicated its willingness to sell China improved Hawk antiaircraft missiles and was considering the sale of GE-F404 and PW-1120 jet engines, Light Airborne

Multi-Purpose System MK-I ASW equipment, and E-2C Hawkeye early-warning aircraft. In addition, the United States had sought to liberalize technology transfers to the PRC from NATO [North Atlantic Treaty Organization] countries and Japan coming under the review of the Coordinating Committee for Multilateral Export Controls (COCOM).

Sino-American military relations became somewhat strained after mid-1987, when the United States decided to place Kuwaiti tankers under the American flag and to provide them with U.S. naval protection in the Persian Gulf. This placed U.S. vessels and sailors under direct threat of the HY-2 Silkworm antiship missiles sold by China to Iran for possible use in blocking the Strait of Hormuz.

For months the United States, aware of the sales through intelligence sources, had asked the Chinese to stop the supply of these missiles to Iran. China, however, repeatedly denied that it had sold the Silkworms to Tehran. The issue simmered until October 1987, when Iran fired several Silkworms, hitting a Kuwaiti offshore oil loading facility and two tankers, one owned by a U.S. company and the other flying an American flag.

In response, the United States announced that it was freezing a review on lifting controls of high-technology items China could buy from the United States. Some components of the F-8II modernization package reportedly were affected. Despite Chinese protests, the freeze remained in effect until Beijing in early March [1988] assured the United States that it would no longer ship Silkworms to Iran. After Chinese Foreign Minister Wu Xueqian met with Secretary of State George Shultz and President Reagan, the State Department announced it was lifting the curbs.

One result of the Silkworm incident is that Sino-American military cooperation has cooled. There is less enthusiasm in the Pentagon to sell advanced weapons and technology to the PRC. U.S. military planners are more sensitive to the possibility of conflicting Chinese and American national interests. There is greater caution on the part of the United States in authorizing arms sales and defense technology transfers to China. . . .

Greater Caution Needed

This shift in the strategic environment in Asia may affect U.S. arms sales to China. Initially, the primary objective of U.S. arms sales was to help the PRC deter a Soviet attack. Now, however, the Soviet threat is diminishing. An attack by Moscow is deterred by a complex set of factors, including China's own limited nuclear second-strike capability, the uncertain response of the United States, and Gorbachev's decisions to improve relations with China and to emphasize Soviet economic growth as opposed to overseas adventurism. . . .

The United States should exercise greater caution in future arms sales to China because it is not the Soviet Union that the PRC is likely to fight or seek to intimidate. Those countries most likely to enter into conflict with Beijing are neighboring states such as Taiwan, Vietnam, and India. And of these countries, the conflict most likely to harm U.S. interests would be a confrontation between China and Taiwan. Hence, in decisions on future arms sales to China, the United States needs to place foremost attention on what the sales might mean to the military balance in the Taiwan Strait. As a corollary, it is in U.S. interests to see that Taiwan continues to maintain an adequate deterrence against a PRC attack. . . .

No Threat Yet

Although the transfer of U.S. science and technology and the sale of arms to mainland China will not enable the latter to pose a threat to the United States and the Soviet Union for a long time to come, it will nevertheless greatly enhance Peking's defense capability and create a threat to the Asia-Pacific nations, especially to those that have already fallen foul of Peking. Peking has time and again declared its willingness to solve regional disputes by peaceful means, but it has never abandoned the intention of using force to solve disputes with neighboring countries. . . . U.S. military assistance to Peking will actually create a greater threat to its security.

Ya-Chün Chang, *Issues & Studies,* April 1987.

It seems clear that the United States should follow a very cautious policy of selling arms to China. The question of whether a certain weapon or technology should be sold needs to be examined from both political and military points of view. As a rule of thumb, ground-based defensive systems are relatively safe to sell to Beijing. However, weapons systems that increase PRC power projection capabilities should be denied. . . .

It is difficult to justify an expanding arms sales program when Sino-Soviet relations are improving rapidly. For the time being, at least, U.S. arms sales to the PRC should be cautious, infrequent, and limited to defensive systems of no threat to China's neighbors.

"U.S. military and technology assistance programs extended to Peking would. . .stabilize the Asia-Pacific in the long term."

The US Should Continue Arms Sales to China

William T. Tow

William T. Tow is a contributor to *Issues & Studies*, a journal of China studies and international affairs published in Taiwan by the Institute of International Relations. According to Tow, China needs arms from the United States to protect itself and also to improve its military technology. Tow contends further that continued sales to China would solidify trade relations between the two countries. Based on these factors, Tow states that the US should continue all military ties with China.

As you read, consider the following questions:

1. Why does China need military aid from the United States, according to Tow?
2. What does Tow contend would happen if the US ended arms sales to China?
3. Why does the author think continued military aid to China is beneficial to both countries? Do you agree? Why?

William T. Tow, "The U.S., Mainland China and Japan: Military Transfer Policies and Strategic Collaborations," *Issues & Studies*, October 1987.

Mao Tse-tung's traditional glorification of protracted warfare, with ideology and morale portrayed as invariably stronger assets than an enemy's technological superiority in weapons and firepower, has now been refused as inappropriate for preparing Peking to face Soviet military power in the north or the Vietnamese war machine in the south.

Communist China's defense science and technology infrastructure, however, has far to go before it even begins to meet the requirements of credible active defense now endorsed by its leadership. U.S. Department of Defense spokesmen estimate that while Chinese units in the northern military regions have enjoyed some improvement in mechanization and firepower since the 1969 Sino-Soviet border skirmishes, Peking's air support and comparative theater nuclear weapons capabilities in this area of operations remain drastically inferior. Indeed, these analysts assert, the gap between overall Chinese and Soviet military power has continued to widen in Moscow's favor over the years with the Russians' addition of mobilized firepower and more combat support units over the years. Communist China's present tactical/theater nuclear weapons (T-TNW) inventory is neither diverse nor sophisticated enough to slow a concentrated Soviet axis of advance and combined arms operations in any future Sino-Soviet conflict and little hope exists for the Chinese to achieve the type of sequential nuclear targeting needed to block a systematic Soviet offensive spearheaded by its own sophisticated T-TNW arsenal. Peking needs advanced anti-tank and anti-aircraft weapons systems to complement its own rudimentary armored and nuclear forces. . . .

Technological Needs

Several key aspects of science and technology (S&T) directly relate to Communist China's long-term aspirations of becoming a first-class military power. Electronics research, for example, is directly applicable to strengthening Chinese command, control, communications, and intelligence (C³I) proficiency as time-critical data processing and advanced electronics instrumentation become more crucial in modern weapons systems' production and operation. While Communist China's performance in the metallurgical industry has been somewhat more impressive—it can now, for instance, recover titanium, vanadium, and other rare earth metals with fairly efficient techniques if judged by Western standards and these materials directly relate to its ability to build modern weapons systems—the quantity and quality of metallurgical end-products in China still falls short of both military and civilian needs. Domestically produced axle bearings, for example, last only a quarter of the distance of those produced in the West while the high-speed drill bits cannot begin to match the durability of those made abroad. Telecommunications equipment is also a premium item within PLA [People's Liberation

ROTHCO

BAS

U.S. – CHINA

Army] inventories as the lack of adequate high frequency radio communications during the Sino-Vietnamese border war fought during early 1979 graphically illustrated. Peking's military satellite communications needs will also become more important as it moves to enhance its overall military modernization over time. . . .

The American role in Chinese military technology planning and organization has increased steadily throughout the 1980s. Although the groundwork for such cooperation was laid initially with Secretary of Defense Harold Brown's visit to Communist China in 1980 (shortly following the Soviet Union's invasion of Afghanistan), the two most important high-level military exchanges between Washington and Peking took place under the Reagan administration, with Secretary of Commerce Malcolm Baldrige's journey to Peking in August 1983 and Defense Secretary Caspar Weinberger's visit a month later. Baldrige was instrumental in pushing through the liberalization of U.S. "dual use" exports (applicable to both civilian and military purposes) while Weinberger established procedures and programs for the subsequent exchange of the military services' senior leaders and technocrats as well as setting into motion a U.S. interagency review process for incoming Chinese requests relating to U.S. weapons technology and end-systems. Subsequently, Communist China's Defense Minister, Chang Ai-p'ing, and its PLA Naval Commander Liu Hua-ch'ing visited the U.S. (June 1984 and November 1985) while Secretary of the Navy John Lehman (August 1984), Chairman of the U.S. Joint Chiefs of Staff General John Vessey (January 1985), and Chief of Staff of the U.S. Air Force General Charles Gabriel (October

1985) reciprocated with trips to Peking....

The majority of U.S. officials and independent strategic observers...contend that qualified U.S. military and technology assistance programs extended to Peking would...stabilize the Asia-Pacific in the long term. Following his return from Peking as part of President Reagan's visiting entourage in April 1984, Assistant Secretary of State for East Asian and Pacific Affairs Paul Wolfowitz related in Congressional testimony that the major American geopolitical rationale behind forging a strategic relationship with Peking is "to put U.S.-China relations on a more stable and increasingly comprehensive basis—one that avoids the extremes of hostility and suspicion without succumbing to the opposite extreme of euphoria and sentimentality." Department of Defense spokesmen, perhaps attempting to explain their past reticence for approving high technology transfers to Peking *carte blanche* in response to pressures by the Department of Commerce or by other trade-oriented bureaucracies, have supplemented Wolfowitz's characterization of U.S. policy interest:

>...Our goal is to have an enduring defense relationship which will move in measured steps. [Communist] China has made it clear to us that it seeks no alliance. Neither is one needed or appropriate from our perspective. Rather [U.S.-PRC] defense relations must mirror the slow but steady growth of the U.S.-[Communist] China political and economic relationships....
>
>...Our position is that, first of all, the mission areas to which the technology applies would have to be evaluated. And then the items requested, themselves, would have to be considered for approval on a case-by-case basis.
>
>...The willingness of the United States to develop a military relationship with the PRC is founded on the assessment that the United States and the PRC share important parallel interests, both globally and regionally. Foremost among these is a common security concern—the growing threat of the Soviet Union. Thus, an objective of U.S. policy is to build an enduring military relationship with the PRC which would support [Communist] China's national development and maintain [Communist] China as a force for peace and stability in the Asia-Pacific region and the world. We believe a more secure, modernizing and friendly [Communist] China—with an independent foreign policy and economic system more compatible with the West—can make a significant contribution to peace and stability.

Military Sales to China

During late 1984, U.S. defense technology-related sales to Peking accelerated following President Reagan's comments offered in June that such transactions would "strengthen the security of the United States and promote world peace." By mid-1986, Washington had approved several military end-items for sale to Peking: advanced gas turbine engines to enhance the PLA's naval modernization (August

216

1984), prototypes of selected explosives as the first component of a planned US$98 million artillery munitions factory complex to be built in mainland China for manufacturing anti-tank and artillery shells (September 1985), and advanced jet fighter avionics and navigation equipment (early 1986). Such military technology transfers have been approved mostly on the assumption now prevalent in Washington that the nature of the Soviet threat in the Asia-Pacific *region* justifies military relations with Peking as part of America's overall *global* strategy.

Strategic Interests

The development of U.S.-China military relations has not been a short-term phenomenon responding to ad-hoc international political-military events. On the contrary, it has been, and continues to be, a fundamental element of overall United States China policy. U.S.-China military relations serve basic U.S. and Chinese strategic interest and contribute significantly to peace and stability in the Asia-Pacific region and the world.

The U.S.-China military relationship consists of three basic elements: High-level dialogues and visits, functional military exchanges, and military technology cooperation. The United States seeks balanced progress in each of these areas. . . .

The current trend in U.S.-China relations is a positive trend which ultimately will contribute to the security, not only of China and the United States, but of our friends and allies as well.

Edward Ross, speech before the Asian Studies Center of The Heritage Foundation, Washington, DC, January 28, 1986.

Other U.S. calculations, however, also play a role in the continued U.S. pursuit of military relations with Peking. A Communist China "secure" from Soviet or Vietnamese military threats would, it is thought by U.S. defense planners, continue to pursue Western economic development models along similar lines to those successfully adopted by the so-called "little gang of four" (South Korea, the Republic of China, Hong Kong, and Singapore) and perhaps somewhat less successfully by other ASEAN [Association of Southeast Asian Nations] states. In this context, mainland China would eventually, along with Japan, form the eventual groundwork for a Pacific Basin of unparalleled wealth and stability during the next century. A militarily formidable China would also provide the strategic basis for a "two front" global deterrent, along with NATO [North Atlantic Treaty Organization] Europe, for checking further Soviet expansion. Continued Washington-Peking military technology ties would also assure Washington that it could extract various *quid pro quos* from Peking in its strategic behavior, such as continued access to tracking stations in Sinkiang for monitoring Soviet missile tests or even gradual access to Communist Chinese ports during future Soviet-U.S. confrontations in the Asia-Pacific theater—an especially appealing prospect if continued instability in the Philippines, for example, were to compromise American basing operations there or if the Soviets were to continue expanding their own basing activities at Cam Ranh Bay and at Danang in Vietnam.

Distinguishing Between Fact and Opinion

This activity is designed to help develop the basic reading and thinking skill of distinguishing between fact and opinion. Consider the following statement: "Former Defense Secretary Casper Weinberger visited China in September 1983." This is a factual statement that can be proved simply by checking newspaper accounts from that time. The following statement, however, is an opinion: "It is in America's hard headed self-interest to help China modernize and relate to the world." Others may disagree and argue that the US should not be involved in China's economic development. There is no reliable way to prove it true or false.

When investigating controversial issues it is important that one be able to distinguish between statements of fact and statements of opinion. It is also important to recognize that not all statements of fact are true. They may appear to be true, but some are based on inaccurate or false information. For this activity, however, we are concerned with understanding the difference between those statements which appear to be factual and those which appear to be based primarily on opinion.

Most of the following statements are taken from the viewpoints in this chapter. Consider each statement carefully. *Mark O for any statement you believe is an opinion or interpretation of facts. Mark F for any statement you believe is a fact. Mark I for any statement you believe is impossible to judge.*

If you are doing this activity as a member of a class or group, compare your answers with those of other class or group members. Be able to defend your answers. You may discover that others come to different conclusions than you do. Listening to the reasons others present for their answers may give you valuable insights in distinguishing between fact and opinion.

O = *opinion*
F = *fact*
I = *impossible to judge*

1. In 1985 China's inflation was the highest it had been in 30 years.

2. Trade between the US and China exceeded $8 billion in 1985.

3. The opinions of China's leaders will undergo important changes over the coming decades.

4. As for Americans, our understanding of China is still limited.

5. China needs to diversify its exports to the United States.

6. US government appropriations constitute about 25 percent of all capital loans made available to the PRC by the World Bank and the International Monetary Fund.

7. Since China emerged from the holocaust of the Cultural Revolution, its national preoccupation has been modernization.

8. The national and revolutionary interests of the People's Republic of China are not compatible with the national and foreign policy interests of the United States.

9. Washington designated the PRC as a most-favored nation.

10. The gap between Chinese and Soviet military power has widened in Moscow's favor with the Russians' addition of mobilized firepower and more combat support units.

11. Communist China's Defense Minister, Chang Ai-p'ing, and the Naval Commander Liu Hua-ch'ing visited the US.

12. A more secure, modernizing, and friendly China—with an independent foreign policy and economic system more compatible with the West—can make a significant contribution to peace and stability.

13. In 1987 Chinese leader Zhao Ziyang advocated closer cooperation between the US and China.

14. It is impossible for the United States to improve China's army with arms sales.

15. China should build its own defense equipment whenever possible.

16. China and Vietnam fought each other over borders in the late 1970s.

Periodical Bibliography

The following articles have been selected to supplement the diverse views presented in this chapter.

John F. Copper — "America's East Asia Policy," *Vital Speeches of the Day*, October 1, 1986.

J. Terry Emerson — "Determining US Relations with China: The Taiwan Relations Act or the August 17 Communique with Beijing?" *The Backgrounder*, November 30, 1987. Available from The Heritage Foundation, 214 Massachusetts Ave. NE, Washington, DC 20002.

Juan Xiang — "Sino-US Relations over the Past Year," *Beijing Review*, February 15-28, 1988.

Louis Kraar — "The China Bubble Bursts," *Fortune*, July 6, 1987.

Martin L. Lasater — "Arming the Dragon: How Much US Military Aid to China?" *The Heritage Lectures*, March 1986. Available from The Heritage Foundation, 214 Massachusetts Ave. NE, Washington, DC 20002.

Martin L. Lasater — "Sino-American Military Relations," *Global Affairs*, Winter 1988.

The New Republic — "Carrying Friendship Too Far," November 25, 1985.

Michel Oksenberg — "China's Confident Nationalism," *Foreign Affairs*, vol. 65, no. 3, 1986.

Christopher E. Paine — "Fuzzy Safeguards for US-China Deal," *Bulletin of the Atomic Scientists*, October 1985.

Thomas W. Robinson — "The United States and China in the New Balance of Power," *Current History*, September 1985.

J. Stapleton Roy — "China: Reform and Future Prospects," *Department of State Bulletin*, December 1987.

Gaston J. Sigur Jr. — "US Policy Priorities for Relations With China," *Department of State Bulletin*, July 1987.

Jia-Lin Zhang — "Assessing United States-China Relations," *Current History*, September 1985.

Chronology of Events

1839-1842   Opium belonging to British merchants is destroyed by Chinese officials in an effort to enforce China's prohibition of opium importing, starting what is commonly called the Opium War. The British respond by attacking several Chinese coastal ports. The Chinese are easily defeated and The Treaty of Nanjing is signed in 1842 which stipulates that several Chinese ports remain open to British trade and also cedes Hong Kong to the British.

1850-1864   Chinese peasants revolt against the Ching dynasty in The Taiping Rebellion. These rebels capture Nanjing in 1853 and make it their capital. The Western powers, fearing a loss of foreign trade, aid the Ching dynasty and defeat the Taipings in 1864.

1856-1860   The Second Opium War breaks out following the Chinese seizure of a British ship in Canton. British and French troops seize the Chinese cities of Canton and Tientsin and compel the Chinese to sign the treaties of Tientsin to which France, Russia, and the US are also party. China agrees to open eleven more ports, permit foreign legation in Beijing, sanction Christian missionary activity, and legalize the importation of opium. China's attempt to block the entry of diplomats in 1859 leads the British and French to occupy Beijing and burn the summer palace there. The Beijing conventions in 1860 force China to make more concessions and the hostilities end.

1894   Civil war erupts in Korea. China and Japan support different sides of the conflict with troops.

1894-1895   In spite of its superior size, China is defeated by Japan in the first Sino-Japanese war. China recognizes Korean independence, cedes Taiwan, pays a large indemnity, and grants Japan the right to manufacture in Chinese ports.

1897-1898   Western powers and Japan partition China into spheres of influence. Britain leases Hong Kong for ninety-nine years.

1899   The US issues its Open Door Policy. Under this policy, treaty ports would be opened for all trade to all nations equally, and Chinese territorial integrity would be officially respected.

1899-1902   Armed bands of peasants known as the Boxers attack Christian missionaries in north China in the Boxer Rebellion. The siege is ended in August 1900 by an international force of British, French, Russian, American, German, and Japanese troops. In 1901 China is forced to make reparations to these countries by paying an indemnity of $333 million, amending commercial treaties to the advantage of foreign nations, and permitting foreign troops to be stationed in Beijing.

1911	Disaffected troops revolt in central China and several southern and central provinces declare independence from the Manchu monarchy.
1912	Emperor Henry Pu-yi abdicates, ending over two millennia of monarchy. The Republic of China is declared.
1915	Japan invades the German-controlled Chinese territory Kiaochow and issues its Twenty-One Demands. Japan orders that it replace Germany in Kiaochow, control Manchuria and Mongolia, and control the main Chinese coal deposits. Japan also insists that other Western powers be excluded from more territorial concessions, and that it guide China's military, commercial, and financial affairs. The demands for control of Chinese policy are dropped, but the remainder of the demands are accepted after Japan threatens to continue its invasion.
1919	After the Versailles Conference awards Kiaochow to Japan, a mass protest movement on May 4 of about 5000 Chinese university students forms and a nationwide boycott of Japanese goods follows. Because of the protests, China refuses to sign the Treaty of Paris. This movement also inspires increased labor organization, political participation by women, and education reforms.
July 1921	Eleven members of the Chinese Communist Party (CCP) meet in Shanghai in what is later called the First Congress of the Chinese Communist Party.
1921-1922	The Washington Conference convenes and France, Japan, Great Britain, and the United States sign the Four-Power Treaty in which Japan agrees to return Kiaochow to China.
June 1923	The Third Congress of the CCP agrees to merge with the Kuomintang (KMT), the nationalist party that rules China. This creates a left and right wing in the KMT.
1926-1928	The KMT party (the nationalists) overthrows the warlord-backed Beijing government and establishes a new government in Beijing in the Northern Expedition. At the outset, the expedition was supported by the smaller communist party (CCP), and was receiving aid from the USSR. By March 1927 the KMT armies take all of southeast China. Disagreements break out between the leader of the KMT, Chiang Kai-shek, and the communist party (CCP). Chiang launches a purge of communists. His troops descend on Shanghai and destroy CCP leadership and organization. Beijing is taken by the KMT in June 1928 and the national government moves to Nanjing.
1931	Japan launches an invasion of Manchuria. Chiang, believing the Nationalist government cannot battle both Japan and the communists, adopts a policy of concessions to the Japanese while intensifying the war against the CCP. Japan occupies Manchuria, Mongolia, and north China.

1934	The CCP, led by Mao Zedong, begins the 5000-mile march to Shensi province to evade Chiang's extermination campaigns against the communists.
1936	Ominous troop movements signal an imminent Japanese invasion of China. In spite of Mao's plea to end the fighting between the CCP and the KMT, Chiang decides to destroy the CCP before focusing on Japan. He sends troops to attack the CCP in Shensi province. The KMT refuses to fight the CCP and kidnaps Chiang Kai-shek. The CCP negotiates Chiang's release on the condition he allow the KMT and the CCP to unite.
1937	Japan attacks near Beijing in July. Nanjing falls to the Japanese in December.
August 1945	Japan surrenders and World War II ends. China regains control of Manchuria and Taiwan.
1946-1949	The CCP and the nationalists (the KMT) battle for the right to govern China. CCP forces overwhelm nationalist opposition and move south while the remnants of the nationalist government flee to Taiwan. The People's Republic of China is proclaimed with Mao Zedong as CCP chairman and leader.
February 1950	A thirty-year Sino-Soviet treaty is signed, granting the Soviets permission to station troops in China in exchange for loans, technical assistance, and the return of part of Manchurian territory.
June 25, 1950	The Korean War begins.
1950	United Nation's forces led by General Douglas MacArthur drive the North Korean army near the North Korean-Chinese border, despite Chinese warnings against approaching the border. China responds by sending armed troops to sweep across the border and rout UN positions. UN forces retreat across recently captured North Korean territory.
1953	The Korean War ends as the principal combatants sign an armistice setting a boundary between North and South Korea at the 38th parallel. China institutes its first five-year plan designed to promote industrialization.
1955-1956	The Chinese government institutes reforms in an attempt to collectivize agriculture. These reforms include dividing the rural population into family cooperatives. Though the majority of the land remains with the cooperative, each family retains its house and five percent of its former land holdings.
1956-1957	Protests and criticism of the government grows intense and many dissidents are sent for reeducation in labor camps.
1957	Agricultural output continues to decline and the government reorganizes cooperatives and seizes small family plots.
1958	China begins the "Great Leap Forward." It abandons the Soviet economic model that emphasizes heavy in-

dustry and instead emphasizes the development of labor-intensive industry.

1959	Widespread violence and rebellion against Chinese rule in Tibet culminates in China forcing the Tibetan ruler, the Dalai Lama, into exile.
July 1960	The Soviet Union withdraws its technicians and ceases to supply tools and equipment for Chinese industrial projects.
1960-1961	The Chinese government returns small parcels of land to families and reorganizes cooperative units. Agricultural production increases. The Chinese Central Committee places less emphasis on developing labor-intensive industry and thus ends the aspirations of the Great Leap Forward.
1964	China is the fifth nation to explode a nuclear bomb.
1965	The Cultural Revolution begins.
1966	All schools and universities in China are closed to allow students to participate in the Cultural Revolution. Students form groups known as the Red Guards and the schools do not reopen for several years.
1967	Red Guards defy orders and take over the municipal government of Shanghai and institute a committee-ruled commune. The new governing strategy fails to provide authority or essential services and Beijing sends the army in to restore order. Red Guards continue to cause problems by infighting and by storming the British embassy until they are sent to the countryside in 1968.
1969	A Soviet patrol is ambushed by Chinese troops near the Ossuri river. The Soviets respond with artillery and tank bombardment of Chinese border villages. China declares the Soviets its principal enemy, and the Soviets compare Mao to Adolf Hitler.
1970	Henry Kissinger, US national security adviser, makes a secret visit to Beijing.
1971	The People's Republic of China gains membership in the United Nations and Taiwan loses its membership.
1972	President Richard Nixon meets with Mao in Beijing. This is the first US attempt to improve relations with Communist China. Twenty countries, including Japan and West Germany, establish diplomatic relations with the People's Republic of China. The US is the only major country that recognizes the Republic of Taiwan as China.
1975	Chiang Kai-shek dies. His son, Chiang Ching-kuo, succeeds him as Taiwan's president.
1976	Mao Zedong dies and thirty high-ranking government and party officials are arrested, including four Central Committee members. These four, including Mao's widow, become known as the Gang of Four and are blamed for the failure of the Cultural Revolution. Hua

	Guofeng assumes the positions of premier, chairman of the Communist Party, and chairman of the military commission.
1978	Deng Xiaoping initiates reforms, which include the dismantling of agricultural communes.
1979	Many political prisoners are released. China begins limiting couples to one child in an effort to control population growth. The US and China establish diplomatic ties. Deng's travels to the US and Japan signal a new opening of Chinese trade and discourse with the capitalist world.
March 1979	After Vietnamese troops invade Cambodia, China orders its own troops to invade Vietnam in order to punish the Vietnamese. The Chinese invasion ends with the capture of the provincial capital of Lang Son.
October 1979	Wei Jingsheng, China's most prominent dissident, is sentenced to fifteen years in jail.
December 1979	The Beijing municipal government forbids the hanging of posters on Democracy Wall, a wall where leaflets critical of the party and the government are posted. Many government critics are arrested.
1982	China's population reaches one billion.
1983	The government launches a campaign against spiritual pollution, intended to restrict foreign culture and morality. The campaign ends when it begins to threaten economic reforms and foreign investment.
1984	Four years of increased agricultural harvests inspire China to implement similar reforms in industry.
1985	Some Communist Party leaders criticize China's economic reforms, citing falling grain production, inflation, and a retreat from communist ideology.
1986	Soviet leader Mikhail Gorbachev calls for better Sino-Soviet relations. University students from a number of cities march to advocate democracy, human rights, and freedom.
April 1987	Portugal and China sign an agreement which returns the colony of Macao to China in 1999.
May 1987	The Dalai Lama gives a speech before the US Congress outlining a five-point plan for Tibetan independence.
July 14, 1987	Martial law is lifted on Taiwan after thirty-nine years, allowing new political parties and ending military censorship.
October 1987	The Tibetan capital erupts in violent protest for independence from China. China responds by cutting Tibet's communication with the outside world.
January 1988	Chiang Ching-kuo, the president of Taiwan, dies. Lee Teng-hui is named successor.
March 1988	The Great Prayer Festival in Tibet becomes a bloody confrontation. Tibetan civilians, led by monks, battle

Chinese and Tibetan police. Sixteen monks are killed as riots engulf the city.

August 1988   China relaxes its one-child policy, allowing couples in rural areas to have a second child if the first is a daughter.

Organizations To Contact

The editors have compiled the following list of organizations concerned with the issues debated in this book. All of them have publications available for interested readers. The descriptions are derived from materials provided by the organizations.

Asia Resource Center (ARC)
PO Box 15275
Washington, DC 20003
(202) 547-1114

Founded in 1978, ARC has worked to increase North Americans' awareness of human rights violations in Taiwan. It provides audiovisual materials, publications, and speakers to schools and other organizations. Its publications include its 1985 report *Martial Law in Taiwan.*

The Asia Society
725 Park Ave.
New York, NY 10021
(212) 288-6400

The Asia Society works to increase American understanding of Asia and its growing importance to US and world relations. One of its many programs is The China Council, part of The Asia Society's Contemporary Affairs Department. The China Council sponsors public education programs and compiles timely publications on China, including an annual update of contemporary Chinese affairs called *China Briefing.*

Asia Watch
739 Eighth St. SE
Washington, DC 20003
(202) 546-9336

Asia Watch was established in 1986 by the Fund for Free Expression to monitor and promote human rights in Asia. It is affiliated with Helsinki Watch and Americas Watch, and has published a number of books and reports, including *Human Rights in Tibet* and *Intellectual Freedom in China: An Update.*

Association for Asian Studies (AAS)
1 Lane Hall
University of Michigan
Ann Arbor, MI 48109
(313) 665-2490

The Association is a group of educators, students, government officials, and others interested in the study of Asia. AAS publishes scholarly research and other material designed to promote Asian studies. It publishes the quarterly *Journal of Asian Studies.*

The Brookings Institution
1775 Massachusetts Ave. NW
Washington, DC 20036
(202) 797-6000

The Institution, founded in 1927, is an independent organization devoted to nonpartisan research, education, and publication in the fields of economics, government, and foreign policy. It publishes the quarterly *Brookings Review,* and various books and reports. A recent book published was *China's Second Revolution* by Harry Harding.

China Books & Periodicals, Inc.
2929 24th St.
San Francisco, CA 94110
(415) 282-2994

China Books & Periodicals publishes books about China and also serves as a distributor for materials published by other companies in America and China. It handles subscriptions for Chinese magazines including *Beijing Review, China Reconstructs,* and *Women of China.*

Christian Anti-Communist Crusade
PO Box 890
227 E. Sixth St.
Long Beach, CA 90801
(213) 497-0941

The Crusade, founded in 1953, sponsors anti-subversive seminars "to inform Americans of the philosophy, morality, organization, techniques, and strategy of communism and associated forces." Its newsletter, published semi-monthly, is free.

Committee for a Free China
PO Box 65012
Washington, DC 20035-5012
(202) 223-8596

The Committee for a Free China works to support and encourage freedom and peace in Asia. It believes the US should maintain close relations with Taiwan and should pressure mainland China to adopt democracy. The Committee publishes *The China Letter* bimonthly.

Foreign Policy Association (FPA)
729 Seventh Ave.
New York, NY 10019
(212) 764-4050

The Foreign Policy Association was founded in 1918 to help Americans gain a better understanding of significant issues in US foreign policy and stimulate constructive and informed citizen participation in world affairs. FPA is non-partisan and not associated with the government in any official way. It publishes a yearly bibliography of their publications as well as books and pamphlets. Some of the Association's writings on China include *Hong Kong and China: For Better or For Worse,* and a chapter on China in *Great Decisions '89.*

The Heritage Foundation
214 Massachusetts Ave. NE
Washington, DC 20002
(202) 546-4400

The Foundation is a conservative public policy research institute. It has published many materials on the People's Republic of China, Taiwan, and Hong Kong in its *Backgrounder* and *Heritage Lectures* series.

Institute of Current China Studies
PO Box 14-19
Taipei, Taiwan, ROC

The Institute publishes *Inside China Mainland*, a monthly newsletter of articles and speeches originating in the People's Republic of China and translated into English. It has also translated and published Chinese dissident writings and has sponsored studies of the Chinese Communist Party.

Maoist Internationalist Movement (MIM)
PO Box 3576
Ann Arbor, MI 48106-3576

The Maoist Internationalist Movement is an international communist group that believes the victorious revolution led by former Chinese leader Mao Zedong should be duplicated worldwide. It is against what is sees as imperialism in both the United States and the Soviet Union. MIM distributes a catalog of books, and has published articles and a book on China's recent economic reforms.

Midwest China Center
308 Gullixson Hall
2375 Como Ave.
St. Paul, MN 55108
(612) 641-3233

The Midwest China Center is a non-partisan, non-profit education institution which promotes understanding and facilitates relationships between the people of the Upper Midwest and of China, Taiwan, and Hong Kong. It maintains a library of Chinese publications and sponsors seminars and lectures. The Center publishes a newsletter and the *Midwest China Resource Guide*.

The Washington Institute
1015 18th St., NW, Suite 300
Washington, DC 20036
(202) 293-7440

The Washington Institute is a research and educational institute that does policy research on China, among other countries. It explores ethical values underlying public policy issues, and believes private and governmental institutions should share responsibility for promoting the common welfare and a strong national defense. The Institute publishes books and pamphlets through its own publishing company. Recent books on China include *Human Rights in East Asia* and *The East Wind Subsides*.

Bibliography of Books

John F. Avedon	*In Exile from the Land of Snows.* New York: Alfred A. Knopf, 1984.
Geremie Barme and John Minford, eds.	*Seeds of Fire: Chinese Voices of Conscience.* Hong Kong: Far Eastern Economic Review, 1986.
A. Doak Barnett	*The Making of Foreign Policy In China: Structure and Process.* Boulder, CO: Westview Press, 1985.
A. Doak Barnett and Ralph N. Clough	*Modernizing China: Post-Mao Reform and Development.* Boulder, CO: Westview Press, 1986.
David Bonavia	*The Chinese.* New York: Lippincott & Crowell, 1980.
Wen-shun Chi	*Ideological Conflicts in Modern China: Democracy and Authoritarianism.* New Brunswick, NJ: Transaction Books, 1985.
Alasdair Clayre	*The Heart of the Dragon.* New York: Houghton Mifflin, 1985.
Ken Coates, ed.	*China and the Bomb.* Nottingham, England: Spokesman, 1986.
Communist Party of China	*Documents of the Thirteenth National Congress of the Communist Party of China.* Beijing, China: Foreign Languages Press, 1987.
Deng Xiaoping	*Build Socialism with Chinese Characteristics.* Beijing, China: Foreign Languages Press, 1987.
Deng Xiaoping	*Fundamental Issues in Present-Day China.* Beijing, China: Foreign Languages Press, 1987.
Craig Dietrich	*People's China: A Brief History.* New York: Oxford University Press, 1986.
R. Randle Edwards, Louis Henkin, and Andrew J. Nathan	*Human Rights in Contemporary China.* New York: Columbia University Press, 1986.
John King Fairbank	*China Watch.* Cambridge, MA: Harvard University Press, 1987.
John King Fairbank	*The Great Chinese Revolution 1800-1985.* New York: Harper & Row, 1986.
David S.G. Goodman, Martin Lockett, and Gerald Segal	*The China Challenge: Adjustment and Reform.* London: Routledge & Kegan Paul, 1986.
A. James Gregor	*Arming the Dragon: US Security Ties with the People's Republic of China.* Washington, DC: Ethics and Public Policy Center, 1988.
A. James Gregor	*The China Connection: US Policy and the People's Republic of China.* Stanford, CA: Hoover Institution Press, 1986.
A. Tom Grunfeld	*The Making of Modern Tibet.* Armonk, NY: M.E. Sharpe, 1987.
Harry Harding	*China's Second Revolution: Reform After Mao.* Washington, DC: The Brookings Institution, 1987.

Lillian Craig Harris and Robert L. Worden, eds.	*China and the Third World: Champion or Challenger?* Dover, MA: Auburn House, 1986.
Thomas G. Hart	*Sino-Soviet Relations: Re-examining the Prospects for Normalization.* Aldershot, England: Gower Publishing Company, 1987.
Liang Heng and Judith Shapiro	*After the Nightmare.* New York: Alfred A. Knopf, 1986.
James C. Hsuing	*Beyond China's Independent Foreign Policy.* New York: Praeger, 1985.
Harish Kapar, ed.	*As China Sees the World: Perceptions of Chinese Scholars.* New York: St. Martin's Press, 1987.
Ilpyong J. Kim, ed.	*The Strategic Triangle: China, the United States, and the Soviet Union.* New York: Paragon House, 1987.
Roy Kim and Hilary Conroy, eds.	*New Tides in the Pacific: Pacific Basin Cooperation and the Big Four.* Westport, CT: Greenwood Press, 1987.
Samuel S. Kim, ed.	*China and the World.* Boulder, CO: Westview Press, 1984.
David Lampton and Catherine H. Keyser	*China's Global Presence: Economics, Politics, and Security.* Washington, DC: American Enterprise Institute, 1988.
Don Lawson	*The Eagle and the Dragon.* New York: Thomas Y. Crowell, 1985.
Liu Binyan	*People or Monsters?* Bloomington, IN: Indiana University Press, 1985.
Ian Mabbett	*Modern China: The Mirage of Modernity.* New York: St. Martin's Press, 1985.
John S. Major and Anthony J. Kane	*China Briefing 1987.* Boulder, CO: Westview Press, 1987.
Roberta Martin, ed.	*China: A Teaching Workbook,* second revised edition. New York: Columbia University East Asian Institute, 1983.
David Allan Mayers	*Cracking the Monolith: US Policy Against the Sino-Soviet Alliance.* Baton Rouge, LA: Louisiana State University Press, 1986.
Roy Medvedev	*China and the Superpowers.* New York: Basil Blackwell, 1986.
Maurice Meisner	*Mao's China and After.* New York: The Free Press, 1986.
Steven W. Mosher	*Journey to the Forbidden China.* New York: The Free Press, 1985.
Andrew J. Nathan	*Chinese Democracy.* Berkeley: University of California Press, 1986.
Dwight Perkins	*China: Asia's Next Economic Giant?* Seattle, WA: University of Washington Press, 1986.
Alvin Rabushka	*The New China.* Boulder, CO: Westview Press, 1987.
Orville Schell	*Discos and Democracy.* New York: Pantheon Books, 1988.
Gerald Segal	*Defending China.* London: Oxford University Press, 1985.

Su Wenming, ed.	*Open Policy at Work*. Beijing, China: Beijing Review, 1985.
Robert G. Sutter	*Chinese Foreign Policy: Developments After Mao*. New York: Praeger, 1985.
Tiziano Terzani	*Behind the Forbidden Door: Travels in Unknown China*. New York: Henry Holt and Company, 1986.
Anne F. Thurston	*Enemies of the People*. New York: Alfred A. Knopf, 1987.
Wang Furen and Su Wenqing	*Highlights of Tibetan History*. Beijing, China: New World Press, 1984.
You Youwen, ed.	*The Work and Life of China's Young People Today*. Beijing, China: China Reconstructs, 1986.
Yu Guangyuan, ed.	*China's Socialist Modernization*. Beijing, China: Foreign Languages Press, 1984.
Yu San Wang	*The China Question*. New York: Praeger, 1985.
Zhang Xinxin and Sang Ye	*Chinese Lives: An Oral History of Contemporary China*. New York: Pantheon Books, 1987.
Zong Wenxian, ed.	*Mao Zedong—Biography, Assessment, Reminiscences*. Beijing, China: Foreign Languages Press, 1986.

Index

236